Christian Names
in Local and Family History

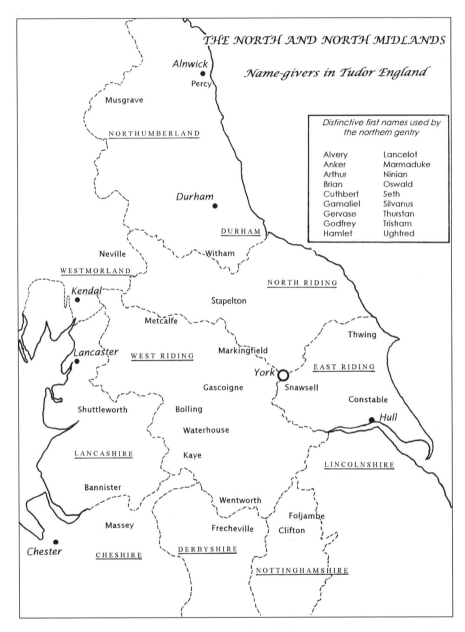

THE NORTH AND NORTH MIDLANDS

Name-givers in Tudor England

Alnwick
●
Percy

Musgrave

NORTHUMBERLAND

Durham
●

DURHAM

Distinctive first names used by the northern gentry	
Alvery	Lancelot
Anker	Marmaduke
Arthur	Ninian
Brian	Oswald
Cuthbert	Seth
Gamaliel	Silvanus
Gervase	Thurstan
Godfrey	Tristram
Hamlet	Ughtred

Neville   Witham

WESTMORLAND

NORTH RIDING

Kendal
●

Stapelton

Metcalfe

Thwing

Lancaster   Markingfield
●

WEST RIDING

York ○   EAST RIDING

Gascoigne   Snawsell

Constable

Shuttleworth   Bolling

Hull ●

Waterhouse

LANCASHIRE   Kaye

LINCOLNSHIRE

Bannister

Wentworth

Foljambe

Massey   Frecheville   Clifton

Chester
●   DERBYSHIRE

CHESHIRE

NOTTINGHAMSHIRE

Distinctive first names were preserved or reintroduced by the status-conscious gentry of northern England in the Tudor period. Some of the most important families are shown here, along with a list of their favourite first names.

Christian Names
in Local and Family History

GEORGE REDMONDS

the national archives

First published in 2004 by

The National Archives
Kew, Richmond
Surrey, TW9 4DU, UK

www.nationalarchives.gov.uk/

The National Archives was formed when the Public Record Office and
Historical Manuscripts Commission combined in April 2003.

ISBN 1 903365 52 X

Jacket illustration:
A Scottish Christening by John Phillip (1817–67)
Roy Miles Fine Paintings/Bridgeman Art Library

Text designed by Geoff Green Book Design, Cambridge
Printed in the UK by Cromwell Press, Trowbridge, Wiltshire

Contents

The plate section falls between pages 78 and 79.

Foreword

Christian names are historically of great interest because they can tell us much about families, communities and culture in past times. Yet the value of christian names as a tool of historical research has been little appreciated. This is largely due to the way modern naming has become increasingly influenced by an individualistic consumer culture, as though christian names were little more than personalised designer labels. Our current christian name-stock is hugely larger than in any previous age and continues to grow as new names are coined or introduced from other cultures. The most popular names form just a tiny percentage of the whole and seem to change from one decade to another at random. Most parents apparently make their choices by leafing through one of the many christian name dictionaries and if you ask parents why they chose a particular name the usual reply is 'because we liked it'.

Go back to the eighteenth century or to any century before then and you are in a different world. The name-stock was small, stable and dominated by a handful of names that have remained exceptionally popular for generations or even centuries. Few choices of name were random or idiosyncratic for most were governed by traditional processes, parents or godparents mostly naming children after themselves or close relatives. A child so named was slotted securely into a social network of familial or communal obligations and loyalties, where relationships were hierarchical and deferential.

This was a world in which continuity was the norm, change was generally slow and where only major social upheavals like the Norman Conquest and the Reformation caused radical changes in the name-stock or in ways of choosing names. Most eighteenth-century names had been continuously in the name-stock since at least 1250 and a few men's names like John and William had maintained an exceptional degree of popularity for all of five centuries. This picture of christian name usage reflects the pre-industrial, pre-Romantic world of our ancestors just as modern ways of naming reflect our current culture with its hectic pace of change, its economic individualism and its increasing egalitarianism and child-centredness.

In short, christian names have their own social history, and in *Christian Names in Local and Family History* George Redmonds sheds new light on this undeservedly neglected subject and demonstrates its special value to anyone interested in the history of regions, communities, families or individuals. He employs two principal research methods. The first is comparative, either with respect to different communities and regions at the same point in time or with respect to a single community or region at different times. By this method he reveals dissimilarities in the name-stock or the patterns of name usage that are highly suggestive of social and cultural differences between places and between generations.

Redmonds' chief sources for medieval comparisons are the poll tax returns of 1377, 1379 and 1381. The recent publication of these county returns gives us for the first time a nationwide database for a statistical survey of men's and women's names at all levels of late medieval society. Redmonds' compilation of forename frequencies, county by county, produces some surprising findings, contradicting many of the usual assumptions about the identity, survival and popularity of medieval personal names. Some names are very clearly regional in their distribution and some that are usually supposed to have been quite common after the Norman Conquest turn out to be rare or even absent in the late fourteenth century until re-introduced by continental immigrants in the fifteenth century. By comparing his own figures for 1377–81 with those of Smith-Bannister for the sixteenth and seventeenth centuries in *Names and Naming Patterns in England*[1] he is also able to chart the real history of these names across the cultural watersheds of Renaissance humanism and the Reformation. For the post-medieval centuries parish registers also offer excellent opportunities for comparative studies. See Chapter 10, for example, where Redmonds' analyses of forenames in Halifax and Leeds in the 1590s point to a sharp difference of religious sympathies between the two parishes.

These comparative studies furnish essential data for Redmonds' second method, one that is pioneered in this book, and which uses a distinctive christian name to trace the social networks of family kinship, patronage and influence. Redmonds has researched many families and communities in which distinctive names occur and the result is an impressive body of evidence which shows how a name can originate with a particular person or family, and how it can spread within and beyond the family through the social influence of its individual members, parents and godparents especially. It becomes abundantly clear that some names assumed to be generally popular were actually peculiar to certain families and their localities.

Studies of this kind depend on having reliable data on names, such as statistical profiles of the name-stock at different times and places and accurate histories of individual names. However, none of the standard dictionaries of christian names fulfil these requirements, and the few general histories that have been

written are insubstantial and extremely variable in the quality of their information. Fortunately recent publications like Cecily Clark's *Words, Names and History*[2],
Scott Smith-Bannister's *Names and Naming Patterns* and the present work are
beginning to provide the kinds of data and analyses that historians need.

Christian Names in Local and Family History is original, scholarly and readable,
and is the first general history of christian names that can be thoroughly recom-
mended to ordinary readers and specialist historians alike. It represents a significant advance in knowledge and methodology, correcting many errors and false
assumptions and revealing much that has lain hidden about the history of
English christian names. Historians will find in it new sources of information
and inspiration. There is still much to be learned about and from this fascinating
subject.

Peter McClure
University of Hull

---

1   See *Select Bibliography* for details.
2   Peter Jackson (ed.), *Words, Names and History: Selected Writings of Cecily Clark*
    (Cambridge, 1995).

Introduction

We take it for granted that we each have a surname and one or more first names, and we are familiar with the conventions attached to them. The first time that I was made to think twice about the system was in East Africa, almost 40 years ago, when I was teaching in a multi-racial school near Nairobi and had a class register that contained names from Asia and Africa, as well as a wide variety of European countries. Strangely enough it was not the more foreign names, such as Mustansir Mamujee or Mwangi Kioi that proved most enlightening about our national custom, but Stephen Morris, a very English combination of first name and surname.

Stephen was an African boy, a gifted athlete and footballer who may have been given his name at a mission school. I remember discussing his prowess with a colleague soon after he came to us, and also our confusion when we discovered that whereas the boy had said to me that his name was Stephen Morris, he had called himself Morris Stephen to my fellow teacher. In the school at that time a boy could be addressed by his surname or by his first name, and we smiled at what we took to be our mistake.

Later though it emerged that the newcomer had simply failed to understand the different functions of the two names. At the school sports day, he was placed both first and second in a field event, having given Morris as his name in one round and Stephen in another. We realised that we ought to discuss with him the separate roles of christian name and surname. Teachers know from experience that you often begin to understand something fully only when you have to explain it to others and so it proved in this case. I found myself thinking much more about our English naming practices.

I soon realised how inaccurate the dictionaries can be when it comes to non-etymological matters and the stimulus to further research was the recognition that they were offering me information about my own first name that differed fundamentally from what I could find out about it in local records. It was a short step from that to checking the data offered on other names and the discovery that many of the entries were just as likely to be inaccurate. It became clear to me that few people had actually bothered to look closely into the frequency of names in earlier centuries, or into naming practices and related topics, but I did little about it for I could see how vast a subject it was and I had other priorities at the time.

For a number of years therefore I was content to introduce christian name topics into my lecture programmes and to write an occasional article on the subject. I hesitated to do more than that because most of the data I was collecting came from sources in Yorkshire and the adjoining counties and I had no picture of christian name use in other parts of England.

However, that changed with the publication of two very important books in the period 1997–2001 (details of both are in the *Select Bibliography*). The first of these was Carolyn Fenwick's *The Poll Taxes of 1377, 1379 and 1381*, a massive resource that presents us with very full information about both male and female first names at a key moment in English history. The second was Scott Smith-Bannister's *Names and Naming Patterns in England 1538–1700*, which includes nation-wide name counts from the mid-sixteenth century and deals also with the role of the godparents and their influence on name-giving. This had long been apparent to me in my own regional work but it was heartening to find that it was true more generally. I was also delighted to discover that the author had the same reservations about first name dictionaries that I have.

Of course two topics of real interest had still not been treated: that is the popularity of first names before 1538, and the influence that the godparents had on the frequency of individual names. These are subjects of enormous significance to historians and students of surnames and I have a direct interest in both. It seemed at last that there was a niche for the regional evidence that I had accumulated.

During our lives we are likely to find ourselves involved in the naming process, directly or indirectly, so it is hardly surprising that we are curious about names, particularly our own and those of our immediate family. When we stop and think about it we soon recognise that our surname is something we normally inherit from our parents, not a matter of choice. It advertises our relationship to them and places us securely within the family: in a wider context, it connects us with our kin and our ancestors, the living and the dead. On the other hand our first names, which are what identify us as individuals, are actually chosen for us, usually from a corpus of traditional names, the national name-stock.

In the past scholars have concentrated on the etymology and earliest linguistic history of those names, and the fruits of their research are the most reliable material in our best dictionaries. Family historians may find these aspects of the subject on the fringe of their interests but the original meaning of a name is an integral part of its identity and one of its most precious assets. There have been times in our history, particularly periods of significant social development or religious crisis, when the meaning clearly influenced the name-giver's choice and we would be unwise to ignore such matters. Moreover the meaning reminds us, no matter how common the name might have become, that its history goes back over countless generations to the person who first used it, establishing a link between today's bearers of the name and the original name-giver.

When we read that John derives from the Hebrew 'Johanan', which is interpreted as 'God is gracious', those words tell us that John came into being many centuries ago, perhaps as a spontaneous expression of joy and gratitude at the gift of a new life. The etymology takes our interest in family history back into the distant past, far beyond what is possible using just the surname: if we are fortunate our surnames can help us to identify an ancestor in the Middle Ages, whereas our first names give us a closer connection with thousands of our fellow human beings, right through the ages and across the world.

Of course the Hebrew language that gave us John is just one of the sources of our first names. Others have origins in Latin, Greek, Gaelic and the Germanic languages; and the Germanic names may have come down to us through Old English or less directly via Norman French. What they all have in common though are their roots in the everyday vocabulary of our ancestors; they derive from ordinary words with uncomplicated meanings. Nevertheless we do not understand names such as Richard, Henry or Robert when we first hear them; we have to learn that each of them has a Germanic origin and is typically made up of two elements, words like 'haim' meaning 'home' and 'ric' meaning 'power', or 'hrod' meaning 'fame' and 'berht' meaning 'bright'. We get some idea of how old such names are when we read that they were no longer clearly understood by scholars at the beginning of the ninth century.

But what also demands our attention is the history of such names once the etymology had been forgotten, for they were subject to new practices and came to acquire new layers of meaning, both within the family and society more generally. For that reason we are interested in the popularity of first names both regionally and chronologically as well as in the motives of the name-givers. Above all we need to understand what lies behind the introduction of a new name or the revival of an old one, and all the circumstances surrounding its use. A first name can tell us something about an individual's or a family's place of origin, whether in some part of the British Isles or other parts of the world, and it can also offer us an insight into networks of families and wider communities, even into aspects of our national history.

It is here, unfortunately, that most reference works have let us down. The opinions they express about when and why particular names were introduced, or how frequent a name may have been in the past, are quite likely to be wrong, based more on impression than on accurate observation and statistical data. The implications behind significant regional and chronological differences are seldom investigated. When such opinions are not challenged they are eventually accepted as facts, and so reappear in every new book on the subject, almost defying us to think otherwise. The lesson for family historians is clear; unsupported statements about even the most commonplace of first names should always be treated with caution, and the evidence should be checked at both the local and personal level wherever possible.

For those who are actively involved in local and family history the few details contained in a dictionary are merely the starting point, and the need for further information increases once we recognise that names have patterns of decline and popularity, and that these reflect changing customs within our society. We quickly understand the potential that our first names have to throw light on past communities, helping us to identify influential individuals, reconstruct sibling groups, and trace more distant family connections. This is a field in which there are new discoveries still to be made and much new ground to be broken – some of it in areas which do not demand specialist linguistic skills. In fact few people are better placed than family historians to become more actively involved in those areas of first name studies, and they will be among the main beneficiaries as more information is made available.

We soon learn that while a name's etymology may be straightforward enough it is much more difficult to catch its wider associations, for the motives behind its use may differ from family to family and from region to region, and they have differed also from one generation to another. For that reason it is the breaks with tradition which can be of particular interest, for they alert us to changes that have taken place within our communities and to the role played in those changes by individuals or groups of individuals. Once we have discovered just when a name fell out of use, or when it was introduced, we have a new insight into the past and a valuable tool that adds a fresh dimension to family and local history.

For several hundred years it was usual in England to call that first name a 'Christian' name, but increasingly there has been a move towards avoiding the word in this context and writers now use terms such as given names, forenames, first names and even baptismal names, largely because modern society embraces many diverse ethnic groups and religions. While I occasionally talk of 'first' names in this present book, I feel no need to avoid the word 'christian' since so much of what is being said concerns name-giving in an essentially Christian context. I distinguish between Christian with a capital 'C', which can be taken to imply a name from a Christian source, particularly the Bible, and the use of 'christian' which can be related more narrowly to the act of christening.

Another term, 'personal names', has long been in use among scholars for names that had been coined in non-Christian traditions and were borne by individuals who either had no surname at all or merely a temporary second name. The term will be used here for names of that kind that survived into more recent centuries, influencing the development of certain types of surname and Tudor naming practices.

The overall aim of the book will be to emphasise the importance of building up a picture of how individual names have fared in the last seven or eight hundred years, even some of those we consider to be commonplace. Topics touched upon will include the social status and precise gender associations of first names, their pet forms and diminutives and their fluctuations in popularity. The material is based on two major research projects, the first an investigation into the history and frequency of first names in the English poll tax returns of 1377–81.

In fact the small number of names in those lists was the culmination of a trend going back to c.1200, and thirteenth-century sources make it clear how many names dropped out of fashion in that period. No doubt that was emphasised as the population declined, especially after the Black Death in 1348–49. It was the period in which many surnames stabilised and English finally emerged as the national language. Since first names were part of those developments, it will be important to discover all we can about their use and the ways in which they influenced surname origins.

The second major theme has to do with naming practices in the northern counties, concentrating on Tudor and Stuart England within the wider chronological context. At the heart of this investigation are the detailed histories of individual first names, selected to illustrate how and when new names entered the name-stock and the influence that individuals and godparents had on naming practices. The two topics are closely interwoven and I believe that the findings will oblige us to redefine what we understand by 'fashion' in name-giving outside the modern period, as well as what we mean when we say a particular name was 'popular' or 'rare'. The findings will also encourage us to look more closely at the significant role of the name-givers and relate that to other social phenomena, particularly in the Tudor and Stuart periods. It will emerge that many more names than we might have imagined have something distinctive in their history.

This is not a book that sets out solely to instruct family historians, but it is my hope that they will find some practical value in it. With that in mind I have tried to provide information about the types of sources that can be used, and to demonstrate the methods employed when investigating first names and the surnames derived from them. Most references are given in notes at the end of each chapter, but there is also a *Select Bibliography* of the most important sources. These are normally referred to in the text by author only.

I particularly wish to promote the idea that each first name, no matter how popular it might be or have been, goes back over the centuries to the first time that it was used. In this sense all first names have a 'pedigree' and a progenitor, and the etymology and early history then become an essential part of our understanding of the name. The influence these matters have had is apparent not just on surname origins, but also on genealogical connections and on the family and society more generally.

Acknowledgements

I was called George after my uncle, who lost his life at the battle of Loos in the Great War. The discussions I had with my father about the name, and about his relationship with this favourite brother, taught me a great deal about the role of first names in family history, and even more about meaning as opposed to etymology. These were valuable lessons, but it was only long afterwards that I came to appreciate their worth.

Partly as a result of that, I have been collecting material on first names for more years than I care to admit to. Along the way I have benefited enormously from conversations with friends, colleagues and students – too many people, I fear, for me to list all their names. Nevertheless, it is that exchange of views that has fuelled my interest in the subject and stimulated my research, and I am pleased to acknowledge here the debt I owe them.

In more recent years I have lectured widely on different aspects of name studies, and one result of that has been a succession of fascinating letters from genealogists and family historians, who have generously shared with me the results of their own research. I have used some of that information in this book, trying wherever possible to credit the source. Unfortunately that is not always possible, so I am grateful now to have this opportunity of saying thank you to all those people who have written to me on the subject. I have valued that correspondence. I particularly wish to draw attention to the contributions of Margaret Barwick, Guy Hirst, Pauline Litton, Marion Moverley, Walter Norris, Rita Savage and Steven Wood. Each of them has done really valuable work on the history of first names in Yorkshire.

My greatest debt is undoubtedly to Peter McClure of Hull: I can think of nobody who is better informed about first names during that transitional period after the Norman Conquest. His meticulously argued articles are ground-breaking pieces of research, not to be measured in terms of their length. They are a source of inspiration and have influenced me greatly. The truth is, though, that Peter's published work represents only a part of the knowledge that he has accumulated, and I have benefited enormously from the conversations we have had on all aspects of name studies. I value too the comments he made on the first draft of this book, not just for steering me away from a few glaring errors, but for many thoughtful and perceptive contributions that cannot easily be recognised in footnotes.

I should also like to thank the editorial staff of the National Archives. In particular, I am grateful to Jane Crompton and Sheila Knight, who read the first manuscript and somehow contrived to find enough in it to go ahead with the project. To Sheila Knight, who has influenced and improved the text in many ways, and to Diana Shelley, who did the final editing, I owe my special thanks.

I delayed writing this book for years, for new material was constantly coming to light, moderating my views on the different topics involved. I wanted everything to be in place before going ahead with the actual writing. Almost inevitably, therefore, I was made aware of a significant new publication just as the text was being completed. When Steven Archer produced his CD-ROM *The British 19th Century Surname Atlas*[1], he supplemented it with data about the frequency of first names in 1881, displaying the information on maps, either by county or poor law union. It is a superb achievement, and a major contribution to the subject. It opens up possibilities that I am unable to pursue at present, but I am delighted that Steven has allowed us to use some of his maps as illustrations. His work should inspire family historians in particular to reassess their views on first names.

Finally, I cannot let this occasion pass without recognising the contribution that my wife Ann-marie has made to this book, especially as she claims to have no particular interest in its subject matter. I am no computer expert, and I often manage to create problems for myself doing allegedly simple things. To my enormous relief she has been able to recover texts that had disappeared, unfreeze one especially reluctant chapter, and generally preserve my sanity. Our relationship appears to have survived the experience.

---

1 See *Select Bibliography* for details.

CHAPTER ONE

A Transitional Period

This investigation into our traditional christian names will concentrate on the years between 1200 and 1400. This was the 'watershed' period in the history of first names in England, a time during which naming practices changed fundamentally and the bulk of our surnames stabilised. As many surnames derive from first names it is clearly important to discover all we can about the changing customs. At the heart of this investigation will be evidence about the names that were falling out of general favour, supported by evidence from the poll tax returns of 1377–81.

The fundamental change in naming practices referred to above was effectively complete by 1379 and it has been written about so often that scholars more or less take it for granted. Even so it will be useful to say something here about the earlier period and examine what was happening to individual names, for it was a significant development in our history, and marked a dividing line between name-giving practices in two quite different eras. The names introduced by the Normans are at the heart of the investigation but the division is not simply between their names and those used by our English ancestors, even though few Old English names survived beyond 1400. Nor can it be said that the names commonly used after 1400 were simply those brought here by the Normans for that would be to ignore the significant contribution made to our national name-stock during the religious revival of the twelfth century.

What made the period from 1200 to 1400 special in name-giving history was the fact that so many names of all kinds dropped almost entirely out of common use and just a small percentage survived, a few rising to extreme levels of popularity. Many of those were names such as Richard, Robert, Henry and William which had indeed been introduced to England by the Normans, but others were truly Christian names, inspired by the scriptures and a renewed interest in the saints. These included John, Thomas and Peter for boys, and Agnes, Elizabeth,

Margaret and Katherine for girls. We may not be able to explain just why a few names came to be so dominant but we can certainly say something about the impact this had on other naming practices.

Early personal names: the impact of the Norman Conquest

The field of personal name studies is extensive, covering all the British Isles and more than 2,000 years of history, with a few of the names going back to a Celtic or Roman origin. If we concern ourselves just with England we still have to come to terms with the names of a succession of invaders, starting with the Anglo-Saxons but taking into account Danes, Irish-Norse, Normans, Bretons and Flemings; many of these groups were Germanic in origin but each had significant national characteristics. Their names can be as foreign-sounding as those we encounter now on our travels abroad, for example, Osketel, Archbishop of York in 956, and Cuthred, King of Wessex in 752, succeeded by Sigeberht and Cynewulf. Women's names may be mentioned less frequently but sound just as alien, e.g. Eormenbeorg, a lady of the Kentish royal house, and Mildburg, her daughter, who founded a monastery at Much Wenlock in the late seventh century.[1]

Some names from that period are better known – Offa, for example – especially if we have walked the old boundary between the lands he claimed and those claimed by the British. We may also remember others from our schooldays, Cnut perhaps, defying the waves, and Godwine, father of Harold. Even so such names were outside our experience when we first heard them and they still have a foreign ring to them, evoking distant lands and a distant past. Just occasionally there are names from that same pre-Norman Conquest period which are genuinely familiar to us, either because they never fell out of use, like Edward and Edmund, or because they have been revived in more recent times. Alfred and Harold, for example, may sound old-fashioned in the twenty-first century but they became popular in the nineteenth century and remained prominent into the 1920s.[2]

Even lists of personal names from the late twelfth century, heavily influenced by the Normans, contain many that remind us of that earlier history. In a pipe roll[3] of 1191, for instance, we have Ulf, Wulfric, Uchtred and Suein alongside William, Walter and Alan, a fascinating mingling of the familiar and the unknown; a corpus of names in the midst of change. We owe that change to the Normans who introduced the conquered English to a whole new range of modified French and Scandinavian forms.[4] From the Normans came Henry, Richard, Hamond, Otes and Turstin, and from their allies in Flanders and Brittany such names as Alan, Brian, Tankard and Baldwin. Before long these began to displace the Old English and Scandinavian names, consigning them to obscurity, if not always to extinction.

There were many more additions in the twelfth century, as the influence of the Church in Western Europe increased. That revival is evident to us in the foundations of great abbeys and the dramatic story of the ill-fated Crusades, but it was responsible also for a significant addition to the existing pool of English and Norman first names. Many came from the Bible, extending the linguistic origins of our everyday names to Hebrew and Greek. The names of saints, not all of them from the Bible, introduced us to such names as Michael, Joseph, Paul, Eve, Sara and Denise. Their legacy is in the abundance of surnames to which they gave rise, a development that P. H. Reaney drew our attention to in *The Origin of English Surnames*.

In fact the variety of names in late twelfth-century records is amazing; at no other time in our history, at least until the modern day, have so many been in use. That was soon to alter and by the mid-thirteenth century the total number of names was steadily declining. Moreover a relatively small percentage of these had begun to predominate and by 1350 the revolution was almost complete, with just a few names at the head of the frequency lists. The very full poll tax returns of 1377–81 prove that a new tradition in naming had been established, and it would last for centuries, continuing to have some impact on name-giving even today. John and William, Alice and Joan are just a few of a distinctive corpus of names that has survived in England for almost a thousand years.

Evidence from the poll tax returns

These rolls cover many English counties in great detail, making it possible to compile frequency tables for names of adult men and women in the period 1377–81. These inform us about naming practices a generation earlier and will be discussed in Chapter 3. They are invaluable in giving us statistical evidence to set against what is already available for the period from 1538 to the present day. Of course it is not just the frequently used names that are of interest, and an effort has been made to gather information about all those that were recorded, some of which defy identification. This evidence will undoubtedly throw light on the circumstances behind the origins of surnames, and the transition more generally from first name to by-name and surname. (By-name is the term we now use for those second names which had not finally stabilised, but which can look identical to inherited surnames.) Some dictionaries unfortunately make no distinction between the two terms, so it is worth remembering that the early examples they quote may have nothing to do with surviving surnames. In such cases the etymologies they offer are often quite irrelevant as far as the genealogist is concerned.

There is also positive evidence in the rolls about the pet forms and diminutives used by the clerks, more commonly for women's names. This topic will be dealt with in Chapter 2, and we shall see that some of our most cherished assumptions may be wrong. We assume, for example, that Maid Marion's real name was Mary, but can we be sure?

Finally, such broad-based statistics provide us with information about the less-common and rare first names, many of them survivors from before 1250, and we can use these to look more closely into our ancestors' spiritual networks in the fifteenth and early sixteenth centuries. They also identify the names that were missing from the records in 1377–81, either because they had fallen out of fashion, or had not yet come into fashion: this 'negative' evidence is vital to our understanding of changes in naming practices in that period.

Evidence from surnames

The value of such evidence emerges once we look more closely at the history of individual surnames. We can start with the East Anglian surname Cobbold, which derives from a personal name and became more widely known as the name of a firm of brewers. A good deal has already been written about Cobbold, for its history and distribution link it firmly with Suffolk. Guppy in *Homes of Family Names in Great Britain* identified it as a Suffolk surname over a century ago[5] and David Hey went further in *Family Names and Family History*, saying that Suffolk has always been its main 'home', although 'between 1327 and 1674 they (the Cobbolds) appear to have migrated from the north to the south of the county'.[6] The question Hey raises about a possible link between Cobbold and the rare Norfolk surname Cobble or Cobbell is of particular interest for it might explain what happened to the Cobbolds noted by McKinley for Norfolk in 1522–5.[7] McKinley's statistical evidence for the sixteenth and seventeenth centuries suggests that Cobbold was exclusively an East Anglian name, for it was unknown in many other counties at that time.[8] It is perhaps surprising to find that topic dealt with in his book on surnames in Oxfordshire rather than in his earlier book on East Anglia.[9]

At this point in the enquiry information about the personal name is needed to throw more light on the origin of the surname, and the negative evidence is immediately helpful. The fact that Cobbold as a first name is missing from the records in 1377–81, at least from those that have survived, points to a much earlier origin for the surname. This is reinforced by David Hey's observation in *Family Names* that five Cobbolds were listed in a Suffolk subsidy roll of 1327, all living near the Norfolk border. That tight-knit distribution supports his view that the families were probably related and shared a common progenitor. In other words all those who bear the name are likely to descend from just one Suffolk man with the personal name.

Fortunately our investigation need not end there, for the history of Anglo-Saxon personal names in East Anglia has been researched by a Swedish scholar, Dr B. Seltén.[10] He identified the Old English personal name as Cuthbeald or Cuthbald, but he found no reference to it in East Anglia earlier than 1219, when the land of 'Alani Cubald' was mentioned in a Norfolk land transfer. We would

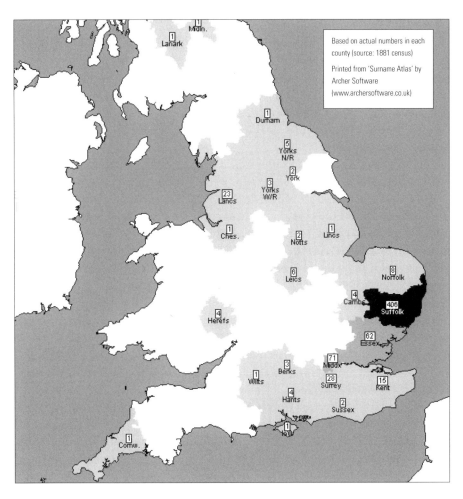

Based on actual numbers in each
county (source: 1881 census)

Printed from 'Surname Atlas' by
Archer Software
(www.archersoftware.co.uk)

1 **The surname Cobbold (656).** The Suffolk surname derives from an Old English personal name. Its main concentration in 1881 was in the Stow/Ipswich area. The spelling Cobbald (42) was much less common and occurred mostly in Norfolk.

describe 'Cubald' here as a by-name rather than a surname and his selection of later examples shows that it had a variety of spellings in Middle English. Among those he lists are Cutebald, Cubald and Cobald, which illustrate different stages in the surname's development. It is noticeable though that many of these were from Norfolk sources and it would be interesting to know if they had links with places near the border with Suffolk. Reaney and Wilson have just one direct reference to the personal name, Cotebaldus de Wigornia, recorded in a Dublin document that dates from before 1200, and several examples similar to those of Seltén dating from 1066, which include by-names. Only one of them is from Suffolk, John Cobald (1309).[11]

It would be possible to examine many other Old English names in a similar way but that is outside the scope of this present book: the story of Cobbold is intended to suggest how a family historian might approach the problem of his or her surname's history, if it appears to derive from a personal name. A brief list of such names, selected from the volumes of the English Surnames Series, indicates the scope there is for research on these lines, e.g. Thurkell, Ulf, Woolgar, Segrim, Edrich, Orm, Utting, Uchtred, Dolphin, Osmond, Cole, Hereward, Gamel, Kettle and Leverich.

Some of these almost certainly had a Scandinavian rather than an Anglo-Saxon origin and where personal names in this category are concerned the published books and articles of Gillian Fellows Jensen are extremely valuable. In her pioneering work she took the trouble to compile detailed lists of personal names, aimed at giving 'an impression of the nature and extent of Scandinavian nomenclature in a section of Eastern England', namely in Lincolnshire and Yorkshire.[12] Her material is drawn from a wider range of sources than Seltén's, taking place-name elements into account, but it has similar advantages, offering us a sequence of spellings from the Norman Conquest and even earlier. The author noted in her introductory chapter that 'the frequency of occurrence of these names diminishes rapidly after the first quarter of the thirteenth century', which suggests that most surnames based on such personal names have a very long history. As an example here we can discuss Auty and its variants, another personal name not recorded in 1377–81.

Guppy does not mention Auty in *Homes of Family Names* but I identified it as a prolific Dewsbury surname in *Yorkshire West Riding*[13] and David Hey's map of its distribution in 1842–6 shows two significant clusters in south-west Yorkshire and in west Lancashire.[14] The zone between these two concentrations includes many of the Lancashire towns which lie close to that part of Yorkshire where the name is common. We would of course expect a name with a Scandinavian origin to survive in that part of the country where Scandinavian influence was most marked, but the fact that there are two concentrations within that much wider area is significant. It highlights what the documentary evidence tells us, for the surname is found in the neighbourhood of Dewsbury from 1287 and in Lancashire from about the same period.[15] A single origin might therefore be unlikely but it should not be ruled out, for major landowners had estates in both counties at that time and families readily moved across the county boundary. In fact the de Lacy family had lands in all three counties where Auti has been recorded.

Gillian Fellows Jensen has about 40 references to the personal name starting with Auti, who witnessed a charter in about 1030 and 'Tochi filius Outi' in Domesday Book. The spellings vary but are commonly Outi and Auti, with an occasional Houti and Awty, and the great majority until about 1230 were located in Lincolnshire. Later though, if we count all the examples of the by-name, it is noticeable how many are found in and around Tickhill in the late thirteenth and early fourteenth centuries, and this small Yorkshire town is only a short distance from Lincolnshire. Auti is first recorded there in 1226 which suggests that the surname may have been hereditary for something like 800 years.

Rare and uncommon names, 1377–81

Old English names were still in use as late as around 1200 but survival beyond that point usually depended on special circumstances. That is certainly true of Edward, Edmund and Edith, the names of major personalities who were canonised and had cult status in the post-Conquest period. The stories of Edward the Confessor and Edmund the Martyr are well known but it is worth remembering that for a long time they were looked on as England's patron saints. Indeed they were 'depicted as two royal patrons of England' in the Wilton Diptych in the National Gallery.[16] Edith is less well known but she was the daughter of Edgar who became king of all England in 959; in her short life she was renowned for her humility and service to the poor. Her name, along with Edward and Edmund, was venerated in the Anglo-Norman period, and all three remained in use throughout the fourteenth century and into modern times.

A few other Old English names were recorded as christian names in 1377–81, among them Aylward (Norfolk), Dunstan (Lincs.) and Gladwin (Somerset), and all these had previously given rise to surnames, most of them probably in the 1200s. They were certainly not common in 1377–81 and were used only rarely afterwards. Equally uncommon were the women's names Gundred (Suffolk), Mildred (Leics.) and Ethelburgh (Essex), although Mildred never quite fell out of use and enjoyed a measure of popularity in the nineteenth and twentieth centuries.[17] It is likely also to be the source of the surname Mildred and possibly even of Milden, derived by Reaney from another Old English name, Mildhun.[18] The return for the Leicestershire village of Cold Overton in 1381 contains the names Milden Watson, Mildred Sheperd and Mildred Planys, and in this context it seems possible that Milden was a pet form of Mildred.

Rather more numerous in 1377–81 were the two women's names Gun(n)ild and Etheldred. The former derived from a Scandinavian personal name, judged by Reaney and Wilson in English Surnames to be the source of the surname Gunnell, and it was well established in Surrey in 1381. It was also found as Gonild and Gun(n)eld in the south-western counties of Somerset and Gloucestershire. Etheldred on the other hand was an East Anglian name in that period, found in the three counties of Norfolk, Suffolk and Essex. It was especially prominent in 1381 in Mildenhall where four women bore the name. The inspiration in this case was probably Queen Etheldred who founded the abbey of Ely and is thought to have been born in Suffolk: scenes from her life are carved on the capitals in the lantern tower of Ely cathedral. I have no evidence of a surname derived from Etheldred but Audrey was the vernacular form, and the fair dedicated to her was known as either St Etheldred's or St Audrey's Fair. The necklaces sold there are said to have been of such poor quality that St Audrey was soon corrupted to 'tawdry'.

A frequent first element in Germanic names was 'Guda', the word for 'god', and a surprising number of these were still in use in 1377–81. Godard, found in Kent, was almost certainly Norman and it was still in use in Sussex in Elizabeth's reign. However, some of the others may have survived from before the Conquest, and are occasionally found in 'clusters', e.g. Godyth (Lancashire), Godlef (Sussex) and Godewyn (Norfolk). In the small village of Weeton near Lancaster, for example, three women bore the name Godyth in 1379, and in Lonsdale the names Goditha de Grenes and Thomas Godithson show how the surname Goodison could have originated. The surname Good must often be from a short-ened form of one of these names since 'Goda' and 'Gode' had survived in many counties, usually as women's names. In Ashford (Derbyshire) William Elys had two servants in 1381, one called Gode and the other Goda.

Godelin(a) is recorded quite frequently as a woman's name in the Kent poll tax returns, especially in the Cinque Ports (originally Sandwich, Dover, Hythe, Romney and Hastings in Sussex). Reaney's two earlier examples are Godelina, in Hampshire (1148) and Simon filius Godelini in Kent (1212), the latter apparently a man's name. Godelena is also found in Essex in 1381, another coastal county, so there is a strong possibility that these were from across the Channel and not Old English. The name was certainly known on the Continent. Godfrey too had a Continental origin and several of those recorded in fourteenth-century sources were described as 'de Brabant' or 'ducheman'.

Another first element which meant 'god' is 'Os' found in three more Germanic names recorded in the poll tax, Osbert, Oswald and Osborn. Oswald is rare, found once in Northamptonshire, but not at all in the northern counties where St Oswald was especially popular. Osborn is also infrequent, the few examples not falling into any significant pattern. However there is some evidence that it could be confused with Osbert, i.e. 'god bright', a more common name used by both the Anglo-Saxons and the Normans.[19] According to Withycombe it occurred principally in Northumbria in the Old English period[20] but Seltén thought that most of his East Anglian examples probably referred to Normans. In fact none of his spellings there points to a native origin.[21] Other Osberts were recorded in several counties across southern England, from Sussex on the south coast as far north as Shropshire and Leicestershire. One group in Great Leighs in Essex in 1381 is of particular interest, for it indicates how Osbert might have given rise to two distinct surnames: Osebertus Bukstrat is followed in the list by his son Thomas Osebert and just a few places lower down is a man called James Osekyn. This diminutive had been recorded even earlier in London and Essex and is a possible source of the surname Hoskins.[22] Another survivor is Anselm and it is worth closer investigation.

Anselm

This is a name with a Germanic origin which is said to mean 'god helmet', but there is no record of it in England before the Norman Conquest and it is first recorded here in 1093 when a monk called Anselm was made Archbishop of Canterbury. The see had been vacant for several years, since the death of Archbishop Lanfranc, and it was this man who was indirectly responsible for Anselm's appointment. In fact Anselm was not a Norman but had been born at Aosta in Lombardy in 1033, of wealthy parents. He moved first to Burgundy with his mother's family and was then attracted to Normandy by the reputation of Lanfranc in about 1060, becoming a monk in the monastery at Bec where he made a name for himself as a scholar.

Lanfranc was later made Archbishop of Canterbury and when he died in 1089 Anselm was seen by many as his natural successor. He was a churchman not a politician and is said to have been reluctant to take the office, but the English clergy left him with little choice. Not surprisingly he soon found himself involved in a series of disputes with both William II and Henry I, and he was twice exiled. Soon after Anselm's death, in 1109, there were attempts to have him canonised, but the cult was initially overshadowed by that of Becket. However, it benefited from a revival of interest in the fourteenth century and that may have helped the name to survive.[23]

Examples of Anselm have been recorded from the twelfth century and Reaney and Wilson's evidence in *English Surnames* shows that it was interchangeable in that period with Ansell. They quote examples of both in the thirteenth century, notably in East Anglia where it gave rise to the surname Ancell. McKinley's work shows that Ancell was a numerous surname there in the sixteenth century and that Surrey was another stronghold in the seventeenth century.[24] As a first name it continued to be used at least up to the end of the fourteenth century and occurs as Ansel at North Tuddenham in Norfolk in 1379. The diminutive form Ancelin is used by two families at Gillingham in Dorset in 1379. Anselm itself is found at Ibstock in Leicestershire and as far north as Northumberland in 1377, but the only significant cluster is in Lincolnshire, focused on Somercotes. It occurs there three times and may have survived much later since 'Anselmo filio Anselmi' is one of those listed in 1377.

Two centuries later Anselm was not uncommon as a first name in that part of Gloucestershire that lies close to the Severn, between Gloucester itself and Stroud. It was particularly well established in the early seventeenth century in Elmore and Whitstone, among families with the surnames Hanman, Bullock, Blanche and Bailey. In King's Stanley a weaver called Anselme Dangerfild had a servant with the same name, Ansellm Bennett, and a neighbour called Ansellm Newman who was a 'tucker' or cloth-fuller.[25] This was a late and very localised popularity, and we do not know whether the name had survived from the Middle

Ages or been revived at a later date. In either case it raises important questions, for it is just one illustration of a more widespread phenomenon.

~

By the fourteenth century many of the names associated with the Normans and their predecessors were no longer in use. They had, however, survived long enough to influence the development of surnames, and the accounts of Cobbold and Auty show that this aspect of their history can be important to family historians. Moreover, a few of those early names had declined but not disappeared completely and there is evidence to suggest that they may have remained in local use well into the Tudor period, possibly confined to one family or small community. Such names would obviously be of interest to genealogists and the circumstances behind their survival and reintroduction will be discussed later. The phenomenon is more noticeable where men's names are concerned but it affected some women's names too, although in their case the family connections are usually less obvious.

Notes

1   The spellings of such personal names differ from one source to another but these references are taken from Sir Frank Stenton's *Anglo-Saxon England* (Oxford, 1971).
2   L. A. Dunkling, *First Names First* (London, 1977). This book contains statistical evidence on the frequency of first names throughout the English-speaking world for the period 1850–1975.
3   Pipe rolls were the annual accounts of crown revenues sent to the Exchequer. They were rolled around rods or 'pipes' for storage.
4   We tend to think of Henry, Robert, Richard and many more as 'French' but they were of course names popular among the Germanic Franks.
5   H. B. Guppy, *Homes of Family Names in Great Britain* (London, 1890).
6   D. Hey, *Family Names and Family History* (London, 2000).
7   R. A. McKinley, *Norfolk and Suffolk in the Middle Ages*, English Surnames Series (Chichester, 1975).
8   The evidence here is confined to Buckinghamshire, Dorset, Norfolk, Oxfordshire, Staffordshire, Suffolk, Surrey, Sussex and Wiltshire but in his volume on Lancashire McKinley noted its absence there also.
9   R. A. McKinley, *The Surnames of Oxfordshire*, English Surnames Series (London, 1977).
10   B. Seltén, *The Anglo-Saxon Heritage in Middle English Personal Names: East Anglia, 1100–1399* (Lund, 1979).
11   P. H. Reaney and R. M. Wilson, *A Dictionary of English Surnames*, revised edn (Oxford, 1997).
12   G. F. Jensen, *Scandinavian Personal Names in Lincolnshire and Yorkshire* (Copenhagen, 1968).
13   G. Redmonds, *Yorkshire West Riding*, English Surnames Series (Chichester, 1973).
14   D. Hey, *Family Names*, p. 206.

15 For example, 1287 Richard Outay of Thornhill, in W. Brown (ed.), *Yorkshire Inquisitions*, Yorkshire Archaeological Society, Record Series XXIII (1898). For Lancashire see R. A. McKinley, *The Surnames of Lancashire*, ESS (London, 1981).

16 D. Farmer, *The Oxford Dictionary of Saints*, 3rd edn (Oxford, 1996).

17 L. A. Dunkling, *First Names First*, p. 190.

18 P. H. Reaney and R. M. Wilson, *English Surnames*, p. 309.

19 See, for example, Seltén, *Anglo Saxon Heritage*, p. 126. In 1381, in Great Leighs in Essex, the two names are found side by side, but that cannot be taken as evidence of confusion. The choices may even have been a deliberate attempt to indicate relationship.

20 E. G. Withycombe, *The Oxford Dictionary of English Christian Names*, 3rd edn (Oxford, 1977).

21 B. Seltén, *Anglo-Saxon Heritage*.

22 P. H. Reaney and R. M. Wilson, *English Surnames*, p. 239.

23 D. Farmer, *Dictionary of Saints*, p. 23.

24 R. A. McKinley, *The Surnames of Oxfordshire*, English Surnames Series (London, 1977), pp. 238–43.

25 J. Smith (ed.), *Men and Armour for Gloucestershire in 1608* (1902 and Gloucester, 1980).

CHAPTER TWO

Tom, Dick and Harry

*I*t was in the thirteenth and fourteenth centuries that most English surnames became hereditary. These served to identify families within the local community and also authenticated an individual's claim to ownership or tenure of land. It was a period of change, as by-names gave way to more permanent surnames, and we can look back on what happened as a major revolution in naming practices. Among the new surnames thus created were thousands that had their origins in the changing stock of first names, and this chapter looks at some of the developments in those years that are of particular interest to family historians.

Identifying first names from Latin, vernacular, and diminutive forms

One of the major problems that researchers face in this subject is the variety of ways in which christian names were formerly presented in the records. It means that each name can effectively have several different spellings, including the vernacular and latinised versions. To these must be added the popular short forms and diminutives, some of which could also be latinised on occasion. Hugh, for example, would usually be recorded as 'Hugo', with 'Hugonis' as the genitive; typical short forms and diminutives included 'Hud' and 'Hul', 'Huchon', 'Hewett' and 'Hewlett'. Nor can we always be sure just how some of the names would have been pronounced, especially a short form such as 'Gil' which might be for Gillian (Julian) or Gilbert. Ironically, because surnames were not latinised, they provide us with much of our information about the vernacular forms of first names in this period.

For the most part the Latin forms were produced by adding –*a* to a female name and –*us* to a male name and these were then declined like ordinary nouns.[1] 'Willelmus', 'Ricardus', 'Margareta' and 'Alicia' are immediately recognisable as

William, Richard, Margaret and Alice, and their advantage is that they clearly identified the sex of the name-bearer. It is essential to remember though that these were scribal conventions and not in everyday use. In fact such conventions are helpful to researchers who work on early documents, for many names were formerly used for either boys or girls. This was true of Richard, Robert and Laurence and I have even come across one 'Briana'. We expect to find 'Johanna' for Joan, the feminine version of John, but need to be careful with Philip, Thomas and Nicholas which were also used for girls. Julian and Christian are a greater danger for they were almost always feminine, as was Douglas in the seventeenth and eighteenth centuries. The following references to 'Philip', some of them latinised and some in the vernacular, will illustrate the point.

Philip – a girl's name

In the poll tax returns the Latin ending clearly identifies Philippa Prodeman of Halstead in Essex and Phelippa Belle of Blakeney in Norfolk as women but, where the vernacular was preferred, we need additional evidence if we are to be sure of the person's sex. There is no problem in a Nottinghamshire will of 1532, where the testator referred to Fillipe Markham of Hawton as 'my doughter', nor in the marriage entry in 1620 of Edward Rossendall and Felope Gaskin of York, but there could be confusion when unfamiliar diminutives were used. It is fortunate therefore that Philot Clark of Northallerton was said to be a spinster in 1641 and Philot Lynas a widow, since there is nothing otherwise to tell us that they were women.[2]

The surnames Philot and Philpot are correctly said in dictionaries to derive from diminutives of Philip but few writers draw attention to the fact that these diminutives were often feminine.[3] Philipot Schikyn of Wadworth in south Yorkshire had a husband called John in 1379, an example that has clear implications for the surname Philpot. This still has a restricted distribution and was said by Guppy in *Homes of Family Names* to be characteristic of just three counties, Kent, Wiltshire and Shropshire. It has also been suggested that 'Pot', as a short form of Philipot, was a possible source of the surnames Pott, Pottell and Potkins, and if that is so these too are unlikely to have numerous origins.

Difficult Latin forms

Not all the Latin forms of men's names ended in –*us*. John and Andrew were 'Johannes' and 'Andreas' whilst Adam and Thomas were unchanged but had the genitive forms 'Ade' and 'Thome'. Unfortunately there are some Latin spellings which bear little resemblance to the English names and these have to be learnt. 'Radulfus' for Ralph is difficult enough but it is even further from the medieval name which was written Rawfe and could be pronounced 'Raw', the 'f' silent.

This was responsible for the surnames Rawes and Rawson and the popular diminutive Rawlin gave rise to Rawlinson. There could be problems too with Denis, James, Geoffrey and Giles, usually recorded as 'Dionisius', 'Jacobus', 'Galfridus' and 'Egidius'. Giles is not thought of now as a female name so the occasional 'Egidia' reminds us how useful the Latin inflection can be. 'Dionisius' and 'Dionisia', our modern Denis and Denise, were almost equally popular in the fourteenth century and either of them might have given rise to the surnames Denison and Dennison. However, it was Dionisia of Linthwaite who was responsible for Dyson, via the short form 'Di', and this, together with frequent late spellings such as 'Dionis', points to possible alternative pronunciations.4 The diminutive Diot produced the unfortunate combination Diot Coke in 1379.

Quite often it is the similarity between a present-day name and its latinised spelling that can be misleading, for the modern pronunciation may have been influenced quite recently by an equivalent name introduced here from the Continent. We are probably aware of this in the case of Philippa, used only from the nineteenth century, but Anna, Eva and Cecilia are less obvious examples. These modern names are identical with the early Latin forms but the final 'a' would not have been pronounced in the past and the names were more probably Anne, Eve and Cecile in the vernacular. Evot and Sissot were common diminutives of Eve and Cecile but Annot, as we shall see, more probably stood for Agnes.

In other cases a name may have been revived in relatively recent times and given what has been called a 'learned' spelling, one that is far removed from the medieval pronunciation. That is true of Matilda and Agatha which are familiar to us now only in these learned forms. The evidence for their earlier pronunciation is in such vernacular spellings as Mald or Maud and Matill for Matilda, and Agace or Agass for Agatha. Surnames such as Mattleson and Agass confirm that, just as the surname Parnell reminds us of the colloquial pronunciation of Petronilla.

There are male names also where the modern pronunciation has moved much closer to the learned version and in these cases we are in danger of not recognising the vernacular form at all. Reginald may be readily identified as Reynold but Nigel is much more difficult: it is based on the latinised spelling 'Nigellus' and is said to have been revived by Sir Walter Scott in the nineteenth century. Its former pronunciation is apparent in the vernacular form Nele, responsible for the surname Neale, and in Nell, which is sometimes the origin of Nelson. Sander and Saunder, which survive in surnames such as Sanders and Saunderson, are shortened forms of Alisander or Alisaunder, typical medieval pronunciations of Alexander.

Because Latin was the language of legal documents it is quite rare to find first names written in the vernacular in earlier centuries but they occur often enough for us to have an insight into how they might have been pronounced. The following are examples from fourteenth-century wills and most of them can be readily recognised: Esteven (Stephen), Phillipe (f), Mauld (Matilda), Elyn, Symond,

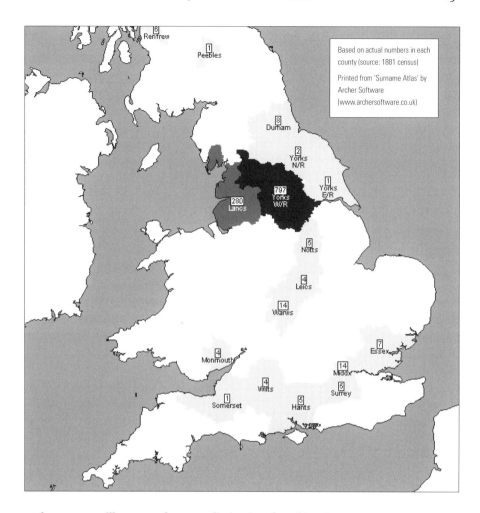

Based on actual numbers in each county (source: 1881 census)

Printed from 'Surname Atlas' by Archer Software (www.archersoftware.co.uk)

2 The surname Tillotson (1158) From a diminutive of Matilda. The progenitor was Tillot de Northwod, who lived in Cowling in 1379, just on the Yorkshire side of the border with Lancashire. The surname's main concentration in 1881 was in a triangle formed by Skipton, Burnley and Bradford.

Robard, Wauter and Piers (Peter). Less obvious are short forms such as Bette, which may have been for Beatrice or Elizabeth (often written Elizabet); Custe, for Custance or Constance; and Munde, possibly for Edmund. It can be very difficult to identify diminutives such as Abelota, Elsete, Levota and Saukin, all found in 1377–81, but several of them gave rise to distinctive surnames, such as Ablett and Sawkins. Tillot, as a diminutive of Till, and probably from Matilda, is recorded in several counties but all the Tillotsons appear to descend from a Yorkshire lady named as Tillot de Northwod (1379).[5]

More readily recognised are Symkyn, Watkyn, Huchoun (Hugh), Paulyn (m) and Beton (Beatrice); Tibot and Ibot were common for Isabel, and Jonett and Janett became frequent for Joan in the fifteenth century. Each name might have several short forms and diminutives and they were of many different types, such as 'Col' for Nicholas, 'Gib' for Gilbert, 'Gep' for Geoffrey, 'Nalle' for Alice and 'Gel' for Gerard. A few such pet forms could be used for more than one name, so that 'Nel' was sometimes for Ellis (m) and sometimes for Ellen.

This is an extremely complicated subject, as one or two recent studies have made clear,[6] but it is an area of first name history where there are still many discoveries to be made and these will undoubtedly throw new light on surname origins. Here I am concerned only with introducing the topic to those who have previously given it little thought, and there are many more examples in Reaney's *The Origin of English Surnames.*[7] We are all familiar with such names in everyday English: typical of the examples we seldom question are the traditional 'Molly' and 'Polly' for Mary, 'Peggy' for Margaret, 'Ned' for Edward and the modern 'Tel' for Terry.

Tom, Dick and Harry

The term 'pet form' may not be familiar to everybody but it describes what we get when a name such as Thomas is shortened to Tom, a practice that we know well and still employ. The pet forms of the male names that were in frequent use in the Middle Ages are possibly more familiar to us than those for the common female names, but even so it is easy to forget how popular such abbreviations once were, not just to describe friends and family members, but right through the language. There are more than 20 references listed under 'Tom' in *Brewer's Dictionary of Phrase and Fable*, ranging from Tom-cat and Tom Thumb to Tom Fool and Tom Noodle, some that we know well and others that we have forgotten.[8] Brewer's explanation informs us that Tom was 'of the ordinary sort', the 'honest dullard', and these qualities are at the heart of most of his interpretations. Tom Tiller, for example, was 'a hen-pecked husband' and Tom the piper's son 'a poor, stupid thief'. Tom, Dick and Harry were 'persons of no note'.

Jack merited even more entries than Tom and was credited by Brewer with a wider range of meanings, some of them directly contrasted with those suggested for Tom, such as his explanation of the 'Jack' in Jackdaw. This was, he said, 'pert, dexterous and thieving', sharper qualities than those attributed to 'the thick-headed, ponderous, male Tom-cat'. In fact 'Jackdaw' is a reminder of how our ancestors formerly personified many of the birds that they would have seen round their houses, including Tom-tit, Jenny-wren, Dicky-bird, the Robin and the Magpie. The list makes it clear that practices other than abbreviation affected our ancestors' first names. Mag is a pet form of Margaret but it has lost the consonant 'r' in the process and Jack is usually for John. The others in that group are diminutives based on pet forms, that is Dicky, Robin and Jenny (Jane). I am

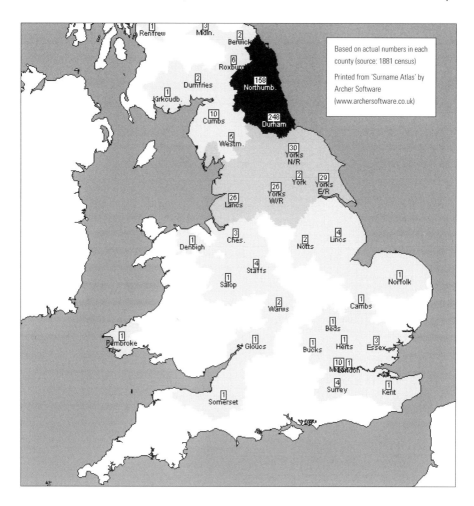

Based on actual numbers in each county (source: 1881 census)

Printed from 'Surname Atlas' by Archer Software (www.archersoftware.co.uk)

3 The first name Robson (597) The distribution of Robson as a first name reflects its distribution as a surname. That is to say it was most popular in Durham (248) and Northumberland (158). Robson Green the actor is from that area.

uncertain just when the final –y became popular but it may have been after most surnames had stabilised as it appears to have had little impact on their development in England. Ritchie and Robbie seem always to be Scottish names and these stabilised rather later.

Even in this very brief introduction to the topic it will have emerged that not all the vernacular forms of our ancestors' first names are immediately recognisable. I cannot imagine that anybody who reads this will need to be told that Dick is for Richard, and yet this involves a change in the initial consonant and the substitution of 'ck' for 'ch'. The latter came about because Richard and Rickard were parallel forms in the Middle Ages, an alternative reflected in the surnames that derive from them. However, the change from Rick to Dick is less easily explained, although it was characteristic of other male names beginning with 'R'. A further change to initial 'H' gave Hick and when we consider that these pet forms also had diminutives it is clear how a common first name could develop a wide range of alternatives, with far-reaching effects on by-names and surnames.[9]

That is obvious if we take a closer look at Robert. We can see immediately how this might give rise to Roberts and Robertson and how the pet form would lead to Robb(s) and Robson and the diminutives to Robbins, Robinson and Robbie. Rhyming forms would produce Dobbs, Dobbin, Dobbinson, Hobbs, Hobson, Hopkins and Hopkinson. Similarly the pet form 'Dodge' for Roger gave rise directly to the surnames Dodge and Dodgson, Hodge and Hodgson, and the diminutives produced Hodgett, Hodgkin and Hodgkinson. Such developments were not confined to the common names nor indeed to male names, and the process is one that is familiar to anybody working on early records. The purpose here though is simply to remind those who are not familiar with such practices what can lie behind latinised forms such as 'Robertus' and 'Ricardus'.

The Tom and Dick of the phrase Tom, Dick and Harry serve to remind us of pet forms in everyday use and they offer an insight into the development of a wide variety of surnames. 'Harry', or 'Herry' as it first appeared, is not a pet form but the French pronunciation of Henry, as the surnames Harris and Harrison confirm. It is possible now to say either Harry or Henry and the inference may be that we have adopted the latter pronunciation from the written form, making it more formal and causing Harry to suffer a decline in status. Similarly Pearce and Pearson are reminders of the French pronunciation of Peter, but here the medieval 'Piers' seems to have been revived quite recently, possibly with the aim in this case of conferring status on its bearer. In fact the history of Peter throws light on several different aspects of first name development and is now treated in more detail.

Peter

Peter was the name given by Jesus to Simon, son of Jonas, and it derives from the Greek word for 'rock' or 'stone', an etymology that most of us remember from our schooldays, when the quotation 'thou art Peter, and upon this rock I will build my church' was first explained to us. Of course the play on words is transparent in French, where 'pierre' without the capital letter means stone. The fact that Peter was regarded as the founder of the Christian church is reflected in the popularity of the christian name and in the number of English churches dedicated to him – well over one thousand according to Withycombe (*English Christian Names*).

Examples of Peter occur in England from 1086 and by the fourteenth century it was popular in almost every part of the country, usually between tenth and twentieth in order of frequency. The vernacular form 'Pers' occurs regularly in by-names and surnames in 1377–81, sometimes alongside its Latin equivalent. In Ecclesfield, for example, an entry for 'Petrus filius Petri' is followed by 'Johannes Pereson', who was possibly the grandson of the first Peter. In Pontefract, five consecutive entries have to do with a tavern keeper recorded as 'Petrus Baylle'. The four entries that follow his name seem all to refer to his servants; they are John, Robert and William Perysman and Alicia, 'seruiens dicti Petri' (servant of the said Peter). The diminutive 'Perkin' or 'Parkin' was responsible for surnames such as Perkins and Parkinson, another reminder that 'Peter' was not the usual medieval pronunciation.

Reaney quotes examples from c.1200 of what we think of as the modern form but this appears to have had little influence on English surnames. Nevertheless it had become an accepted alternative by the sixteenth century, e.g. Peter alias Pears Pennatt of Essex (1600).[10] References to 'St Petyr', from c.1400, may have played their part in this.[11] An entry in 1567, in the register of St Denis in the city of London, informs us that an abandoned baby boy was found there in December and named 'Petter Denis' because he had been found on St Peter's day.[12] Another influence may have been the pronunciation used by immigrants from the Low Countries, evidenced in names such as Peter Brabaner (1379), Deryk Peterson (1467) and Peter Adryanson (1485): Peterson might therefore sometimes have a Continental origin.

Withycombe in *English Christian Names* stated that the Reformation struck a blow at Peter's popularity, because it was 'so closely associated with the Papacy', but the decline is scarcely noticeable, and Peter continued to be in the top 25 as late as 1700. It certainly remained in regular use in some families of Catholic recusants, possibly as a covert way of demonstrating where their sympathies lay, although that would be difficult to prove. In the will of a priest called Peter Dyneley, written in English in 1541, there were bequests to three of his godchildren, named as Peter Webster, Peter Hall and Peter Helde.[13] The Dineleys remained staunch Catholics and suffered later as recusants, so these factors may have influenced their choice of the name and its pronunciation.[14] The fact that they used it also for their godchildren is evidence of a practice that will be discussed at greater length in Chapter 4. A footnote to the marriage entry for Peter Snawsdell or Snawsell in 1611 makes an unusual point when referring to several families regularly listed as recusants:

> Peter was a name common in the families of Ingleby, Slingsby, Vavasour, Dolman, etc. A hundred and fifty years ago every beneficed Clergyman who had been a Fellow of Peterhouse, Cambridge, was styled by his families (sic) 'Peter', in lieu of his proper baptismal name.[15]

There is another tantalising reference in Adel parish registers where a man was referred to in 1652 as 'Simon alias Peter Bland'. It seems an almost deliberate reminder of the apostle's change of name. In fact christian name aliases are not uncommon but most of them simply reflect confusion about which name was intended, e.g. Ellen alias Eleanor, Edward alias Edmund. The problem with Margaret and Margery however goes much deeper.

Margaret and Margery

Margaret derives from a word meaning 'pearl', and its popularity in the Middle Ages is generally attributed to the legends surrounding St Margaret of Antioch, although St Margaret of Scotland also bore the name. Margery had the same origin but derived from the vernacular French pronunciation and there are differing views on how early it came to be thought of as distinct from Margaret. In a recent article Peter McClure brought new light to bear on this matter and on the short forms used for the two names in early documents.[16] For instance he was able to show that in Nottinghamshire 'Magota' was normally for Margery, although previously it had been thought of as a diminutive of Margaret. His work raises important questions about whether the names enjoyed separate status in the fourteenth century and also about the exact pronunciation of Margery at that time. He obliges us to think again about the precise interpretation of surnames such as Madge, Maggot, Magson and Mogg.

The issues in this case have not been finally resolved, so in the frequency lists, which are discussed later, there are separate totals for Margaret and Margery, as well as for the abbreviations Mag' and Marg' and the diminutive Magota. The statistics will show how common one or two of these variations were and that has clear implications for the overall popularity of both names. McClure's thought-provoking article obliged me to look much more closely at all the entries for Margaret and Margery in the poll tax returns and some of these pointed to another possible area of confusion.

In a small number of the returns the clerks entered the names of certain individuals twice or even three times in succession. I am uncertain why that was but there were often slight differences in the entries and these discrepancies can serve to identify pet forms and abbreviations. For example in Stockerston in Leicestershire the servant of a lady called Emma Wade was named first as Margereta and then as Margeria; in Saddington the short form Marg' was for Margeria whereas in Barwell it was for Margareta. It might be argued that these were mistakes by the scribes, or lack of attention to detail, but they occur frequently enough for that to seem unlikely. In Appleby Parva a woman named Magota Bocher was also entered as Marg' Bucher and in Asfordby the daughter of Secilia de Dalby was called both Mag and Mariori (i.e. Marjory, an alternative form of Margery). More surprising were entries in Nailstone (Leics.) and Westmeston (Sussex) which have Marion and Mariot as diminutives of Margaret or Margery, not of Mary. The following examples give a better idea of the nature of the evidence:

Nailstone	Westmeston
Henrico Waren' ux' [and his wife] 4d	Johannes Crippe 4d
Henrico Wareyn ux' [and his wife]	Johannes Crippe
Joh' fil' eius [his son] 4d	Johannes Creppe
Johanne filio eius [his son]	Mariona Mariote 4d
Alicia Tayd 4d	Margeria Mariote
Alicia Tayde	Marioria Mariote
Marg' Haubel 4d	
Mariota Haubel	

The surname Marriott is chiefly found in the north Midlands but it may have more than one origin and without more evidence we cannot know whether it derives from Mary or Margery/Marjory. The much rarer Marrison is found in roughly the same area and is recorded in Nottinghamshire from the early sixteenth century: here again we have to consider that either Mary or Margery might be the source.

Surnames derived from first names

Dictionaries provide us with numerous examples of surnames derived from common first names, but few genealogists take the trouble to look more closely into such origins, thinking that there can be nothing distinctive about surnames such as Thomlinson, Hicks and Harris. Such assumptions can be misleading and there is usually something in a name's history that is worth investigating, no matter how commonplace it might seem. The history of Joseph, and the surnames derived from it, will illustrate that point.

Joseph

The meaning of Joseph is not in doubt and most reference works identify it as Hebrew in origin, meaning something like 'Jehovah adds', possibly referring to another child. It is so familiar to English speakers that it is difficult now to imagine a time when it was not in everyday use, and yet that was the case. Its history from the sixteenth century has been profiled by Scott Smith-Bannister, whose tables in *Names and Naming Patterns* show that it was not among the 50 most common English names when parish registers started in 1538, but that it was coming into regular use by the 1560s and 1570s. From then on there was a slow but steady rise in its popularity and by the 1650s it was the tenth most popular name in England. It maintained that position and improved on it, occupying eighth place in the decade 1690–1700. Joseph remained a favourite through the eighteenth and nineteenth centuries and it has never completely disappeared, although there have been fluctuations in its popularity in more recent times.

Its absence from the frequency lists of 1538–59 is a vital clue to its earlier history, and our attention was drawn to that by Withycombe who said that 'its general and widespread use...dates only from the seventeenth century'. The truth is that Joseph, along with many other biblical names, was deliberately reintroduced into the name-stock in the mid-sixteenth century, as Englishmen were being exhorted to choose names from the Holy Scriptures.[17] Its revival coincides roughly with that of Mary so it may be the New Testament Joseph who was the inspiration, but obvious alternatives are Joseph of Arimathea and Joseph the patriarch, written about in the book of Genesis.

In medieval England the name was usually spelt 'Josep' and Withycombe saw a possible influence there of the Italian 'Giuseppe', as 'many of the medieval *Josephs* were Jews' from Italy. In fact there is no evidence that any of those who bore the name in 1377–81 were Jews and the influence was from across the Channel, directly or indirectly. That may have played some part in the name's early distribution.

It was certainly an uncommon name in 1377–81 and we could make an impressive list of all those counties where no examples at all were recorded. The few that were listed are found mostly in east- and south-east England with one small but significant 'cluster' in the Liberties of the Cinque Ports in Kent – originally Romney, Hastings, Hythe, Dover and Sandwich. In this section of the return the names Josep Elys, Josep Younge and Josep Palmer are recorded; three individuals who were obviously close neighbours and possibly kinsmen. Elsewhere there are individuals with the name in Norfolk, Lincolnshire, East Yorkshire and Northamptonshire. In even earlier records there are occasional examples of 'Joseph' in Sussex, Suffolk, Hertfordshire, Cumberland and Yorkshire, and one at least as far back as 1086, but references before the mid-sixteenth century are so rare that it is worth looking in closer detail at the fourteenth-century evidence, for this was when many surnames were stabilising.

The surname Jessop

The distribution of Josep in 1377–81, as a by-name or surname, is roughly in those areas where the few references to the first name occurred, with examples in Yorkshire, Kent, Sussex, Hampshire and Rutland. One exception to that is William Josep of Weston in Somerset. One or two of these names may already have been hereditary and it would be wrong to imply that these 'Joseps' should be linked directly with one or more of the people in the returns who were named Joseph, even where the first name and surname are found close together, as in Kent. However, there is evidence to suggest that some of the surnames could have had their origins about this time. For example Richard Josepp was taxed on the Isle of Wight in 1379 and his servant was called Thomas Josep. This entry need not imply kinship between the two men and it raises questions about the exact nature of the name's origin. Elsewhere, for example, it has been shown that a servant or apprentice might derive his surname from his master.[18]

There is also evidence in Yorkshire at this time for the transition from by-name to surname, and the vowel change from 'Josep' to 'Jesop'. In 1375 William, the son of Baldwin Josep, granted lands in the West Riding township of Cumberworth to his brother John, and four years later their names were entered in the poll tax as William Josop and John Jesop, both paying four pence. In title deeds to the family's property these two spellings alternated through the fifteenth century, until Jessop became the conventional spelling by around 1500: it eventually ramified strongly in that part of the county.[19] The progenitor Baldwin may have been a recent arrival from the Continent, as may some of the 'Joseps' listed in 1377–81.[20]

The extraordinary part of this surname's history is that Kent and Yorkshire were for centuries at the heart of its distribution, and Guppy in *Homes of Family Names* identified Kent as the major 'home' of Jessup only a century ago. He found other Jessups just across the Thames estuary in Essex, but these may be connected with a family recorded in a Suffolk subsidy roll in 1524.[21] David Hey included Jessop in his survey of Sheffield surnames, finding that 1,778 subscribers were listed in the 1986 UK telephone directories, of whom 32% were in Yorkshire and 21% in East Anglia (Essex and Suffolk).[22] His analysis of Jessop/Jessup deaths in the 1842–6 period is more detailed but still identifies major concentrations in Kent, Yorkshire and the eastern counties of Lincolnshire and Norfolk. In 1881 over half the 3,553 Jessops were in Yorkshire and there were significant concentrations also in London (416) and Lincolnshire (212). Jessup, with a total of 834, was rare in Yorkshire but numerous in Kent (228), and in East Anglia and Lincolnshire (325).[23]

These are artificial areas in one sense and the London evidence no doubt masks the extent of the ramification in Kent and Essex. Similarly, a breakdown of the Yorkshire figures would show how rare the name was generally in the county compared with the enormous ramification around Cumberworth where it originated. It is still true in England, in the twenty-first century, that a single-origin surname can be concentrated in a relatively small area, close to where it originated, and the same principle applies to names which have two or three origins, for they too are often found in good numbers close to where they first stabilised. That point has already been made with Philpot, Tillotson and others, and Jessop and Jessup can be seen to belong in that category, once their distinctive patterns of distribution and early history have been determined.

Jessop is therefore precisely the type of English surname that could benefit from DNA analysis, and the Y chromosomes of males called Jessop and Jessup would surely provide us with a much more accurate idea of how many distinct families there are. The probability is that some of the very early by-names soon became extinct and that we are searching for at most three or four significant progenitors called Joseph. Indeed, there is no reason now why those Americans who descend from the John Jessop/Jessup who settled in Massachusetts in the 1630s should not finally identify which English family he belonged to.

~

We know far more about the surname Jessop once we have examined its links with the rare first name Joseph, but it is just one example. The fact is that many surnames derive from uncommon first names and this clearly has important implications for some family historians. However, the study of first names throughout their history concerns all family historians, for they are the means of identifying our ancestors correctly. The phrase 'Tom, Dick and Harry' did not pass accidentally into common usage; it related to practices that were once taken for granted. It is our key to an understanding of the pet forms and diminutives that were formerly in everyday use, particularly when surnames were stabilising.

Notes

1   C. T. Martin, The Record Interpreter (1892, facsimile 2nd edn: Chichester, 1982). This work contains the Latin forms of places, surnames and christian names, pp. 345–464.
2   J. C. Atkinson (ed.), Quarter Sessions Records, The North Riding Record Society IV (1886), p. 196.
3   P. H. Reaney noted that his only example of Philot was feminine. See 'Phillott' in P. H. Reaney and R. D. Wilson, A Dictionary of English Surnames (Oxford, 1997).
4   G. Redmonds, Huddersfield and District, Yorkshire Surnames Series 2 (Huddersfield, 1992).
5   G. Redmonds, Yorkshire West Riding, English Surnames Series I (Chichester, 1973).
6   P. McClure, 'The Interpretation of Hypocoristic Forms of Middle English Baptismal Names, Nomina 21 (1998), pp. 101–31. G. Redmonds, Surnames and Genealogy: a New Approach (Boston, 1997, reprinted 2002), pp. 42–9.
7   P. H. Reaney, The Origin of English Surnames (London, 1967). He has a useful introduction to the topic in Chapter 7, pp. 149–56.
8   E. C. Brewer, The Dictionary of Phrase and Fable (1870, reprinted 1988).
9   For the most recent discussion of Jack and other pet-forms see P. McClure's article in Nomina 26, 'The Kinship of Jack: I. Pet-forms of Middle English personal names with the suffixes –kin, –ke, –man, and –cot'.
10 C. B. Norcliffe (ed.), 'Paver's Marriage Licenses', Yorkshire Archaeological and Topographical Journal X (1889), p. 178.
11 For example, 'the college kirk of Saynt Petyr in Rypon', Testamenta Eboracensia, Surtees Society XLV (London, 1864).
12 J. C. Cox, Parish Registers of England (1910, reprinted 1974), p. 63.
13 G. D. Lumb (ed.), Testamenta Leodiensia, Thoresby Society XIX (Leeds, 1913), p. 47.
14 H. Aveling (ed.), 'The Catholic Recusants of the West Riding of Yorkshire 1558–1790', Proceedings of the Leeds Philosophical and Literary Society X, Part VI (1963), pp. 287–90.
15 C. B. Norcliffe (ed.), 'Paver's Marriage Licences', YAJ XII (1893), p. 157.

16 P. McClure, 'Middle English Baptismal Names', *Nomina* 21, p. 118.

17 C. W. Bardsley, *Curiosities of Puritan Nomenclature* (1880, reprinted 1996), p. 44.

18 P. H. Reaney and R. M. Wilson, *English Surnames*, p. xiv.

19 G. Redmonds, *Huddersfield and District*, Yorkshire Surnames Series 2.

20 The Continental connection is clear in the case of Baldwin Teutonicus or le Tyeys (1236), the ancestor of the Tyas family. Tyas, the family's surname, was Old French for 'German'; this was latinised as 'Teutonicus'.

21 P. H. Reaney and R. M. Wilson, *English Surnames*, p. 255.

22 D. Hey (ed.), *The Origins of One Hundred Sheffield Surnames* (Sheffield, 1992).

23 S. Archer, *The British 19th Century Surname Atlas* (2003), CD-ROM.

CHAPTER THREE

The Popularity of Christian Names

The growth and decline in popularity of christian names must be seen in the context of England's total population, and yet that is a topic where there seem to be very few certainties. Estimates for c.1350, in the aftermath of the Black Death and the earlier years of decline, vary considerably, but it is generally agreed that a period of stagnation followed and that the upward trend resumed in the later fifteenth century. Totals of something under three million in 1350, and twice that figure by the end of the seventeenth century, are only informed guesses, but they are a reasonable enough guide to the size of the population from the point of view of naming practices. An important point to bear in mind is that each name that was introduced into the name-stock, or revived after a period of obsolescence, was initially borne by just one person, and in each case there was a name-giver.

The use of the word 'popular'

In discussions about christian names it is almost impossible not to employ words such as 'popular' and 'rare', and it is unfortunate that writers in the past have sometimes used the terms in a misleading way. That was true of Withycombe in *English Christian Names*, and she was also apt to describe a name as 'a favourite', or to say that it was 'used a great deal', or was 'not uncommon'. Although she occasionally commented on regional usage, she actually provides us with little insight into the local popularity of most first names, and I am not alone in thinking that her views about the popularity of names in the past seem to have been based more on impression than on statistical data.

It is true that she occasionally used statistics, for she did so in the introduction to her dictionary, mainly to demonstrate that from the thirteenth century 'a comparatively small number [of names] were borne by an increasingly large proportion of the population'. She included tables which listed the most common names for men in the period 1550–1799, and for women in 1600–1799, but had only three names in each category and these few figures are really quite inadequate. It might be argued that it was never her intention to carry out a survey of christian name popularity but the topic features so prominently in her work that we are obliged to criticise the lack of evidence and her unsupported claims. She provided very few examples from the fifteenth century, although it is a key period in first name use, and little information on the frequency of the less-popular names for either sex. Nor was any real attempt made to investigate changes in naming habits, either from one period to another, or from one region to another.

The shortcomings of earlier dictionaries were identified by L. Dunkling and W. Gosling in *Everyman's Dictionary of First Names*. They criticised writers in general for dealing with the subject 'in a haphazard way' and also went some way towards putting matters right by carrying out what they described as 'massive name counts nation wide'. Those lists were said to cover the period 1600–1800 and the writers used evidence from them when commenting on individual names. Disappointingly, the actual frequency tables were not published, so we are not in a position to comment on them or to make local comparisons. Nor did they use statistical evidence for most of the Tudor period, and yet these were arguably the most important years in the history of our modern first names.

The opportunity to look more closely into English naming practices and first name popularity was not taken up by P. Hanks and F. Hodges in *A Dictionary of First Names*. Their introductory comments on such matters are often superficial, as when they link 'fashion' so closely to popularity, implying that the name-givers' motives now and in the Middle Ages can be directly compared. Equally disappointing is the single paragraph devoted to 'English coinages since the seventeenth century', for many such names were introduced much earlier than they claim and practices differed from parish to parish. That might be excused if the essays on individual names in that category made a real contribution to the debate, but sadly they too often repeat the errors found in earlier works. The authors provide us with information on more recent practices in the English-speaking world and a comparative survey of names in other European languages but we are told little that is new about the earlier history of English first names.

More recent publications have taken this aspect of the subject far more seriously, and Scott Smith-Bannister's *Names and Naming Patterns* breaks new ground in several important areas. For example it contains a wealth of valuable statistical data against which more regionally-based information can be measured, and prominence is given to the role of the godparents in the giving of names, an influential practice that has for too long been ignored.[1] From the point of view of family historians and genealogists it is unfortunate that Smith-Bannister says little about the history of less popular first names in that period but that is not a criticism, for the author had quite different priorities. His achievement is that he has laid the foundations for a thorough investigation into the first names themselves. In the chapters which follow there will be constant reference to Smith-Bannister's book which has frequency tables in the appendix for both male names and female names. These cover baptisms in the period 1538–1700, and they list the 50 most common names decade by decade, using statistics drawn from a cross-section of 40 named English parishes. However, to say 'most common' in this context could be misleading for, in one or two cases, fewer than 50 names were recorded in a decade and those at the bottom end of the lists were never numerous.[2]

A definition of 'popular', 1377–81

The growth and decline in the popularity of individual names, and the reasons for that, are major themes in this present book, and as the words 'popular' and 'rare' will inevitably be used, they should be meaningful terms. It is proposed therefore to suggest precise criteria for their use in 1377–81, as a firm basis for the conclusions in this chapter. To that end frequency tables for male names from 10 counties and female names from 10 counties have been compiled from the poll tax returns of 1377–81 and are shown below.[3] In each case 1,000 male names and 1,000 female names have been counted. These lists can be commented on individually or combined to give a total of 10,000 (see Appendix 1), allowing us to say whether a name was popular locally or generally. It was thought desirable to have lists from different regions but because fewer women's names are given it was not always possible to find 1,000 names in a specific county. The Dorset list had therefore to be supplemented with a very few names from neighbouring Hampshire, and to find 1,000 names in north-west England it was necessary to combine the territories that make up modern Cumbria. The poll tax returns used for Yorkshire are from *The Yorkshire Archaeological and Topographical Journal* V (female names) and IX (male names).

Because those who were being taxed were adults, the names testify to practices a generation earlier. The lists provide us with statistics to set against those of Smith-Bannister for the later centuries (see Appendix 2), but there is unfortunately no documentary source for the fifteenth century to match the poll tax returns and parish registers, so some regional statistics have been compiled for use in the short term.[4]

We are immediately struck here by how few names there are in each list (see pp. 30–33), for all those that were recorded more than once have been included. In fact the overall total is so small that there are difficulties in defining 'popular' satisfactorily. However, for use in this section, and as a proposal for how we might tackle the problem, a six-tier classification has been devised. It is based on the statistical evidence but some consideration has also been given to matters such as the size of the population in the wake of the Black Death, and the possible

CLASSIFYING POPULARITY 1377–81

	Classification	No. out of 1,000	Percentage
1	Extremely popular	100 & upwards	10% and over
2	Very popular or very common	40–99	4% to 9.9%
3	Popular or common	20–39	2% to 3.9%
4	Quite popular	6–19	0.6% to 1.9%
5	Infrequent	1–5	0.1% to 0.5.%
6	Rare	less than 1	less than 0.1%

extent of one person's family and acquaintances. We need to think how that might have differed in rural and urban communities and within the different administrative systems of the day. The population may have been small, and in some regions scattered, but our ancestors would have expected to meet people on a regular basis at the town well, at the corn mill, at market, at church, at the manorial court, and in those towns where the assizes and quarter sessions were held. The catchment area for these would in some cases have been extensive, bringing each person into contact with names from across a wide area.[5]

Popular male names for the period 1377–81

We are accustomed to thinking of our first name as something that identifies us personally, chosen as a distinguishing characteristic, so the overwhelming frequency of just a few names in 1377–81 raises fascinating questions about how distinctive John, William and two or three more were and what the motivation of the name-givers might have been. At the other end of the scale are the numerous names classed as infrequent or rare, significant because many of them became popular in later centuries and we do not always know when or why. Detailed studies of individual names should throw light on that topic and it will be important in each case to see whether regional frequencies mirror those at the national level.

Fewer than 80 identifiable names were recorded in the 10 counties surveyed, a very small number by modern standards, and of these only 15 qualified as popular, that is with an overall count over 0.5%. Many names that we might have expected to be popular were in fact infrequent, including Stephen, Philip, Laurence, James and Matthew, and among those classified as rare were Edward, George, Bartholomew, Martin and Christopher. Anthony and Bernard were 2 of the more than 20 identifiable names which were recorded just once in the consolidated total of 10,000. Many more were not recorded there at all, although they had given rise to surnames in previous centuries and would later return to favour. Among the best known examples are Arthur, Charles and Leonard.

The overwhelming popularity of John and William, representative of the two

FIRST NAME FREQUENCY 1377–81

With the exception of the figures for Yorkshire the source used for these frequency tables is Carolyn Fenwick's two-volume transcription of the English poll taxes for 1377, 1379 and 1381.

MALE NAMES

E. Yorks. 1379	%	Berks. 1381	%	Essex 1381	%	Devon 1377	%	Gloucs. 1381	%
John	33.4	John	39.8	John	45.9	John	31.4	John	38.6
William	21.3	William	16.2	William	13.8	William	15.8	William	18.1
Thomas	13.0	Richard	8.7	Thomas	7.5	Richard	10.6	Thomas	10.4
Robert	9.8	Robert	7.9	Richard	6.1	Thomas	7.1	Richard	9.4
Richard	5.0	Thomas	6.2	Robert	6.1	Robert	7.0	Robert	5.5
Henry	2.6	Henry	4.3	Walter	3.4	Walter	6.5	Henry	3.3
Adam	2.3	Walter	3.9	Roger	2.4	Henry	4.7	Walter	3.0
Roger	2.1	Roger	2.2	Henry	2.2	Roger	3.0	Nicholas	2.0
Nicholas	1.8	Nicholas	2.1	Geoffrey	1.7	Adam	1.8	Roger	1.4
Peter	1.3	Ralph	1.1	Stephen	1.7	Geoffrey	1.5	Hugh	1.0
Walter	1.1	Geoffrey	0.9	Nicholas	1.2	Nicholas	1.3	Philip	0.8
Stephen	0.8	Hugh	0.7	Simon	1.0	Ralph	0.9	Geoffrey	0.7
Simon	0.8	Adam	0.7	Edmund	0.7	Peter	0.8	Ralph	0.7
Denis	0.7	Peter	0.7	Ralph	0.7	Stephen	0.7	Reginald	0.7
Alan	0.7	Reginald	0.6	Gilbert	0.7	Simon	0.7	Gilbert	0.7
Geoffrey	0.6	Stephen	0.5	Peter	0.6	Reginald	0.5	Simon	0.4
Hugh	0.6	Simon	0.4	Laurence	0.4	Michael	0.4	Laurence	0.4
Ralph	0.3	Philip	0.4	Andrew	0.3	Gervase	0.3	Adam	0.3
Gilbert	0.3	Laurence	0.3	James	0.3	Gilbert	0.3	Peter	0.3
James	0.2	Andrew	0.3	Alexander	0.3	Hugh	0.3	Stephen	0.3
Philip	0.2	Alexander	0.3	Giles	0.3	Andrew	0.3	Alexander	0.3
		Denis	0.3	Hugh	0.3	Laurence	0.3	Michael	0.2
		David	0.3	Adam	0.3	Gregory	0.3	Alan	0.2
		Gilbert	0.2	Benedict	0.2	Matthew	0.3	Stacy	0.2
		Maurice	0.2	Edus	0.2	Edward	0.2		
		Edward	0.2	Lucas	0.2	James	0.2		
				Michael	0.2	Martin	0.2		
				Reginald	0.2	David	0.2		
						George	0.2		
						Hamond	0.2		

N. Lancs. 1379	%	Leics. 1379	%	Sussex 1377/79	%	Warwicks. 1379	%	Shropshire 1381	%
John	32.3	John	33.6	John	40.7	John	35.2	John	22.3
William	19.4	William	19.2	William	19.0	William	19.4	William	21.2
Thomas	10.6	Robert	12.3	Thomas	8.2	Thomas	10.5	Thomas	12.4
Richard	8.3	Thomas	8.6	Robert	8.1	Richard	9.6	Richard	10.5
Robert	7.9	Richard	8.0	Richard	6.9	Robert	5.2	Roger	5.9
Adam	5.9	Roger	3.3	Roger	2.9	Henry	4.4	Henry	4.3
Roger	4.5	Henry	2.9	Walter	2.4	Roger	2.9	Robert	4.3
Henry	3.0	Nicholas	2.5	Henry	1.7	Walter	2.2	Hugh	4.2
Nicholas	1.1	Hugh	1.7	Adam	1.4	Simon	2.1	Adam	2.6
Peter	0.7	Adam	1.2	Simon	1.4	Nicholas	1.9	David	1.7
Gilbert	0.7	Ralph	0.8	Nicholas	1.3	Adam	1.3	Philip	1.4
Ralph	0.6	Walter	0.8	Ralph	0.8	Geoffrey	0.9	Nicholas	1.1
Simon	0.6	Geoffrey	0.8	Geoffrey	0.7	Ralph	0.5	Geoffrey	0.7
Michael	0.6	Simon	0.7	Peter	0.6	Hugh	0.5	James	0.6
Edus	0.6	Peter	0.7	Hugh	0.6	David	0.5	Ralph	0.5
Hugh	0.5	Reginald	0.3	Stephen	0.4	Peter	0.4	Reginald	0.5
Walter	0.4	Bartholomew	0.3	Matthew	0.4	Edmund	0.4	Benedict	0.4
Laurence	0.4	Alan	0.3	Giles	0.3	Laurence	0.3	Jena	0.4
Philip	0.3	Laurence	0.3	Gilbert	0.2	Denis	0.2	Walter	0.3
James	0.2	Gilbert	0.2	Denis	0.2	Alexander	0.2	Edmund	0.3
Benedict	0.2	Ive	0.2	Alan	0.2			Stephen	0.3
Elias	0.2			Reginald	0.2			Madok	0.3
				Nigel	0.2			Griffin	0.3
								Lewk	0.3
								Eyvyn	0.3
								Houkin	0.3
								Houde	0.2
								Alexander	0.2

FEMALE NAMES

Staffs. 1377	%	Dorset 1379/81	%	Gloucs. 1381	%	Kent 1381	%	Cumbria 1377/79	%
Alice	20.6	Joan	20.3	Agnes	20.3	Joan	24.3	Agnes	16.7
Agnes	15.8	Alice	16.6	Alice	19.8	Alice	14.2	Alice	16.6
Joan	7.9	Agnes	9.5	Joan	12.8	Agnes	9.1	Joan	9.3
Margery	7.8	Christine	8.9	Marg'	8.9	Isabel	7.2	Matilda	6.7
Julian	5.1	Edith	8.4	Matilda	8.5	Christine	6.5	Emme	5.3
Matilda	4.2	Matilda	7.4	Isabel	3.6	Margery	5.7	Isabel	4.8
Marg'	3.5	Marg'	4.2	Julian	3.6	Julian	3.1	Margaret	4.4
Isabel	3.1	Julian	3.0	Christine	3.3	Matilda	3.1	Ellen	4.2
Felice	3.0	Isabel	2.1	Emme	2.7	Margaret	2.7	Christian	2.9
Edith	2.9	Emme	1.6	Ellen	2.6	Cecile	2.5	Mariot	2.6
Sybil	2.7	Lucy	1.4	Edith	1.8	Emme	2.0	Cecile	2.5
Margaret	2.6	Ellen	1.4	Cecile	1.4	Ellen	2.0	Magot	2.2
Ellen	2.0	Cecile	1.0	Sybil	1.3	Denise	1.9	Margery	2.2
Emme	2.0	Amice	1.0	Elizabeth	1.1	Sarah	1.5	Katherine	1.7
Isolde	1.7	Margaret	1.0	Isolde	1.0	Godelene	1.1	Marg'	1.6
Petronille	1.7	Is'	0.9	Amice	0.7	Mabel	1.1	Beatrice	1.5
Cecile	1.5	Denise	0.8	Mag'	0.7	Amice	1.0	Elizabeth	1.5
Katherine	1.1	Margery	0.8	Felice	0.6	Beatrice	0.6	Julian	1.4
Avice	1.0	Katherine	0.7	Katherine	0.5	Idony	0.6	Annabel	0.9
Christian	0.9	Eve	0.6	Magot	0.5	Felice	0.5	Avice	0.7
Elizabeth	0.8	Magot	0.6	Lucy	0.5	Lucy	0.5	Tillot	0.7
Rose	0.7	Avice	0.6	Marin	0.4	Lora	0.5	Ellot	0.6
Lettice	0.7	Lettice	0.5	Sarah	0.3	Petronille	0.5	Anot	0.6
Amice	0.7	Isolde	0.5	Denise	0.3	Custance	0.5	Evot	0.5
Denise	0.7	Ibot	0.5	Emot	0.2	Katherine	0.5	Ibot	0.5
Anne	0.6	Elizot	0.4	Lettice	0.2	Lettice	0.5	Godith	0.5
Mary	0.6	Sybil	0.4	Marion	0.2	Gunnora	0.4	Marion	0.4
Eleanor	0.6	Felice	0.3	Rose	0.2	Helwise	0.4	Alina	0.4
Eve	0.5	Ammot	0.3	Avice	0.2	Wymark	0.4	Mag'	0.4
Lucy	0.3	Mabel	0.3			Colet	0.4	Merg'	0.4
Beatrice	0.3	Eleanor	0.3			Marion	0.4	Sybil	0.4
Mabel	0.3	Beatrice	0.3			Ibot	0.4	Mary	0.3
Hawise	0.3	Sarah	0.2			Annabel	0.3	Custance	0.3
Constance	0.2	Gunnora	0.2			Clemence	0.3	Till	0.3
Maiot	0.2	Orenge	0.2			Martha	0.3	Amy	0.3
Sarah	0.2	Marion	0.2			Agatha	0.2	Eve	0.3
		Thomesia	0.2			Anne	0.2	Emmot	0.2
		Clarice	0.2			Justine	0.2	Marcery	0.2
		Christian	0.2			Floria	0.2	Amice	0.2
		Mag'	0.2			Millicent	0.2	Isolde	0.2
		Elizabeth	0.2			Isolde	0.2	Edith	0.2
						Eleanor	0.2	Elisot	0.2
						Obraya	0.2	Sibot	0.2
						Edilda	0.2		

Leics. 1381	%	Lincs. 1377/81	%	Norfolk 1379	%	Warwicks. 1379	%	S. Yorks. 1379	%
Alice	20.3	Agnes	12.2	Margaret	14.4	Alice	21.9	Agnes	16.1
Agnes	14.0	Joan	11.8	Alice	14.0	Agnes	15.8	Alice	15.9
Emme	9.3	Alice	11.5	Agnes	13.8	Joan	9.0	Joan	15.9
Joan	7.6	Emme	7.4	Matilda	8.0	Matilda	8.3	Matilda	8.0
Amice	6.2	Ellen	6.9	Katherine	6.0	Marg'	4.8	Isabel	7.9
Matilda	5.5	Marg'	6.8	Emme	5.6	Margery	4.6	Cecile	6.7
Isabel	4.1	Matilda	6.0	Isabel	5.2	Isabel	4.5	Margaret	4.4
Marg'	4.0	Isabel	4.0	Joan	5.0	Julian	3.4	Magot	4.4
Ellen	3.9	Katherine	3.8	Marg'	3.2	Emme	3.1	Elizabeth	2.9
Margery	3.6	Elizabeth	2.6	Beatrice	2.7	Is'	2.5	Beatrice	2.3
Avice	2.5	Sarah	2.0	Christian	2.5	Margaret	2.0	Ellen	2.1
Cecile	2.3	Margaret	1.9	Cecile	2.4	Ellen	1.8	Emme	1.9
Katherine	1.5	Cecile	1.7	Margery	2.3	Amice	1.6	Denise	1.8
Sarah	1.4	Is'	1.5	Sarah	1.7	Christian	1.5	Julian	1.8
Felice	1.4	Beatrice	1.5	Is'	1.3	Katherine	1.5	Avice	1.2
Beatrice	1.3	Evita	1.4	Julian	1.1	Felice	1.3	Christian	0.9
Margaret	1.2	Mar'	1.2	Ellen	0.9	Sybil	1.3	Idony	0.8
Julian	0.8	Christine	1.1	Avice	0.8	Elizabeth	1.1	Sybil	0.6
Rose	0.8	Magot	1.1	Mabel	0.7	Rose	1.1	Custance	0.6
Christine	0.7	Margr'	0.9	Lucy	0.6	Cecile	0.9	Katherine	0.5
Clemence	0.7	Isolde	0.9	Amice	0.6	Edith	0.8	Rose	0.4
Denise	0.7	Custance	0.7	Agatha	0.5	Anne	0.8	Lora	0.4
Isolde	0.6	Lucy	0.7	Sybil	0.4	Magot	0.7	Petronille	0.3
Elizabeth	0.6	Margery	0.6	Christine	0.4	Christine	0.6	Isolde	0.3
Petronille	0.5	Anne	0.6	Magot	0.4	Annabel	0.5	Margery	0.3
Mabel	0.5	Marion	0.5	Marion	0.3	Isolde	0.5	Lettice	0.3
Lettice	0.5	Julian	0.5	Mariot	0.3	Beatrice	0.5	Sarah	0.2
Mag'	0.4	Idony	0.5	Rose	0.3	Petronille	0.4	Amice	0.2
Lucy	0.4	Ivet	0.5	Levot	0.3	Sarah	0.3	Sibot	0.2
Sybil	0.2	Osanne	0.5	Dulcia	0.3	Eve	0.2		
Marion	0.2	Goda	0.5	Clarice	0.3	Clemence	0.2		
Sabine	0.2	Ibot	0.4	Helwise	0.3	Idony	0.2		
Elie	0.2	Samia	0.4	Eleanor	0.3	Lucy	0.2		
		Helwise	0.4	Aveline	0.3				
		El'	0.4	Lettice	0.2				
		Amice	0.3	Petronille	0.2				
		Eve	0.3	Anne	0.2				
		Eleanor	0.3	Annabel	0.2				
		Agatha	0.2	Elizabeth	0.2				
		Petronille	0.2						
		Dulcia	0.2						
		Lecia	0.2						
		Colet	0.2						
		Iglesia	0.2						

major influences on English naming practices since the Norman Conquest, is apparent here in every part of England. In Essex, for example, there were 459 Johns and 138 Williams; in Gloucestershire the totals were John (386) and William (181); in Devon, where the predominance was least marked, there were 314 Johns and 158 Williams. The next most popular names were Richard, Robert and Thomas, although not necessarily in that order in each region. Together these five names accounted for between 72% of the male population in Devon and 82% in East Yorkshire. It is true that Robert slipped into seventh place in Shropshire but that was affected by the county's position on the border with Wales. Indeed it was Welsh influence there that helped David into a relatively high position.

Overall there were just three names in the 'popular' category; Henry, Roger and Walter, and it is at this level that the regional tables begin to show marked differences. In north Lancashire, for example, Walter was in seventeenth position with a total of 4, whereas in Devon it was sixth with 65. Adam was quite popular generally but it was recorded just 3 times in Gloucestershire and 59 times in North Lancashire. Hugh was represented just 3 times in Essex and Devon but 42 times in Shropshire. These figures provide evidence of significant regional differences in distribution, even among names with a degree of popularity generally, and this has implications for genealogists and those interested in surname origins. More than one third of the men counted in 1377–81 were called John, a remarkable statistic that puts the name in a category of its own.

John

John is a Hebrew name, a shortened form of Johanan, and it is said to mean either 'God is gracious' or 'Jehovah has favoured', depending on which dictionary you consult.[6] The meaning 'Jehovah' is there in many other Hebrew names such as Joel, Joseph, Jonathan and Joshua, but John, unlike them, is spelt with an 'h' which preserves the etymological connection.

Its rise to popularity in England can be traced to the early part of the thirteenth century, but it is said to have been in common use among eastern Christians earlier than that, which may support the suggestion that returning crusaders contributed to its success. It is certainly noticeable how rare John was in charters before 1200 and how much more frequent it had become by about 1250.[7] After that its claim to be the most popular English name in history is reinforced by sound evidence, for it dominated the frequency lists right across the country in 1377–81 and remained at the top through the sixteenth and seventeenth centuries. It was only in the nineteenth century that it was overtaken at times by William, that other perennial favourite, and even then it continued to hold second position.

Even if it were true that John's growing popularity in the early thirteenth century owed something to the crusaders they were only a small percentage of the total population and could not have been directly responsible for the name's widespread success. We are left wondering therefore just how it spread to all classes of society, for that is what happened. It is traditional to attribute that sudden surge to the religious revival more generally, particularly to the venera-tion of individuals like St John the Baptist and St John the Evangelist, but nobody has satisfactorily explained how that worked in practice. Unfortunately we have too little information about naming practices in that period.

What is not in doubt is the uninterrupted prominence of John among the more influential members of society. It is said that no fewer than 500 English churches bear a dedication to St John the Baptist and another 181 to St John the Evangelist. Other possible influences include scores of other saints, 23 popes, 8 Byzantine emperors and a number of kings. Nor was the popularity of John just an English phenomenon, for it seems to have been to the forefront right across Europe. The popularity of parallel names, like Iain in Scotland and Ieuan in Wales, also testifies to its success. Moreover, its overwhelming frequency as sur-names were stabilising means that we have scores of names across England and Wales that can be interpreted as 'son of John', notably Jones and Johnson. However, some Johnsons were from continental Europe, immigrants who arrived in this country without a surname and whose fathers were called John. David Postles identified Peter Jonessone and William Jonessone as aliens in Devon in the mid-fifteenth century,[8] and there are many more in other sources.[9]

First name sources after the Conquest

The lists for 1377–81 confirm what was said earlier about the dramatic change in naming habits in the post-Conquest period: for only Edmund was among the top 30 names that had an Old English origin. Like the less common Edward, it sur-vived because it was the name of a popular saint and gained Norman approval. In fact the Norman influence is evident almost everywhere, most obviously in the frequency of names with a Germanic origin, that is William, Richard, Robert, Henry, Roger, Walter, Hugh, Geoffrey and Ralph. It is evident also in less-fre-quent names such as Gilbert and Reginald, and the Breton Alan.

The influence of the Church is apparent in Adam, from the Old Testament, and the names of the apostles and saints, especially John, Thomas, Simon and Peter. Stephen, Philip, James, Matthew and Andrew were much less prominent, as were the names of the archangel Michael and the non-scriptural saints Denis and Laurence. Nicholas, whose cult was widely known in France and England in the tenth century, was quite popular; he is remembered, if not always recognised, as Santa Claus. The inspiration behind Alexander is less certain: there were early saints called Alexander but another likely source was Alexander the Great, whose heroic deeds lived on in the popular romances.

Changing fashions from 1377 to 1700

The evidence from Smith-Bannister's frequency lists in *Names and Naming Patterns* has been used to present profiles of first name popularity over the period 1377–1700, and these appear in Appendix 2. In those cases where the statistics are uniform throughout, the profile can be easily summarised. For example the names that dominated the first five places in 1377–81 remained at the top until 1700, i.e. John, William, Thomas, Richard and Robert. John was always in first place, followed by William and Thomas, not always in that order. Other names that maintained their popularity were Henry and Nicholas, although both lost some ground in the seventeenth century. Roger, Walter, Hugh, Simon, Ralph and Peter were in decline and the profiles chart the sometimes uneven course of each name's history. The loss in favour suffered by Adam and Geoffrey, missing from most of the lists after 1538, was far more dramatic.

Many names that rose to popularity between 1377 and 1538, and then remained prominent through to 1700, are those of saints. The most successful were Edward, George and James but Christopher, Francis and Anthony were not far behind. They had all been comparatively obscure in 1377–81, so their improved positions are worth looking at in more detail, especially as much of what has been written about them is inaccurate.

Edward, George and James, 1377–1700

Edward is made up of two elements meaning 'prosperity' and 'guardian', and it has been described as the most successful of all the Old English names, even more so than Edmund. Much of that success must be due to Edward the Confessor, who was the last undisputed Saxon king of England and whose name was esteemed by the Angevins and Plantagenets. Indeed it was Henry II who pressed for Edward's canonisation which was obtained in 1161. His grandson Henry III honoured Edward's memory when he commissioned the building of a magnificent new shrine in Westminster Abbey, and this was completed in 1269 after 25 years' work. Henry also named one of his sons Edward, in a gesture that seemed to aim at reconciling the English and the Normans. As a result, there was an Edward on the English throne for over a century, from 1272 to 1377.

It is usual therefore to credit Edward the Confessor with the name's success, but the timing of its rise to popularity is hardly mentioned. It was actually rare in the fourteenth century and yet from 1538 to 1700 was regularly among the most frequent names in the country. Its high point was between 1580 and 1639 when it consistently occupied sixth place. The picture from 1380 to 1538 is much less clear, although evidence in Yorkshire puts it in tenth place by the end of the fifteenth century. It would be nice if that reflected Edward's role as one of England's patron saints but that is not the case. Although he had that honour in 1351 at the siege of Calais, along with Edmund of East Anglia, it was St George who came to be recognised as the country's main champion in the fifteenth century.

In fact Edward's popularity from 1538 to 1700 was paralleled by that of George, which was also in the first 10 throughout the whole period. Initially it was just one or two places behind Edward but after the Civil War the positions reversed and it featured consistently in sixth or seventh place. That popularity is hardly surprising: St George had emerged as England's major patron saint by 1415, when Archbishop Chichele made his feast one of the principal events of the year. That was after success at Agincourt, an event that Shakespeare chose to celebrate in Henry V's memorable invocation. It is worth noting that George is a non-scriptural saint's name and that its popularity survived the Reformation. In fact Withycombe seemed quite unaware of George's early history and claimed in *English Christian Names* that it was 'rare until the advent of the House of Hanover in 1714'. The same opinion was expressed by Reaney in *Origin* and Hanks and Hodges in *First Names*.

James is known to have been used in England in the late Middle Ages, if only because it gave rise to several surnames, but it was not popular in 1377–81, when it occupied twenty-second place with a frequency of 1 in every 500. It was in tenth position in 1538, and it maintained and increased that popularity through to the end of the century, moving up to sixth or seventh by the 1640s. It has been said that its success began after the accession of James Stuart to the English throne in 1603, but the statistics show how wrong that is, and it seems more likely that it can be traced to the disciples of that name or the cult of St James of Compostella. There is a reference in Chaucer's *Shipman's Tale* to Seint Jame, a spelling that may reflect the influence of the Spanish 'Jaime'. The final 's' stabilised later.

Francis, Christopher and Anthony

Three other names of saints made their mark in this period. The first of them, Francis, is a good illustration of how confusing the information is that we are offered in the major dictionaries. According to Hanks and Hodges it was introduced into England in the early sixteenth century, whereas Withycombe quotes two examples in Norfolk in the 1490s and says the name was not much used in the seventeenth century. In fact Francis occurs in Essex, Norfolk and Yorkshire in the fourteenth century and was extremely successful between 1538 and 1700, never lower than thirteenth in popularity from 1560. The major influence in that period was probably St Francis of Assisi but some examples, especially the earliest ones, may have been nicknames meaning 'Frenchman'. St Francis himself had been baptised as Giovanni or John but was later called 'franciscus' because he spoke French fluently. The feminine Francisca was also in use from the fourteenth century.

Christopher was recorded only twice in the sample of 10,000 from 1377–81 but it was in fourteenth position by 1549 and more or less maintained that level of popularity until the last decade of the seventeenth century, when it dropped to twenty-first. Statistics for Lancashire and Yorkshire show that it had already established itself among the top dozen names by the 1430s, a date that reflects the importance attached to St Christopher's cult at that time. The name means 'Christ bearer' and the legend in which St Christopher carried Christ across the stream was a favourite wall painting in English churches from the fourteenth century.[10] It was usually on the north wall of the building so that it would be seen by people as they passed through the porch and these images may have contributed to Christopher's success.

There was only one Anthony recorded in the sample of 1377–81 and through the fifteenth century the name was much less attractive to name-givers than Christopher. Its success was most marked between 1538 and 1629, when it was regularly ahead of Christopher, and it had a high point towards the end of Elizabeth's reign. It did not drop entirely out of fashion after that but was never higher than twentieth for the latter part of the seventeenth century. The inspiration was probably St Antony the Great, the Egyptian ascetic who was known in Britain well before the Norman Conquest, but whose cult enjoyed wider popularity as a result of the Crusades. His legend is depicted on the backs of the stalls in Carlisle Cathedral.

New names from the Bible in the period 1538–1700

A very significant group of names that came to the fore in this period was drawn from the Old Testament, with Daniel and Samuel the first to make an impact. They are at the bottom end of the frequency lists from 1538–49; this is much earlier than has usually been said, earlier even than in parishes such as Halifax where Old Testament names were later extremely frequent. They both steadily increased in popularity through the sixteenth century and seventeenth century and Samuel was regularly in ninth or tenth position after 1640. In that period Samuel was rivalled by Joseph which had become prominent rather later, first occurring in the 1560s. It would clearly be important to know more about just when and where Daniel and Samuel first came into use and the reasons behind their choice.

In fact Joseph was the most successful of several Old Testament names that enjoyed a revival during the second half of the sixteenth century. Abraham was the earliest, followed by Isaac, Nathaniel and Benjamin, and the last of these emerged as a really popular choice after the Restoration. Several names that all had 'J' as their initial letter, such as Jonas and Jonathan from 1610 and Joshua from 1630, were less significant. Both Jacob and Jeremiah also belong to that period but the evidence for their use can be more complicated. Jacob could be confused with 'Jacobus' for James, and Jeremiah or Jeremy with Jerome, the name of a saint. The frequent use of the initial 'J' may be coincidental but it is noticeable how often siblings were given these names and the impression is that some parents were influenced by the alliteration. The lists contain other biblical names in this period but their use was more intermittent and none of them was particularly popular generally, i.e. Gabriel, Mark, Luke, Paul, Barnabas and Timothy.

Popular female names from 1377–81

In the poll tax returns for some counties the names of the wives are omitted and this makes it difficult to compile satisfactory frequency lists, as noted in the section above, A definition of 'popular', 1377–81. Furthermore the evidence shows that clerks readily used abbreviations that could stand for more than one name and, since these cannot be identified, the totals in a few cases are seriously affected. The most obvious problems are Marg' for either Margaret or Margery and Is' which could be for either Isabel or Isolde. Less important numerically was 'Cris' which could be for either Christian or Christine, two names that are usually listed separately in dictionaries. There may have been no distinction, for the daughter of Robert de Gowtby of Noseley in Leicestershire was first named Christiana and then Crystina.[11] Perhaps the spellings represented scribal preferences, since Christine was particularly frequent in the south coast counties of Kent and Dorset but missing from some counties in the Midlands and North, where Christian was more usual.

The clerks also employed many diminutives, and it has been thought safer to list these variations independently. Magot is the most important of these but Mariot, Marion, Ibot, Evita, Colet, Evot, Annot and Ammot are others that affect the overall counts. This helps to explain why the list of women's names is longer than the men's but, even if we ignore the abbreviations and diminutives, there were still more female names in use, and more of them were 'popular'. Part of the reason for that is that there is no woman's name to compare with John, even though its counterpart Joan was extremely popular.

The most important influence on girls' names after the Conquest was that of the virgin saints, Agnes, Margaret, Julian and Cecile, and these were popular in every part of the country. The very English-sounding Ellen derives from Helen, probably St Helen, the mother of the Emperor Constantine: a British origin was claimed for her by Geoffrey of Monmouth and dedications to her are common in parts of northern England in particular. For example, St Helen's in Lancashire took its name from the chapel of ease that was at the heart of the town's late development. Also quite popular were the female saints Katherine and Beatrice, whilst Felice and Denise are likely to have been influenced by the corresponding male names. Edith is the only name to have survived from the Old English period and the inspiration here seems certain to have been Edith of Wilton, another virgin saint. She was the illegitimate daughter of King Edgar and is famous for having refused to be queen. Instead she built an oratory to St Denys and that may have contributed to the later use of Denise for girls.

Sybil is in some ways a surprising name to find in popular use, for the 'Sibyllae' were pagan prophetesses. There were thought to be 10 of them altogether but the best known was probably the one consulted by Aeneas before his descent into the lower world. It was because the 'Sibyls' were considered to be mouthpieces for divine revelations that the name became acceptable among Christians, and it was eventually brought to this country by the Normans. It was marginally less popular in 1377–81 than the biblical names Elizabeth and Sarah, both of which had uneven distributions. For example Elizabeth was far more prominent in Yorkshire and Lincolnshire than it was in Kent and Norfolk, whereas Sarah was in regular use in the south and east but rare elsewhere. Of course a different and more complex picture may emerge when name-counts have been completed for every county, but these early statistics suggest how easy it might be to form a wrong opinion about a name's local frequency.

Other important names in the lists had a Germanic origin but were brought here by the Normans. Of these Alice was the most remarkable, regularly in first or second place, but Matilda too was very popular. Emma and Avice are two others that are usually said to be from short forms of Germanic compounds, but in the latter case the etymology is disputed by some scholars. Also Germanic in origin is Isolde whose tragic story was familiar to our ancestors through the medieval romances. In this case too the numbers fluctuated from one region to another but the abbreviation Is' may have been responsible for that. It was used also for Isabel which was common in every part of the country. The remarkable thing is that Isabel is in origin a pet form of Elizabeth, and the two names may occasionally have interchanged as late as the sixteenth century.[12] Withycombe noted that the wife of a Berkshire yeoman was named Isabel in his will in 1542 whereas she was called Elizabeth when she died two years later.

Other regional concentrations worth noting are Edith in Dorset, Felice and Petronille in Staffordshire and Amice in Leicestershire, but a close examination of the evidence reveals significant small 'clusters' right down the list. Typical of these are Goda (East Anglia), Godelena (Kent) and Osanne, the last of these found only in Spalding in Lincolnshire. It derives from 'Hosanna', a Hebrew word used as an appeal to God for deliverance, which was adopted into Christian worship as a more general expression of praise. We are familiar with it through the Bible and it occurs as 'osanne' in Chaucer's *Tale of the Man of Lawe*: 'Mary I mene, doghter to Seint Anne, Bifore whos child aungeles singe osanne'. Less well known is its use as a baptismal name from the twelfth century, possibly to commemorate a birth on Palm Sunday. The earliest examples have been noted in Dorset and Herefordshire and it occurred often enough to serve as a by-name.

Typical of these are 'Reginaldus filius Osanna', in the pipe roll of 1180, and Richard Osan of Shelley in 1277.[13]

Changing fashions 1377–1700

Some of the names recorded in 1377–81 failed to establish themselves or else declined rather abruptly, often well before 1540. These included the successful Germanic names Isolde, Matilda, Emma and Avice, the biblical Eve, the saints' names Felice, Petronille and Denise, and Latin Lettice and Idony. Many more remained in common use while others were introduced, and here we can make some obvious comparisons with male naming practices. These are most obvious in the vastly increased popularity of names from the Bible. Mary can be listed here or among the saints' names, but more obviously biblical successes were Sarah, Hannah, Susanna and Martha, all of them among the top 10 most popular names by the end of the seventeenth century. Others that came into regular use were Rebecca, Judith, Rachel, Esther, Ruth, Deborah and Lydia, most of them first used in the mid-sixteenth century. Two successful saints' names, revived in the fifteenth century, were Dorothy and Barbara. The so-called Puritan names had little impact, although Charity, Constance, Faith, Patience and Prudence are all recorded occasionally and Grace, which had a much longer history, was successful from about 1540.

Another difference in the way that women's names developed in this period, is in the treatment of variant forms and diminutives. Aspects of that topic have already been touched on in discussions about Margaret and Margery, Christian and Christine, Ellen, Eleanor and Helen, Elizabeth and Isabel, for these demonstrate how some variants gained independent status. Moreover scribes regularly recorded the diminutives of women's names in official documents, so that Magot, Mariot, Ibot and Evita were all in the top 50 in the poll tax returns. If the line between the 'official' form of a woman's name and its various alternatives was indeed less rigidly drawn, that might reflect on the status men attached to their names and on their more dominant role in society generally. In any case it has implications for both the frequency and development of women's names.

In the men's tables it was the consistency of those at the very top between 1377 and 1700 that was most remarkable and there is nothing directly comparable where women's names are concerned. We can point to something similar between 1650 and 1700 when Mary, Elizabeth, Anne, Sarah, Jane and Margaret consistently occupied the top six places, but the essential difference is that Margaret was the only one that had maintained its popularity since 1377.[14] Several of the other names had actually been uncommon or rare in 1377–81 and Jane as an alternative for Joan had made its first appearance in the fifteenth century. In 1477, for example, Dame Johan Thurlande of Nottingham bequeathed 'a standyng maser...with an egle over the toppe of the coveryng' to John Rochford:

he was the son of her daughter Jane who must therefore have been named no later than 1450.[15]

Joan was extremely popular between 1377 and 1580, but then began slowly to lose ground, especially after 1660. However it was still in tenth position at the end of the century, just five places below Jane which shared the same origin and their combined popularity is very significant. We must also take into account though the growing importance of Janet in the sixteenth century. It was initially a diminutive, and featured occasionally in the poll tax returns, e.g. Jenetta Schakebollok of Hilborough in Norfolk (1381), but the fact that sisters could be called Jane and Jenett in the sixteenth century confirms Janet's growing independent status – as do sixteenth-century aliases such as 'Jehan alias Jenatt'. Other aspects of this subject are now touched on in the accounts of Alice, Agnes and Mary.

Alice

On the face of it Alice was the most popular woman's name in the poll tax returns, but a will of 1393, written uncharacteristically in English, suggests that it may have been less frequently used than its diminutive Alison. Jon of Croxton of York was the testator and he made bequests to Alison of Wappelyngton, to Alison, the wife of his brother Richard, to Alison Smalbane, and to Alise of Lastyngham.[16] Clearly the diminutive was very popular at that time, at least in York. Alice was still in the top four or five until c.1570, at which point it began slowly to lose favour. In 1559, Richard Clarke of Ellerker in the East Riding referred to three Alysons in his will, including his mother and his daughter, and the evidence generally suggests that the diminutive may still have been the more common form of the name.[17]

It is possible that references to 'Alice alias Alison' from the mid-sixteenth century point to the emergence of the diminutive as an independent name, but about that time Alice was in any case falling out of favour. It is difficult to quantify that loss of popularity, especially as Alice was still the twelfth most common English name in the 1690s, but that relatively high position can be misleading. In Leeds, for example, where Alice was eleventh in order of popularity in 1697–8, just 4 girls were given the name, as opposed to 53 who were called Mary and 43 called Elizabeth.

Withycombe in *English Christian Names* said that Alison 'was still common in England in the seventeenth century, especially in the North country', whereas Alice 'fell into general disuse' in the same period. Hanks and Hodges (*First Names*) expressed the opinion that Alison had 'virtually died out in England in the fifteenth century', and survived only in Scotland, but that was clearly not the case. Dunkling and Gosling in *Dictionary of First Names* comment on its revival in the 1930s when it once again became more popular than Alice.

Agnes

Agnes was the second most popular woman's name in 1377–81 although in some regions, Dorset and Kent for example, it was well behind Joan. It no doubt owed some of its popularity to the cult of St Agnes, a Roman maiden martyred in 304, but even so it remained in the top four or five places right through Elizabeth's reign and was still in regular use in 1700. It had two Latin forms, Agnes and Agneta, and it is the former that has influenced the modern pronunciation: the abbreviated Agn' could stand for either of these.

The vernacular pronunciation is represented by spellings such as Annis and Annas which are found frequently enough right through its history. In 1379, for instance, Annas Stele was taxed in the Warwickshire village of Bulkington and Annis Pyemont was baptised in Rothwell in west Yorkshire in 1762. Annot, sometimes latinised as Annota, was a very common diminutive, and these vernacular forms gave us the surnames Annas, Anness, Annatt and Annott. Of course Annot might also have been a diminutive of Anne and it would almost certainly have contributed to the confusion that existed in the sixteenth century between the two names.

Withycombe quotes from an interesting legal dispute, late in Elizabeth's reign, in which it was argued that Agnes and Ann were in fact the same name, but the judgement was that they were distinct and this was reinforced in another case in the early seventeenth century. Nevertheless many people did not distinguish between the two and the names are frequently written as an alias in the sixteenth and seventeenth centuries. Typical examples are 'Agnes alias Ann' Kitson of Birstall in 1627, and 'Annis or An' Booth of Kirkburton in 1670. The confusion is first apparent in references to the saint, for St Agnes day was referred to as 'Seynt Anne daye' in 1481,[18] and the chapel on Foss Bridge in York was sometimes St Anne's and sometimes St Agnes's.[19]

In cases where the alias is not given researchers, especially family historians, need to go through the evidence very carefully, for it is often only a sequence of references that provides evidence of the confusion. In 1718, for example, Chiney Mason married Agnes Leech of Eastby near Skipton but she was called Anne in 1725. In this case the husband's very unusual first name helps to confirm the identification. In 1601 the coroner at Horsham in Sussex returned a verdict of death by natural causes on Agnes Michilborne but R. F. Hunnisett, the editor of *Sussex Coroners' Inquests*, notes that she had been called Ann Michilborne just two years earlier.[20] This confusion, over such a long period, raises questions about how we should interpret the relatively few examples of 'Anna' in the fourteenth century.

Regional records point to an increased use of Anne in the fifteenth century and it was consistently more popular than Agnes from 1580, regularly occupying third place in the tables. The way in which the two names were used as alternatives in that period seems likely to have played some part in the reversal of fortunes.

Mary

Mary was in forty-ninth position in the frequency list for 1377–81, occurring only nine times, and this statistic emphasises how unreliable the dictionaries can be about well-known names. We are told by Hanks and Hodges in *First Names* that 'Mary is the most popular and enduring of all female Christian names, and that its popularity [has been] almost completely undisturbed by the vagaries of fashion that affect other names'. That statement, and some of the assumptions behind it, must be challenged. More 'popular' than Mary by 1377–81 were Godelena, Helwise, Idony, Avice and Dionisia (Denise). Even Dunkling, who has been more aware than most of the need for accurate statistical evidence, said in *First Names First* that Mary was probably one of 'the five most frequently used girls' names at the end of the fourteenth century', but that was certainly not true.

Withycombe, on the other hand, who was far more cautious about Mary's popularity in earlier centuries, appears to have presumed that the name's associations with the Blessed Mary and more particularly with Queen Mary, would have brought about its decline, and she wrote that it 'suffered an eclipse after the Reformation and was seldom used during Elizabeth's reign'. In fact, in some parishes noted for their militant Protestantism, it was in Elizabeth's reign that Mary became one of the most frequent girls' names. In 1571, for example, of 178 girls baptised in Halifax, no fewer than 26 were called Mary. Only Susanna was more common – and that by the narrowest of margins. Smith-Bannister's lists show that the dramatic change in Mary's fortunes had actually taken place by about 1540 when it was the seventh most common girl's name in the country and that popularity increased steadily between 1540 and 1700. In fact Mary occupied second position overall from 1600 and first position from 1650.

It was shown in Chapter 2 that Marion and Mariot could be diminutives of Margery, and that link was not known when I commented some years ago on Mary's frequency in 1379. The reality is therefore that it was probably even rarer than I suspected.[21] The possibility that the diminutives might be used for both Mary and Margery clearly complicates the early history of both names and more work needs to be done on their relationship in that period.

~

This chapter has been concerned with defining what we mean by 'popular' and with the statistical evidence relating to christian names in the period 1377–1700. It has also touched on the early history of popular names and their sources and on the linguistic developments of popular female names in particular. The intention now is to look more closely at the practices that lie behind the statistics and the role of the name-givers.

Notes

1 See also W. Coster, *Baptism and Spiritual Kinship in Early Modern England* (2002).

2 One or two entries in the lists puzzle me. For example, I note that Julian is listed as a boys' name although in my experience it was more usually a girls' name in that period. I am also surprised to find Martha as a boys' name and it is not always clear to me why some names are listed separately, e.g. Hester and Esther.

3 C. C. Fenwick, *The Poll Taxes of 1377, 1379 and 1381*, Parts 1 and 2 (Oxford 1998, 2001). Not all the names have been identified. Edus, for example, a male name in the returns, was earlier a female name.

4 These include over 500 male names in a rental of 1443 for the Honor of Clitheroe (Lancs.). W. Farrer (ed.), *The Court Rolls of the Honor of Clitheroe*, I (Manchester, 1897), pp. 497–507. Also, 1500 male and female names have been drawn from fifteenth-century Yorkshire wills.

5 It might seem strange to have a category described as 'rare' in which there are no names but in the conflated county lists many names have total counts under ten.

6 P. Hanks and F. Hodges, *A Dictionary of First Names* (Oxford, 1990) and E. G. Withycombe, *The Oxford Dictionary of English Christian Names*, 3rd edn (Oxford 1977).

7 E.g. R. Holmes, *The Chartulary of St John of Pontefract*, Yorkshire Archaeological Society, Record Series XXV, XXX (1899, 1902).

8 D. A. Postles, *The Surnames of Devon*, English Surnames Series (London, 1995), p. 180.

9 G. Redmonds, *Surnames and Genealogy: A New Approach* (Boston, 1997), p. 116.

10 D. Farmer, *The Oxford Dictionary of Saints*, 3rd edn, (Oxford, 1992).

11 The pet form was 'Kit', in use long before Christopher became popular, and this probably explains the very local distribution of the surname Kitson. Spellings such as 'Kyrchyan' and 'Kirchin' were used in the north in the sixteenth and seventeenth centuries, similar to 'Kyrstyan', discussed by Withycombe.

12 Similarly Eleanor had the same origin as Helen and Ellen, and aliases which involve these names suggest that some people at least were aware of the links.

13 W. P. Baildon (ed.), *Court Rolls of the Manor of Wakefield*, YAS XXIX (1901), p. 174.

14 Its doublet Margery was also highly placed throughout much of the period but then slowly declined in the seventeenth century.

15 *Testamenta Eboracensia*, Surtees Society XLV (1864), p. 184 n.

16 *Testamenta Eboracensia*, Surtees II (1836), pp. 184–6.

17 J. Kaner (ed.), *Goods and Chattels 1552–1642* (Hull, 1994), p. 60.

18 *Testamenta Eboracensia*, Surtees XLV, p. 245.

19 A. G. Dickens, 'A Municipal Dissolution of Chantries at York, 1536', *Yorkshire Archaeological Journal* XXXVI (1947), p. 169.

20 R. F. Hunnisett, *Sussex Coroner's Inquest, 1558–1603* (London, 1996), p. 139.

21 G. Redmonds (ed.), 'Christian Names in the West Riding, Part 2', *Old West Riding*, New Series, 15 (1995), p. 15.

CHAPTER FOUR

Parents and Godparents

T he frequency tables show that a relatively small number of names achieved popularity in the period 1350–1700, and that a high proportion of those which did so were
consistently very numerous. The loss of some names in that period was compensated
for by the introduction and revival of others and this chapter concentrates on the name-
giving practices that underlie both the continuity and new choices. Consideration will
be given to the influence of the gentry and to the respective roles of parents and godparents within the wider community.

Inherited names

The stability in the national name-stock can be explained, in part, by the tradition
which the English developed under the Normans, of one generation passing its
names on to the next, certainly among the nobility and the gentry. Evidence for
that can be found in even the earliest documents and it was obvious enough to be
commented on by local historians. In 1714 Ralph Thoresby wrote of the
Gascoignes 'that they affected to have the eldest Son to be of the same Name with
his Father for many generations and, as a result, there were no fewer than fifteen
Williams in a lineal Descent'.[1] In other cases two names were alternated over the
generations. For example the estates of the Currers of Kildwick passed from
Hugh to Henry, then from Henry to Hugh and so on without a break, until Henry
Currer died without issue in 1757. The succession then passed to Henry
Richardson whose mother had been a Currer.

This practice ensured the continued use of less popular first names, and the
survival of others long after they had become generally unfashionable. For
example Samuel Margerison, who edited Calverley parish registers in 1880,
wrote that the Dawsons of Wrose, a village between Leeds and Bradford, had
'religiously preserved the family name of Martin', so that there had been 'not

fewer than thirteen generations of Martin Dawsons', a traditional use of the name throughout a period when it enjoyed little general popularity. Indeed it was rare in 1377–81, in fortieth position, although it performed slightly better in Elizabeth's reign and was usually in the thirties. After that it declined further until it re-emerged as a popular name in the 1950s.

The detailed pedigrees of gentry families confirm the importance of parental influence in their case, but we know less about the custom in families lower down the social scale, particularly in the pre-parish register period when so few names were in use. In any case we know now that the godparents were a major influence on name-giving during the late medieval, Tudor and Stuart periods, and some examples of that have already been quoted. More will follow, but statistics quoted by Smith-Bannister in *Names and Naming Patterns* leave us in no doubt about how important the custom was, with over 85% of boys named after at least one godfather in the 1550s and 1560s. That was not necessarily true everywhere and the percentage was considerably less from about 1620, although still in excess of 45% in the 1690s. The pattern was similar where girls were concerned and the significance of this is not just that godparents played a leading role in naming children but that frequently it was their own names that were passed on.

Smith-Bannister was cautious in his treatment of this subject, since the results depended on what he rightly describes as a 'patchwork of evidence'. Nevertheless he was confident that the figures were representative and described them as 'thoroughly compelling'. As the influence of the godparents waned during the seventeenth century so that of the parents increased, for both boys and girls, 'although the pace of change was uneven from one parish to another', and the evidence suggested that fathers rather than mothers were exerting more influence.

The following references from Leeds illustrate how important the practice was from 1700 at all levels of society, especially in preserving names that were less common:

> 1735, 1 May: Abiathar baptised, son of Abiathar Roome.
> 1736, 3 April: Patrick baptised, son of Patrick Ryley.
> 1740, 25 February: Willoughby baptised, son of Willoughby Wood.
> 1744, 2 January: Marmaduke baptised, son of Marmaduke Ayreton.
> 1749, 25 April: Major baptised, son of Major Judson.

As the population increased, this desire for continuity from one generation to the next would have a more far-reaching effect. The names of the parents might be given to one son and one daughter, but each child might then wish to keep faith with the parents' names. In that way a family which ramified within a particular area could be ultimately responsible for the more widespread use of their pre-ferred names, influencing and even creating a local fashion. I was once asked to trace a man called Eli Sutcliffe in the township of Stainland, by a client who was confident that the name would prove to be distinctive. The census returns of 1851 showed that Eli and Hannah Sutcliffe were living there along with their ten-year-old son Eli, but among their immediate neighbours were Eli and Rebecca Sutcliffe, and Eli and Elizabeth Sutcliffe. Moreover three neighbouring Sutcliffe families had children named Eli, aged one, five and ten. A distinctive name was expanding here in one family.

Siblings with the same name

This is perhaps the time to look at the circumstances in which surviving siblings bore the same christian name, a phenomenon that was not uncommon in the sixteenth and seventeenth centuries, and is disturbing now to family historians, especially if the name was common. For example, Thomas Adde of Kexbrough, who died in 1567, was the father of Thomas Adde the elder and Thomas Adde the younger;[2] two of Isabel Wood's six children, named in her will in 1564, were 'John, myne Eldest sone and John my second son';[3] on 27 April 1644, two sons of Mr Richard Horsfall of Storthes Hall were named Richard, 'beinge twindles'.[4] J. C. Cox, in *Parish Registers of England*, has even quoted several examples of three brothers with the same given name and we cannot help wondering how families dealt with that situation.

In fact it is not uncommon in earlier records to come across brothers called John where the younger of the two was regularly described as Jenkin, the diminutive serving to establish that he was John 'junior'.[5] It must be suspected therefore that men such as Jenkyn Mawde (1540) and Jenkin Greetam (1625) had older brothers also called John. The most explicit evidence of this practice that I have seen is in a Swaledale will of 1580, in which Agnes, the widow of Ralph Alderson, expressed a wish that her goods should be equally divided between her three children, John, Jenkin and Phyllis. She then continued:

> ...and also I will that Jenkin my sonne shalbe ordered and governed by John his brother and if the said Jenkin do refuse to be ordered by the said John that then the said Jenkin shall clame no benefytt by this my will but the said John to have the orderinge of the same to the use of the said Jenkin.[6]

These examples all concern boys, and there is rather less evidence to indicate that girls' names were affected to the same extent, although several cases have been noted. The historian J. Horsfall Turner, the author of *Idle in Olden Times*, quoted the will of Robert Clarkson of Idle in 1577, in which he made bequests to two daughters called Anne. Similarly, in 1612, William Wilkinson of Slaidburn left 20s to Margaret his eldest daughter but only 8s 4d to Margaret the younger.[7] In Howden, in 1563, the burial took place of Jennett and Jennett, the daughters of Anthony Newes.[8] In view of such evidence it is important for historians and genealogists to note that terms such as 'elder' and 'younger' were not used just to separate the generations but could refer to siblings, even to twins.

Smith-Bannister suggested that this 'irritating habit' might be attributed to the practice of naming children after their godparents, whilst others have specu-lated that fathers were responsible, over-anxious perhaps to ensure that their name should continue into the next generation. The work of Robert Anderson, a prominent American genealogist, throws new light on the same custom in New England. Having studied more than a dozen examples, almost equally divided between boys and girls, his conclusion was that in every case where surviving children bore the same name it was because they were half siblings, that is to say they did not have the same mother. In most cases the names of the brothers were the same as the name of the father but his interesting theory was that 'when a man had children by two wives, the second wife might wish to honor the hus-band by bestowing his name on one of her children by him, even though a child by the first wife might also bear the name'.[9]

However, that cannot always be the explanation, for there are other instances in which full siblings bore the same name, a point that Robert Anderson made himself when discussing New England families whose children had been named in Old England. We should not be surprised perhaps that the same name could be given to sons born to different mothers, to legitimate and illegitimate sons, even to twins, and it was probably to be expected if a son bearing the favoured name died but, in cases which do not fall into these categories, we should take account of the godparents' influence.

The influence of the local community

The new names which came into the lists in the period 1350–1700 were not all of one kind. A few had been in use previously but appear to have benefited from changes in fashion, locally or more generally; others were names brought back into favour after centuries of neglect, and a small number were freshly coined, representative of parental choices which cannot always be explained. However, evidence brought forward later will show that the local popularity of some first names can be traced back to one person, and it is therefore that person's motive which matters. Indeed, the extent to which an individual or one family could influence naming practices within a local community may have been under-estimated.

The reality is that the increased use of a first name was not necessarily con-fined to the family unit, but could take place within the wider network of kins-folk, servants, friends and neighbours. The importance of 'neighbourliness' in the Tudor period has already been commented on by Mildred Campbell in *The English Yeoman*, and it went far beyond what we now understand by the word. In the sixteenth and seventeenth centuries a good neighbour carried out functions in the community 'that are today performed by nurses, physicians, social workers, secretaries, real estate agents and lawyers', not just out of altruism, but because it was essential if the village was to be a harmonious place to live in. Neighbours helped one another out in legal and business matters, acting as 'sureties', 'umpires', 'witnesses' and 'arbitrators', knowing that they would in turn need such services themselves. Although their behaviour was partly dictated by self-interest it had far-reaching consequences that influenced every aspect of daily life:

> The spirit of good fellowship which neighborliness bred permeated and helped to shape the most colorful and attractive features of social relationships. It pervaded the atmosphere of community gatherings. It was present when men sang songs and drank ale at the village tavern. It caused groups to linger on the steps of the parish church on Sunday morning while women exchanged receipts for marchpane and quodinack of plums, and men talked of their crops and the weather.[10]

These groups formed communities within the larger community, and there are numerous direct and indirect references to them in early sources. They could be bound together by religion, like the groups of Catholic recusants recorded in Barwick near Leeds in 1604.[11] The list there was headed by a gentleman, Mr John Gascoigne, and it included his wife Anne, nee Ingleby, and his mother Maud, nee Arthington, both also from recusant gentry families. Below him in the list were Laurence Wilson, the 'master of his colemyns', Edward Bennet 'his milner at Hillom' and Thomas Thompson his shepherd. Others named were the wives of his men servants and four of his women servants, including Elizabeth Wortley, 'thought to be a dangerous recusant in persuading'. Such a community might cut across both family and class and it was not contained in one township. No doubt the same was sometimes true where Puritan zealots and seventeenth-century dissenters were concerned.

An entry in Leeds parish register for 1584 appears to identify another such group, stating that Richard Lumbye of Leeds, an excommunicated Catholic, had 'dyed at Chappilltowne...and was by his kynsfolks and neighbours brought towards the churche to be buryed'. A confrontation of several days followed between 'hys frends' on one side and the churchwardens and curate on the other, during which time a licence was sought, and refused, at York; eventually Richard was buried, even though it is not clear where. This was a close-knit group but it seems unlikely that all Richard's family and friends were avowed Catholics, although they may have been sympathisers.[12]

There would have been factions in every parish, some brought about by divided loyalties, others the result of shared beliefs, or shared interests and occupations. For example, in the late sixteenth century, my own township of Lepton was divided between two lordships, each based in an adjoining township, some of the tenants owing suit to Mr Kaye of Woodsome, the others to Mr Beaumont of Whitley. More importantly, perhaps, some of the men in the township were clothiers whereas others worked at the iron forge, under a manager who was not a local man. In the manor rolls of the period there are several injunctions which seem to single out the unpopular practices of these 'smithymen'. There were also coal miners or colliers in the township and here, as elsewhere in parts of the old West Riding, these men formed independent groups, quite often at variance with neighbouring colliers. The quarter sessions rolls contain many examples of disputes which reflect such divisions, some of them extremely violent.[13]

In fact court records of various kinds provide very clear evidence of the sometimes bitter feuds which divided families and whole communities. J. S. Purvis, in his work on ecclesiastical records, has shown often enough how a dispute about tithes, or even about pews in the church, could split the parish down the middle and then smoulder on for years, erupting from time to time in violent and bloody affrays. One such affair, in 1556, was ostensibly about where a family should sit in church but, as the witnesses came forward, it became increasingly clear that the quarrel was connected in some way with a defamation suit and, before that, with an argument over peat-cutting rights.[14] Phrases such as 'with his own folkes' or 'with his partakers and adherents' alert us to the existence of those factions and remind us how the term 'kinsfolk and neighbours' helped to identify the Catholic recusants in Barwick.

Other similar phrases refer to kindred and friends: Sir Robert Skargill was said in a Star Chamber case of 1531 to be 'a gentilman of grete landes, kynred and frendes withyn the contrey', whilst Francis Parkin requested in his will that his farm be let 'to none but...frendes and kynfolkes at Lund' (1554). There is also evidence though that kinship was no guarantee of friendship. An indenture of award in 1456 related to 'variances and debates' between two parties of gentlemen in the Mirfield area, each with their 'kin and friends', and it is noticeable that there were men called Beaumont in both factions.[15]

In other Star Chamber cases the reference was to kindred and 'alliance', the latter term seeming to identify a more loosely knit group of relatives. In 1541 William Knevet was said to be 'greatly frynded, akyn and alyed' in the county and Sir Nicholas Fairfax was surrounded in 1534 by 'so many of his consanguinyte and alians' that an ordinary man could have no justice.[16] The will of Robert Hirste of Leeds (1499) tells us of another distinction that might be drawn: 'to Elizabeth Jopis my alyance, for hir good service v marke; to Alison Forster my servaunt for her service...xs'.[17]

The spiritual community[18]

Another dispute, in 1534, between John Standishe of Lancaster and Robert Bekkett of Burton in Lonsdale, used a term which in this present context may be even more significant than 'friends' or 'alliance', one that on examination gives us a closer insight into such communities. On that occasion Robert Bekkett's supporters were said to include 'tenauntes and inhabitantes of the maner, beyng of there alye and *affinyte*', all sworn to uphold an unlawful act.[19]

The significant word here is 'affinity', which echoes a much earlier document. It was Cox in *Parish Registers* who wrote that Cardinal Ximenes had used his influence in 1497 'to secure the registration of the baptism of children throughout Western Christendom', as part of an attempt to 'correct the laxity of morals whereby divorces had become frequent'. It was claimed that this had been possible 'on the score of alleged spiritual relationship or affinity arising out of acts of sponsorship', that is to say that any two people wishing to dissolve their marriage were able to do so by pleading successfully that it was invalid because of a spiritual relationship between them. Cox reminds us that 'godparents were regarded by the Catholic church as spiritual parents who were spiritually related to each other and to the infant of whom they were sponsors, within the prohibited degrees'. The divorces alluded to by the cardinal were possible when there were no records to test the truth of the allegation, as a result of which it became general in some countries for the names of the sponsors or godparents to be registered at the time of baptism.

Visitation articles during Mary's reign reminded the clergy to keep the register with the names of the godparents and, where those entries survive, they give us some idea of the intricate connections which linked families in the parishes of Tudor England. David Hey has already drawn our attention to the significance of the word 'country' in this period which could refer to a local region rather than to England.[20] Now it is important for local and family historians to recognise the existence of these smaller, local communities or 'networks', for, in conjunction with other information, they can help us to identify individuals and follow their movements, not just from one village to another or between manors, but even from one country to another. The English origins of many emigrants to New England have been traced through associates who travelled with them or with whom they communicated after their arrival. One of the keys to these networks is undoubtedly the names they bore, both surname and christian name, and accurate information about the regional use of such names is bound to help the researcher.

The term 'kith and kin' now means little more than the word 'kin' on its own, but in the past it is likely to have identified the 'affinity' just referred to, a community in which the godparents were crucial. When an individual accepted the role of godparent, that automatically cemented a spiritual bond between the godparent and the child and between the two families. The alternative word 'godsib' (i.e. related through God), emphasised that bond and was still used frequently in that sense in the sixteenth century. In November 1561, for example, Robert Hudson of Barkston fell sick and drew up his will.[21] In it were the words 'I gyve to my gotsip Robart Man, for his paynes takynge in drawynge of this my last will, and also for makyng my new lease betwixt Mr Barkeston and me, 3s 4d'.

The fact that the two 'gotsips' had the same christian name is very significant, as we shall see, but their relationship was clearly one between friends and colleagues which involved close mutual support. That intimacy is apparent in the much earlier example of Chaucer's Wife of Bath (c.1390); she was called Alisoun, as was her 'gossib' who, she said, 'knew myn herte and eek my privetee bet than our parisshe-preest'.[22] The change in spelling which gave us modern 'gossip' took place before the word acquired its more pejorative meaning, for Lancelett Threlkeld was described in an inquisition post mortem of 1490, as the 'gossip' of Lancelett Hoton of Hutton in Cumberland. Again it is important to notice the date and the fact that both men had the same christian name.

There are some parish registers where the names of the godparents have survived and those for the second half of the sixteenth century are vital to our understanding of naming practices in Elizabethan England. One of the most obvious ways in which the social and spiritual bond could be made apparent was for the christian name of one or more of the godparents to be given to the new-born child, so it was not unusual, as we have seen, for 'gossips' to have the same name. This custom is often clearly evidenced in the registers and it enabled a name, in a generation or two, to become characteristic of an extremely localised community, one which reflected the network of kinship and the common interests which bound families together within an alliance or affinity. At the same time the personal name they had in common helped to identify the group to the outside world. The first name Giles, adopted by the Kaye family of Lancashire and Yorkshire, will illustrate these points.

Giles

Giles was a rare name in England in the fourteenth century and there were just two in the 21,000 names for the West Riding in 1379. Nor was it recorded in those returns of 1379–81 which survive for Lancashire. By 1545, however, it was enjoying localised popularity in both counties, in a number of parishes on either side of the border, although the full extent of its expansion is not yet entirely clear. In Staincliffe Wapentake, for example, a territory which covers much of lower Ribblesdale, Giles was the twenty-fourth most frequent name in the list of adult males taxed in 1543, with 12 examples in a total of 2,335.[23] This relative popularity was more localised than the statistics suggest and it does not appear to have been part of a national trend, since the name is absent from Smith-Bannister's list of 1538–49.

The first recorded Giles Kaye, described as 'of Bury' in Lancashire, is mentioned in a violent family dispute which came to a head in 1472, in the Yorkshire parish of Almondbury.[24] This man was almost certainly the Giles Kaye who was mentioned six years later in the will of Sir John Pilkington, the head of a gentry family with extensive estates in both Yorkshire and Lancashire: he named Giles Kaye as a person in his service, along with Giles Lingard.[25] The Kayes themselves were a gentry family with branches in both Bury and Almondbury and, because the names of the godparents survive in the Almondbury register from 1558 to 1601, we can see how Giles came to be used more widely among their kith and kin:

> 1560, 3 August: Giles baptised, son of Humphrey Armitedge; godfathers Giles Kaye and Giles Langfelde.
> 1565, 17 June: Giles baptised, son of Giles Kaye off Lane; godfather Giles Kaye.
> 1573, 10 May: Giles baptised, son of John Hanson; godfather Giles Kaye.
> 1590, 9 February: Giles baptised, son of Thomas Croslande; godfather Giles Kaye.

In the sixteenth century Giles was used by at least 15 families in that parish, but it became traditional with one or two only, most notably with a family bearing the unusual name Dollive. Their use of it suggests that the link with the Kayes must date from at least about 1520, for Giles Dollyf of Wakefield and Giles Key (sic) of Almondbury were both listed in the subsidy of 1545.[26] There are several leases and other documents which emphasise the close connection between the two families and one practical result of this for the family historian is that Giles serves as a key to the Dollives' distribution for something like 200 years. Again though it is the inclusion of the names of the godparents in the register which emphasises how close the two families were:

> 1564, 20 August: Dorothy baptised, daughter of John Dolyffe, godparents Giles Dolyffe and Dorothy Kaye.
> 1577, 10 February: Dorothy baptised, daughter of Giles Dolyffe, godmother Anne Kaye.

Dollive is a very rare surname now, even in Yorkshire where it originated, and the evidence of the Almondbury registers suggests that the family moved out of the parish about 1590. We know something of their movements, for a Giles Dolliffe died intestate in Hull in 1601[27] and a later Giles Doliffe, mentioned in a quarter sessions indictment, was living in Halifax in the 1690s. At this stage the perception of a direct link between these men and the families in Wakefield and Almondbury rests entirely on the unusual surname and christian name they shared.

The decline of Giles in that part of Yorkshire in the seventeenth century is apparent from the records, although it did not immediately fall out of favour with the Kayes and there were three Giles Kayes named in the hearth tax return locally in 1672, in Lepton, Shelley and Walton. In Almondbury it had little lasting influence on naming habits and not many of the families who used it in the sixteenth century did so into a second generation. By 1650 just a few old men in the parish bore the name.

It is clear that within certain periods a name such as Giles can be used by researchers, along with a surname, to locate a person's place of origin and identify which branch of the family he might belong to. Of course, the value of first names as a finding aid diminishes if they became generally popular and more widely distributed. Nevertheless, a few names in current use can still be used in that way, for they have never achieved widespread popularity and were first chosen by the families centuries ago. It is the role of the godparent that makes such names a valuable tool for historians and it seems certain that the custom was well established before 1550.

The early name-givers

Several significant points have emerged from this history of Giles. Not only were the Kayes an influential gentry family but they chose to demonstrate their influence through the names given to their numerous godchildren. As a result Giles became a relatively popular name for a short period within the parish. The fact that Giles Lingard had been named alongside Giles Kay in 1478 suggests that the custom was already in place by 1450. It will be seen later that other christian names passed from the Kaye family to their kinsmen and tenants, notably Judith, Arthur and Laurence.

There is, of course, no parish register material for the period 1450–1550 to confirm the naming connection between godparents and godchildren but some evidence, both direct and circumstantial, can be found in deeds, wills and court rolls. For example, James Witle (i.e. Whiteley) of Rishworth drew up his will in 1534 and made his son Georgie Witle an executor; a second Georgie Witle, the son of Ranalde, inherited 20 sheep. These two bequests draw our attention to a name used within the immediate family but the names of the overseers of the will were Georgie Godley, Georgie Hoill and Georgie Crosle, and their shared christian name is surely evidence of the Whiteleys' wider circle of kith and kin, a relationship which may be further emphasised by the consistent use of the diminutive, and which must go back to the earliest years of the century.[28] George was a rare name in England in 1377–81 but was popular in some regions by about 1550 and this will demonstrates one way in which that expansion was taking place.

Other wills take the practice back even further, certainly into the late fifteenth century. In 1500 a Cheshire lady named Dame Jane Strangways left 40s to each of her five god-daughters; their surnames were Ashton, Dutton, Middop, Ingham and Kirk and all five had the christian name Jane.[29] In the will of William Holleroode (i.e. Holroyd), also written in 1500, the name that catches our attention is Edward, another that had been rare in 1379. After making bequests in favour of the church, a local chapel of ease, the vicar and 'the makyng of Sowerby brige', the testator gave £7 to each of his brothers, John, Thomas and Edward. These were followed by gifts of money to Edward Wodhede, Edward Shepley and his brother, and Edward Maude, the bastard son of Edmunde. William then made his wife 'executrice att the ouersight and discrecion of Edward Waterhouse and George Haldesworde'. William Holleroode may have been childless but he was not without family, and it is the christian name Edward in the will that gives us an insight into his kith and kin.[30]

It was the name of William's brother in the above case that was the key to his affinity and there is an example, just over a hundred years later, in which a sister's name plays a similar role. By then Judith was a favourite with some branches of the Kayes in Almondbury parish, and several girls were given the name in the late sixteenth and early seventeenth centuries: one of these was the sister of Arthur Kaye and, in his will of 1607, he left £8 6s 4d to her under her married name of Fenay. However, he also left 40s to his god-son Arthur Hawksworth and 20s to each of his god-daughters, Judith Crosland and Judith Johnson.[31] The register shows that when they were baptised it was Arthur, not Judith Fenay, who was a godparent. Nevertheless it seems clear that they were named in her honour.

Sometimes, where there is no direct documentary evidence of a connection between individuals, the only clue is the christian name itself. In 1377–81, for example, Laurence was an infrequent name but it occurred several times later in situations which seem to place it at the heart of an affinity. In the legal documents referred to earlier, when Giles was being discussed, four of the main participants in the family feud of 1472 were called Laurence: their surnames were Overall, Beaumont, Alderley and Kaye. The Kayes were at the centre of this dispute and Laurence had been a family name for generations, certainly since 1376 when it was infrequent generally. In 1498, in a second and quite unrelated matter, a Lancashire gentleman called Laurence Townley was granted land in Rimington by his neighbour Laurence Shuttleworth who then appointed Laurence Smyth as his attorney, probably a further example of how 'gossips' supported one another in a practical way.[32]

Other types of document can draw our attention to significant concentrations of uncommon first names. For example a subsidy roll for 1545 listed three men from the tiny hamlet of Morton near Bingley who all had the first name Sander (Alexander),[33] and in a sixteenth-century tithe rental for Nesfield near Ilkley there were three Costins, a very rare first name.[34] A sequence of title deeds for the Shibden and Brighouse corn mills contains the names of three gentlemen, Leonard Lacy, Leonard Beaumont and Leonard Ramsden (1533–1576). Leonard had not been recorded locally in 1379 but it was becoming more popular in the sixteenth century and it draws attention here to the possible social connections of men involved in a financial transaction.[35]

The history of Brian, an exceptionally rare name in 1377–81, provides explicit evidence of how such a name might become popular. It has a Celtic origin, and came to be used by the Stapeltons after they were connected by marriage to Brian fitzAlan, one of the great Barons of Richmondshire.[36] The Stapeltons had extensive estates in Yorkshire, and were one of a very few English families to use the name Brian in the fourteenth and fifteenth centuries. In 1461 Brian Stapelton made bequests to his son Brian and to his godsons, Brian Redman and Brian Smyth – early evidence of how the name was beginning its expansion among the family's kith and kin.[37] They continued to play a central role in its development. In 1596 Bryan Stapelton took possession of lands in Moor Monkton that had formerly belonged to his grandfather, Sir Bryan Stapelton: one of the closes (enclosures) was actually called Brian Riddinge, and the witnesses included Bryan Murgetroyd and Bryan Hallewell. In a confirmation deed, dated 1597, Bryan Spynck and Bryan Tate were the witnesses.[38] Brian was in regular use in Yorkshire in 1538–1700, but it is missing from Smith-Bannister's frequency lists for that period.

These first name 'clusters' are unlikely to be the result of coincidence. Denis, or Dionisius as it was written in Latin, was another name that had become rare by c.1550 – rare generally that is – for it was a favourite with many families in Kildwick parish. When William Oglethorpe sold off his property there, from 1596, the purchasers included men with the following surnames: Cockshott, Coates, Barrett, Garforth, Robinson, Eastburn, Mitchell, Lund and Davy. In every case the christian name was Denis.[39]

It is difficult to say how old this custom might be. The evidence above takes it back into the fifteenth century and there are occasional examples from the early fourteenth century. The tight-knit distribution of rare names such as Osanne and Thurstan in 1377–81 may be further evidence that it was already well established in the fourteenth century, in which case, of course, it may help to explain why the name-stock was so small.

~

In medieval and Tudor society there were groups of families in each parish who might be linked in a variety of ways; socially and economically, by shared beliefs and manorial ties, or spiritually through the godparent relationship. The examples in this chapter show that such links are often evident in a shared christian name, one that was sometimes very distinctive in its own region but not popular generally. The spiritual ties began to weaken in the seventeenth century but individual families sometimes kept faith with a distinctive name, ensuring its survival through the eighteenth and nineteenth centuries. It is a development of potential value to historians and genealogists and it will now be scrutinised more closely in accounts of names from different categories.

Notes

1   R. Thoresby, *Ducatus Leodiensis* (1715, 2nd edn 1816), appendix, p. 142.
2   S. O. Addy, 'The Addy Family of Darton', *Yorkshire Archaeological Journal* XXVII (1924), pp. 166–96.
3   From a will in the Borthwick Institute of Historical Research, York, Vol.17: Fol. 345.
4   F. A. Collins (ed.), *The Parish Registers of Kirkburton, 1541–1654* (Exeter, 1887), p. 246.
5   P. H. Reaney in *Origin* noted that where father and son bore the name the son was referred to as 'Janekyn', i.e. 'John junior'.
6   E. K. Berry (ed.), *Swaledale Wills and Inventories, 1522–1600*, Yorkshire Archaeological Society, Record Series CLII (1998), p. 235.
7   C. Spencer (ed.), *Slaidburn and Bowland Wills and Administrations*, 4 (Preston, 2001), p. 28.
8   G. E. Weddall (ed.), *The Registers of the Parish of Howden, 1543–1702*, Yorkshire Parish Register Society XXIV (1905), p. 33.
9   R. C. Anderson, 'Siblings of the Same Name in Colonial New England', *Names, Northeast* III (1981), pp. 31–40.
10 M. Campbell, *The English Yeoman under Elizabeth and the Early Stuarts* (Yale, 1942, reprinted 1983), p. 386. 'Marchpane' was an earlier form of marzipan, but I am unable to explain the meaning of 'quodinack'.
11 A. G. Dickens, 'Recusancy in Yorkshire, 1604', *YAJ* XXXVII (1951), pp. 24–48.
12 S. Margerison (ed.), *Leeds Parish Church Registers, 1571–1612*, Thoresby Society I (Leeds, 1891), p. 129.
13 See G. Redmonds, *Huddersfield and District under the Stuarts: Seventy Years of Law and Disorder* (Huddersfield, 1985).
14 J. S. Purvis, 'A Note on Pews and Stalls', *YAJ* XXXVII (1951), pp. 162–94.
15 See J. Lister (ed.), *Yorkshire Star Chamber Proceedings*, 4 YAS LXX (1927), p. 131 for Skargill; H. Thwaite (ed.), *Abstracts of Abbotside Wills, 1552–1688*, YAS CXX (1968), p. 4 for Parkin; A. S. Ellis (ed.), 'Yorkshire Deeds', *YAJ*, XIII (1895), p. 77 for the Mirfield case.
16 J. Lister, *Star Chamber Proceedings*, p. 55 and p. 9.
17 *Testamenta Eboracensia* 4, Surtees Society LIII (1869), p. 161.
18 The most recent book on this subject is W. Coster, *Baptism and Spiritual Kinship in Early Modern England* (Aldershot, 2002).
19 J. Lister, *Star Chamber Proceedings*, p. 9.
20 D. Hey, *Family Names and Family History* (London, 2000), pp. 126–31.
21 G. D. Lumb (ed.), *Testament Leodiensia, 1553–61*, Thoresby XXVII (Leeds, 1930), pp. 347–8.
22 I am grateful to Peter McClure for drawing my attention to this reference.
23 R. W. Hoyle (ed.), *Early Tudor Subsidies and Assessments, 1510–1547*, YAS CXLV (1987).
24 Kirklees Archives, West Yorkshire Archive Service, Whitley Beaumont WBL/12.
25 *Testamenta Eboracensia* 3, Surtees XCV (1865), pp. 238–40.
26 *Miscellanea*, Thoresby IX and XI (1899, 1904).
27 *Wills in the York Registry, 1594–1602*, YAS XXIV (1898).
28 J. W. Clay (ed.), *Halifax Wills: 1389–1514* (privately printed, n.d.).
29 *Testamenta Eboracensia* 3, Surtees XCV (1865), p. 186.
30 J. W. Clay, *Halifax Wills*.
31 G. Redmonds, *A Calendar of Yorkshire Deeds in Kansas* (privately printed, 1999), pp. 38–9.

32 R. P. Littledale (ed.), *Pudsay Deeds*, YAS CVI (1916), p. 262.

33 *Miscellanea*, Thoresby IX (1899), pp. 132–3.

34 C. T. Clay (ed.), *Yorkshire Deeds 5*, YAS LXIX (1926), p. 94.

35 *Ibid.*, pp. 11–13.

36 H. E. Chetwynd-Stapylton, 'The Stapeltons of Yorkshire', *YAJ* VIII (1884), p. 223.

37 W. Brown (ed.), *Yorkshire Deeds 3*, YAS LXII (1922), p. 89

38 W. Brown (ed.), *Yorkshire Deeds 2*, YAS L (1914), p. 131.

39 *Yorkshire Fines, 1594–1603*, YAS VIII (1890), pp. 53, 151, 152.

CHAPTER FIVE

Names from the Twelfth Century

In the twelfth century the name-stock in England was particularly rich and varied. It included Old English and Old Scandinavian names, often referred to as 'insular' names, as well as those brought here by the Normans and their followers; others had been introduced during the religious revival. Many of these progressively fell out of favour in the thirteenth century, although for different reasons, and the few that dominated the frequency lists of 1377–81 were the more popular Norman and Christian names. It is a phenomenon that has long been familiar to writers on the subject, who tend to emphasise how many names had disappeared and to comment on one or two rare survivors. In fact many more survived than has been realised and this chapter looks more closely at how that happened.

Surviving names from the eleventh century and earlier

We might suspect that more names survived than has been realised, for Smith-Bannister has Oswyn, Avery and Fulk at the lower end of his lists in the sixteenth century. None of those were prominent in 1377–81, although Fulk occurred in several counties and was well established in Lincolnshire. The reality is that we know very little about such names, for their success was for the most part very localised and little effort has been made to trace their history between 1300 and 1540. Far too often it has simply been said that a particular name 'died out altogether' or 'was revived in the nineteenth century', statements which often fail to stand up to close examination. Occasionally, it is true, Withycombe (English Christian Names) or Hanks and Hodges (First Names) say that a name 'lingered on in remote corners' or 'continued to be used by a few families', but the circumstances of that continued use, and the influence that such names had locally, are seldom investigated.

The place to start such an investigation is Lancashire for it has been said that names in this category continued to be used longer there than in most parts of England. It was a theme that Richard McKinley returned to on a number of occasions, although such names were important to him only for the light they threw on surname origins, and he did not look more closely into their histories. Among the examples he quoted were Thurstan, Sagar, Ottiwell and Orm, which helped to persuade him that 'in Lancashire, personal names of Scandinavian and Old English origin remained in use to later periods than in most parts of England'.[1] This has been a widely-held view, for Withycombe mentioned it in her remarks on Thurstan, and Hanks and Hodges identified Ughtred as a Shuttleworth family name.

McKinley seemed to be suggesting that in Lancashire names of this type were used from before the Conquest or immediately afterwards, until the seventeenth century at least, and that the county was unusual in that respect. If it were true it would be of particular interest to historians and genealogists for it would imply that for a very long period there were unique naming practices in that region. A closer look at the histories of individual names throws new light on the subject.

Thurstan

This name was brought directly to England by Scandinavians over a thousand years ago and it may never have fallen out of use. Less directly it arrived here via the Normans, who were after all of Scandinavian descent, and the Norman influence on the pronunciation is evident in the case of Turstanus Banastre, whose family was connected from c.1160 with Owersby, near Market Rasen in Lincolnshire.[2] This possible dual origin is important, for it explains why Thurstan was in widespread use in many parts of England as late as the thirteenth century, not just in those counties formerly controlled by the Danes. It survived long enough to give rise to by-names and surnames, and typical of these are John Turstein in Somerset (1250) and William Thurston in Wiltshire (1297).[3] As a result the surname is not particularly characteristic of the Danelaw, although popular enough in East Anglia, and it is actually more common now in Worcestershire than it is in Yorkshire.

Of course it was not unusual for such personal names to survive in occasional use into the thirteenth century and to give rise to surnames, but the interesting thing about Thurstan is the range and number of references long after 1300. Late examples have been noted in Worlaby (Lincolnshire), Hull (Yorkshire), Shernbourne (Norfolk), Derby and Bakewell (Derbyshire), Godalming (Surrey) and Coventry (Warwickshire), most of these in the poll tax returns of 1377–81 or later. However, Lancashire appears to have been its main 'home' from the late fourteenth century, particularly the southern part of the

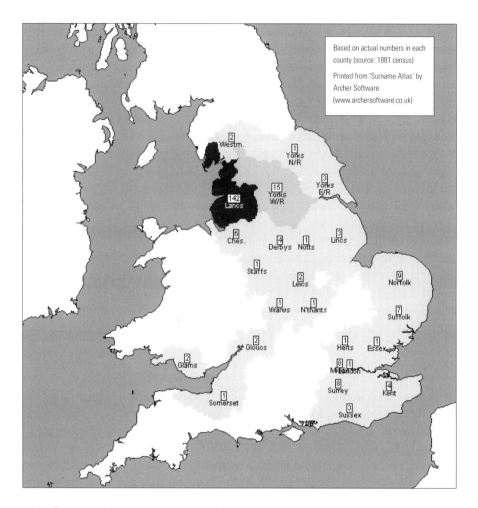

4 The first name Thurston (229) It is surprising to find that Thurston survived until so recently and that Lancashire was still its main home in 1881 (142). There were also 39 Thurstans and over half of these were in Lancashire also.

county, and Richard McKinley found several examples there in the sixteenth and seventeenth centuries.[4]

Although he did not look closely into how Thurstan survived as a first name after 1300, the clue to its history may lie in his account of the Banister family already referred to. Their early descent is far from clear but the surname appears to have been hereditary from the twelfth century at least, when a Richard Banester held land in Cheshire and Shropshire. The first Thurstan Banister on record was probably one of his sons and his personal name was not unusual at that time. However, its use in later generations is significant and other Thurstan Banisters have been recorded at intervals over several centuries. In the thirteenth century the family acquired an estate in Makerfield, south Lancashire, and it was there that Thurstan was locally popular in 1379, used by the Byroms, Leylands, Birkheads, Baxters, Simpsons and Morsalls. This was probably a tight-knit group of the Banisters' kith and kin, for there were none in the other Lancashire hundreds; this means that Thurstan had survived regionally thanks to one family, not because naming practices in Lancashire were different from those elsewhere. In fact Thurstan also survived in Suffolk in the sixteenth century.[5]

Nevertheless, during the fifteenth century Thurstan spread from Lancashire, and possibly also from Derbyshire, into west Yorkshire, and by the early sixteenth century there were significant concentrations around Penistone and Huddersfield, sometimes in families like the Kayes of Woodsome who had strong Lancashire associations.[6] The Duchy of Lancaster had important estates in both counties and that may explain some of the connections.[7]

Thurstan's distinctive history makes it interesting to genealogists whenever and wherever it is found, especially after 1700 when only occasional examples are recorded. For example, the surnames Lindley, Linley and Lindale occur in Leeds parish register between 1718 and 1748, and they are separately indexed. However, we can be reasonably sure they are references to the same person since Thurstan was the first name in each case. For the local historian it throws light on the previously unexplained place-name Thirstin, located in that part of Honley township where John Beaumont came into possession of land in 1573. His wife, Agnes Matley, had formerly been married to Thurston Matley of Bradfield near Penistone, and it seems likely that the property was named in his memory.

Ottiwell

The other rare names mentioned in connection with Lancashire were Ughtred, Orm, Sagar and Ottiwell, and the last of these, a Norman name, is worth looking at in more detail. Reaney found it in Essex (1169), Lincolnshire (c.1150) and Norfolk (1207) but it may never have been popular and its absence from the poll tax returns suggests that it had fallen completely out of fashion by the late fourteenth century. That seems to fit in with what McKinley discovered, for he comments on its rarity in England from the thirteenth century. However, when he says that it was widely used in Lancashire from the fifteenth century, he seems to imply that it had never dropped out of fashion there, and that is far from certain.[8]

In fact Ottiwell is found in Lancashire and Yorkshire from 1480, and soon afterwards in Nottinghamshire.[9] From c.1520 it occurred much more frequently, never quite becoming popular, but familiar to researchers on both sides of the Pennines well into the eighteenth century. It was particularly prominent in the vast parish of Rochdale, used there in 1642 by families called Taylor, Hill, Worrall and Whitworth. Just across the county boundary there were Ottiwells from the mid-sixteenth century in a group of Almondbury families that included the Gledhills,

Charlesworths, Marsdens and Hoyles. The Ottiwell Marsden who lived in Marsden in 1561 was probably responsible for the place-name Ottiwells, usually explained as 'Otto's well'.[10] In several of these families the name became traditional and in Coverdale, further to the north, there was a succession of Ottiwell Ryders between 1582 and 1755.[11]

The early Yorkshire references occur over a wide area but a connection with Lancashire can be inferred where families had a distinctively Lancashire surname, for example Gorrell, Howarth, Platt, Whitworth and Broadbent.[12] In the case of Otuel Schofield of Saddleworth (1545) the link is more explicit, for although he bore a Rochdale surname and lived on the Lancashire side of the Pennines, the township was in Yorkshire and that is where he was taxed. Many families had branches in both counties, for people moved freely between these border parishes, united by the landscape and various social and commercial interests.

It is the re-emergence of Ottiwell therefore that poses a problem, for there are no obvious links between the first families who used the name. It may be that one family was responsible initially, as in some cases described later in this chapter, but we have no evidence for that. One possible clue is that Ottiwell was the name of an allegedly illegitimate son of Hugh de Lacy and this family formerly had extensive estates in Lancashire and Yorkshire.[13]

Uhtred

The Old English name Uhtred has a quite different history, for its use in east Lancashire can be traced directly to Ughtred Shotilworth who was a freeholder in Ightenhill and Padiham in 1443.[14] Its earlier history is unclear but as examples of the name have been recorded in Pennine parishes in the mid-fourteenth century it may never have fallen completely out of use.[15] There are references to it into the eighteenth century at least and many of the spellings suggest that it was unusual enough to be a problem for most ministers. These include Huldred (1543), Hughetryde (1571), Ultrid (1738) and the very unusual Hugheinden (1571).[16] Unlike Thurstan and Ottiwell it seems to have remained very uncommon, but in some respects that increases its value to the local historian.

Other families known to have used Uhtred in that part of Lancashire are Hothersall, Parker, Glover, Hyde, Huntington and Hodgkinson, and in two of these the first name provides a valuable genealogical clue. In the case of Glover, which is a widely distributed and not very distinctive surname, it points to a direct connection in the sixteenth century between Ughtred Glover of Burnley and Ughtred or Uldred Glover of Bingley in west Yorkshire, a link that would normally be very difficult to prove. In the case of Oughtred Hodgson of Slaidburn it alerts us to a contraction of Hodgkinson that is sometimes evident in a direct alias, e.g. 1570 John Hodgekinson alias Hodgson of Hull.[17]

Hamlet

Names in this category occur in other counties and it would be wrong to consider Lancashire as unique in this respect. For example the name Hamo or Hamon(d) is another Norman name with a Germanic origin still in use in 1377–81.[18] Although it was not common generally at that time it is recorded in the coastal counties of the south and south east, from Devon round to East Anglia. Both forms of the name were well represented in Kent, especially in Canterbury and the Cinque Ports, and it remained in regular use there into the early seventeenth century.[19] Once again the suspicion must be that continuing migration from the Low Countries had helped it to survive, e.g. in 1377 Hammus Flemyng of Colchester.

The more distinctive 'Hamlet' is a double diminutive of this name, but it has no direct connection with Shakespeare's Hamlet which had an Icelandic origin. However, there may be an indirect connection if Withycombe's theory is correct. She suggested that English translators would have been familiar with Hamo and its diminutives and that this may have influenced the spelling of the Shakespearean name. When I first came across the diminutive in Yorkshire I knew nothing at all about it and was curious to know where it had come from. The very fact that it was so unusual finally helped me to trace its origins.

The person I had seen mentioned in the records was Hamlet Kennerley, first referred to in 1593, when he was indicted at Slaithwaite manor court for his part in an affray. Local parish registers tell us that he was twice married and that he was buried at Almondbury in 1624, but he apparently had no children by either wife and he remains a shadowy figure who lived for over 30 years somewhere between Elland and Huddersfield. Fortunately his surname was also uncommon at that time, and the unusual combination allows us to identify him in the records, no matter how the clerks wrote his name. For example, when he married Ann Aynelaye in 1594, his surname was given as Kennerslaye, and in his father-in-law's will (1610) he was Hammett Kenorley.

Hamlet's surname was actually a colloquial variant of Kenworthy, a development that appears to have no obvious linguistic explanation. From the late sixteenth century the two spellings occur side by side in the records without any explicit connection but then, in 1718, the alias 'Kenworthy vulgo [commonly known as] Kennerley' appears in the register. This entry confirms the colloquial pronunciation and also suggests that Hamlet Kennerley may have moved into the region from Cheshire, where Kenworthy is a common surname. It derives from the Cheshire place-name Kenworthy which had the same alias, so Kennerley was clearly not a pronunciation that developed in west Yorkshire.

Closer investigation into Hamlet Kennerley's first name serves to link him with a particular locality and a possible kinship group, for Hamo, and its diminutive Hamlet, had been used by the Masseys of Hale in Cheshire since the Norman

Conquest. More importantly there are deeds which prove that this family's many land interests included one in Elland where Hamlet Kennerley's name featured in the parish register in the 1590s. There were other gentry families in Cheshire and south Lancashire who used the name, including the Hydes, Holcrofts and Ashtons, and the likelihood is that all of them had close ties with the Masseys.

Anker

Anker is unusual enough to be of interest to historians and genealogists, particularly in family records of the sixteenth and seventeenth centuries, but it can be a problem that such names are seldom in the standard reference works. It was an isolated example of the name in one village that first attracted my attention but the investigation into its history threw new light on kinship patterns and migration over a much wider area.

The starting point is a man called Anchar Stansfall, who was godfather to Alice Tweddel in Almondbury in 1588. Both these surnames were new to the parish and there is no clear indication where the families might have come from. The spelling Stansfall is misleading for it looks like a variant of Stansfield which is a relatively common surname in that area. One clerk certainly had the local name in mind when he named a later Anker Stancefield as the overseer of the poor in 1690. Fortunately there are other entries such as Stansall and Stanser which point clearly to a derivation from Stancill, the name of a hamlet much further to the south, close to the border with Nottinghamshire. It is an area that has no obvious links with Almondbury.

In Almondbury, or more correctly in Farnley Tyas, that part of the parish where the Stansall family lived in the late sixteenth century, the name Anker soon passed to their kith and kin. It was used for a time by families called Thewlis and Tyas, once even as a girl's name. Because it is so rare it is also unfamiliar to transcribers, who have sometimes mistaken the 'n' of Anker for a 'u' – it is very easily done – and as a result references such as Auker Thewlis are not unusual in printed sources. The common alternative spellings, Anchar and Anchor, have proved misleading in quite a different way. For example, Anchor Wood in Farnley Tyas was said by one place-name expert to be where a hermit or anchorite once lived,[20] whereas it really commemorates Anchor Stansall who lived close by. The farm he occupied is still called simply 'The Wood'.

One clue to the earlier history of Anker is the location of the place-name Stancill, close to Nottinghamshire, for records show that the name was once more widely used there than in Yorkshire, particularly by gentry families such as the Frechevilles and the Wentworths.[21] It had been used by the Frechevilles from the thirteenth century and remained a favourite with them into the sixteenth century at least.[22] Despite the distance involved the link with Almondbury is easily established, for both the Frechevilles and the Wentworths were related to the family who held the lordship of Farnley Tyas. Their surnames are first recorded in the Almondbury register shortly before Anker Stansfall arrived in the parish and it seems probable that he was a tenant of one or other of these families. We are left to wonder if other men, whose names were less distinctive, had followed the same route. None of this touches on the name's earliest history and etymology but it is the Old Picard form of a Continental Germanic name and this is actually where the surname Frecheville also originated.[23]

Alfred or Alvery

We might have expected the Old English name Alfred to have had special meaning for the native population, thanks to the exploits of Alfred the Great. Ironically, though, its continued use after 1066 almost certainly owed more to the conquering Normans than to the English. It had spread in earlier centuries from England to France, enjoying special favour in Brittany, and there is no doubt that many of those who bore the name in post-Conquest England were Normans.[24] Typical early Latin forms include Aluredus and Alveredus, whereas Alverey, Auveray and Averay were Norman-French spellings, and they tell us how the name was being pronounced. Occasional spellings such as Alfridus and Alfredus might seem to suggest an English rather than a Continental origin but those individuals were elsewhere called Alverey or Averey and a direct link with Saxon England seems unlikely. Certainly the Norman version of the name prevailed, and it remained in occasional use in some parts of England into the fourteenth century, late enough to give rise to the surnames Averay and Avery.

Although it had fallen out of favour by 1377–81 a few examples were recorded in East Anglia and Oxfordshire and isolated examples such as these can have fascinating local histories. In Dewsbury, for example, Alvery achieved some local popularity in the sixteenth and seventeenth centuries and, when we examine the circumstances behind that, the evidence actually points to a man called Alvery de Suleigny. There is no evidence that he ever lived in the county, but it is certain that in the thirteenth century he held land in Manston, a locality just to the east of Leeds.[25] From him the property passed to the de Manstons, along with the personal name, and they kept faith with it well into the fifteenth century, possibly until their surname became extinct towards the end of the century.

By that time, though, Alvery had already passed from the Manstons to their kith and kin. The clue to that is in a deed of 1433 in which Alvered Manston granted the manor to John Nevyll, a conveyance which had the surnames Norfolk, Moore and Gascoigne among the witnesses.[26] All three surnames then reappear alongside Manston in a variety of documents. For example, Alvered Manston made his will in 1439, when Alveredus Northfolk was a beneficiary, and in 1488 Alvered More witnessed the settlement of the manor. It is true that no genealogical evidence has yet been found to connect these families with the Manstons, but they were certainly linked socially and geographically and Alvery at that time was found only in this part of the county. Another prominent gentry family to use the name were the Mauleverers and they were directly connected by marriage to the Manstons.

However, the most important alliance in that period, at least in terms of Alvery's subsequent history, was the one between the Manstons and the Gascoignes, evidenced in a variety of documents from the early fifteenth century. Reference has already been made to the deed of 1433 but the two families are linked also in a grant of 1418 and in Alvered Manston's will of 1439. The Gascoignes eventually came into possession of the manor when Robert Gascoigne married Robert Manston's daughter, and the long-standing relationship was sealed when the Gascoignes also 'inherited' the first name Alvery. The family's pedigree shows that it remained a favourite choice for more than 500 years.[27]

Until the sixteenth century the history of Alvery in Yorkshire is relatively easy to follow, for the name was so uncommon. However, the Gascoignes were an influential and well-connected family and through them it spread much further afield. Sometimes the link is explicit: Alvery Birkby, for example, was the son of James Birkby, a man who held land in Dewsbury and York in the 1560s and whose wife had Gascoigne ancestry. In the case of the Pease family of Kippax, with whom Alvery was popular from c.1450, the links can only be inferred at this stage, but the two families were close neighbours for generations.

Another gentry family with strong Gascoigne connections were the Copleys of Soothill and Batley, and there were several Alverys in their family tree in the sixteenth and seventeenth centuries. They were almost certainly responsible for the more general but short-lived popularity that the name enjoyed in and around Dewsbury, a local distribution already alluded to: among the families who used the name there in the sixteenth century, occasionally also for girls, were the Akroyds, Goodalls and Armitages. What is also noticeable is that after the Copleys acquired the lordship of Cowling, a township at the western end of Kildwick parish, over 20 miles from Dewsbury, Alvery became popular for a time there also, used by the Aldersleys, Barretts, Laycocks and others.

Alvery continued to be used in various West Riding parishes in the eighteenth century, often in areas where the Gascoignes or the Copleys had interests, but the direct links with those families have not been traced. Moreover there is evidence that it survived from the fourteenth century in other parts of England, and it is likely to have a quite independent history in East Anglia, Oxfordshire and Nottinghamshire. Even so two things are clear, firstly that Alvery de Suleigny played an important part in the name's survival and secondly that its history in Yorkshire lasted from the thirteenth century to the nineteenth century, late enough to coincide with the revival of Old English Alfred.

Alfred may have a single Germanic origin but if we take into account the Old English and Norman sources, as well as its late revival, there are at least three separate strands in its history in this country. The different spellings allow us to keep these apart but there are other names for which that is not so easy. Godfrey, for example, is similar to Alfred in that it had a Germanic origin and was brought here by the Normans, but its history throws up some important differences.

Godfrey

Godfrey's etymology is not in doubt for it is an Old French form of Continental Germanic Godefrid, composed of two characteristic elements. There is evidence of its use by Flemings, French and Normans but little to suggest that it was popular in England in the Middle Ages, a claim made by Withycombe in *English Christian Names* and Hanks and Hodges in *First Names*. It was certainly missing from most counties in 1377–81 and it seems likely that some of the occasional examples in East Anglia and the south-east, notably in Sussex, may have had a Low Countries link. This source of Godfrey may have been overlooked, but when we look more closely at those who bore the name in the fourteenth and fifteenth centuries, it is surprising how often the Continental connection is explicit. For example there are several men referred to as Godfrey Braban in 1377–81 and a weaver called Godfrey de Ulenbergh in 1367. Even more explicit was the name of a York freeman in 1466, i.e. Godfrey Arnaldson, 'ducheman', whereas at other times the connection is merely implicit, e.g. 'Godefridus, servant of John Braban', a weaver taxed in Stow on the Wold in 1381. The Duchy of Brabant, an area now divided between Belgium and the Netherlands, was obviously an important source during that period.

References in those years have obvious implications for surname derivations but they also emphasise how rare by then the Norman 'Godefrei' may have been. Nevertheless it seems to have survived in the Midlands in some gentry families, among them the Foljambes and the Bosvilles who may have been related. Otherwise it remained very rare and that is emphasised by its absence from the national frequency tables for 1538–1700. Once again though a local usage draws attention to its significance for family historians, this time in west Yorkshire. The hearth tax returns for 1672 show that whilst Godfrey was a rare name in the county generally, it was relatively popular in and around Holmfirth. The table below records the occurrences of Godfrey in a group of ten townships, four representing the Holmfirth area, and the remainder from neighbouring parts of west Yorkshire.

The fact that Godfrey was not recorded at all in Dewsbury, Bradford, Halifax and Huddersfield speaks for itself, since none of these towns was very far from Holmfirth. Equally impressive are the negative totals for the adjoining townships of Saddleworth and Almondbury, especially as Meltham, Honley and Crosland

1672	Male population	Godfrey	
Dewsbury	97	0	
Bradford	188	0	
Halifax	365	0	
Huddersfield	127	0	
Holmfirth	311	21	
Meltham	64	7	Holme Valley
Honley	78	3	
Crosland	68	2	
Almondbury	103	0	
Saddleworth	243	0	

were all in Almondbury parish.[28] The figures emphasise how discrete the ramification was in that part of the county and they demonstrate also how misleading the statistics in the national frequency tables can be. On this evidence, Godfrey was popular in Holmfirth but unknown in most neighbouring parishes.

Holmfirth was partly in Almondbury and partly in Kirkburton, for the town had grown up round the chapel of ease, and it straddled the boundary that separated the two parishes. In what seems at first like a coincidence Godfrey was first recorded in both parishes in 1568, once by the Greens and once by the Armitages, and it became an immediate favourite locally, used by up to 30 other families in the next 25 years. For most of that time there were no adults called Godfrey, so the name could not be passed directly to a newly-baptised child by a godfather. Nonetheless the affinity of the families concerned is implicit in the baptismal entries.

We can illustrate that via the Armitages, one of the two families that had introduced Godfrey into the Holme Valley in 1568. The name was immediately taken up by several other Armitage families, notably at the 'Armitage' to which they owed their surname, but also by branches in Crosland, Fulstone and Netherthong. The parish registers reveal just how central these families were then to the wider use of the name, for they acted as godparents when Godfrey passed to the Swallows, Beaumonts, Brooksbanks, Baileys, Tyases and Waterhouses. Several of these families then contributed to the expansion themselves.

We still cannot be certain how Godfrey first came to be used by the Armitages but it is likely to have been through a direct connection with Godfrey Bosville, whose family held the lordship of Gunthwaite near Penistone. This manor lay just to the south of the Holme Valley and Godfrey Bosville's steward there in the 1560s was John Ermyttage. A family called Green also had a son named Godfrey in 1568 and, significantly, a Roger Grene witnessed a deed that involved both Bosville and Armitage in 1562.[29] The close relationship between these families is confirmed in other local documents, so if we could now link the Bosvilles and the Foljambes then we should have established Godfrey's Holme Valley 'pedigree'.[30]

The fact that a supposedly commonplace first name can be so distinctive locally certainly has important implications for local and family historians. For example when an Englishman called Godfrey Armitage arrived in New England in the 1630s, his surname clearly announced his Yorkshire origins, whilst his christian name placed him in the Holme Valley. By comparing records on both sides of the Atlantic it is evident that he was the Godfrey Armitage of Hagg in Honley who was baptised at Almondbury on 2 February 1612.

Some brief histories

Alvery and Godfrey are just two of many north-country names that survived through the thirteenth and fourteenth centuries, and a few of those that enjoyed more than local success can be dealt with briefly. Marmaduke, for example, had never been common in the Middle Ages, but it was popular in east Yorkshire with the Constables and Thwengs, and came to have a much wider distribution among gentry families in the sixteenth century. From that base it increased in popularity and was eventually accepted as a traditional name in yeoman and gentry circles right across the county.

Also prominent was Guy, said by Withycombe in *English Christian Names* to have been driven out of use because of its associations with Guy Fawkes. That was not the case in Yorkshire where it was traditional among gentry families in low-lying parts of Nidderdale and Wharfedale. The influence there of the Fairfaxes, Wilstrops and Palmeses resulted in its adoption by numerous families of much lower status, including the Lindleys, Coultons, Haxbys, Watertons and Hudsons. Several of these continued to use the name into the nineteenth century at least.

Less well-known is Amer, prominent for centuries in Denby, near Penistone. The key to that history may be Aylmer or Adomar de Valence, the Count of Pembroke, who is well documented until his death in 1316. At least one family connected with him adopted the name and he is known to have had interests in Yorkshire.[31] So far though no evidence has been found to link him and Aymer or Adomar Burdet, the fourteenth-century Denby landowner who was probably responsible for Amer's long-term survival. Those alternative spellings of his name are found again in the period 1456–83, when a later Aymer or Ademer Burdett witnessed several south Yorkshire deeds.

The simpler variant 'Amer' eventually became the conventional spelling and it was a favourite with the Burdetts into the seventeenth century at least. In the 1530s, for example, Amore Burdhed was named in a Star Chamber case, accused of armed intrusion into Birthwaite Hall near Barnsley.[32] In 1660 another Amer

Burdett featured in a dispute with the Beaumonts of Whitley; he was taxed in 1672 as Emor Burdett.[33] Long before that, however, some of their neighbours had started to use the name and by about 1550 it was relatively popular in that part of the county. Among them were the Dentons, Rawsons, Listers, Beaumonts and Marsdens. Further afield it was used by the Hinchliffes, Shaws and Battys in Holmfirth as well as the Hampshires and Oxleys in Emley and the Lockwoods and Jenkinsons in Barnsley.

The name never became generally popular, but it is noticeable that once it had been adopted by a family there was a tendency for it to be retained. For example there were Amers in the Rich family of Thurlstone in the seventeenth century and when Lydia Rich married John Green of Yateholme, a family with gentry connections, they named their eldest son Emor. He died in 1761 but there were other Emors in the family into the nineteenth century.[34]

Many more names from the thirteenth century survived with varying degrees of success. They include Otes in Lancashire, Hardolph and Harold in Nottinghamshire, and Bertram in Northumberland. In Yorkshire were Baldwin, Conan, Warren, Joselin, Asculph and Costin, the latter a pet-form of Constantine favoured by the Maudes. Through them it enjoyed some popularity in parts of Airedale and Wharfedale. Less obvious survivors are names such as Herbert, Arnold, Lionel and Nigel, which were rare in 1377–81 but are familiar to us now because they have been revived more recently. Theobald could be included here, usually spelt 'Tedbald' by the Wallis family but 'Tedbar' in and around Kirkburton, where it was used by the Tinkers, Hinchliffes, Moorhouses, Tyases, Barrowcloughs, Hobsons and others.

Mauger and Serle

I suspect that not all the twelfth-century names found in the Tudor period were genuine survivals, and a few may have been deliberately revived by gentry families who believed that the names' antiquity gave them status. We have long known how important the family surname was to the Tudor gentry; now we must also take into account their attachment to the personal names of their ancestors. Mauger and Serle will serve as examples.

At first it seems that Mauger can be compared with Alvery, Anker or Godfrey. It was certainly brought here by the Normans and was traditionally used in the Vavasour family who had a large estate in Lower Wharfedale. Withycombe commented on their descent 'from one Mauger who held lands in vavasoury in the reign of Henry I' and stated that they used the christian name into the eighteenth century. The connection between the surname and the nature of the family's tenancy is well attested, but her suggestion that they used Mauger continuously for over 600 years may be misleading. There can be no doubt that it was used by them in the Middle Ages and then again from the sixteenth century, but I find no evidence for its use in the intervening period. Indeed, so far as I can establish, it was a family name initially for less than 300 years.

When Sir Charles Clay discussed the Vavasours' origins he made two claims, firstly that they descended from a certain Malger who held land at the time of the Domesday survey and secondly that this man's descendants included one Mauger le Vavasour whose father died c.1190.[35] I find others with the name as late as 1332[36] but none at all in the poll tax returns or fifteenth-century records, even though a wealth of family documentation has survived. However, the name reappears in the records from Elizabeth's reign and it must be suspected that it was deliberately revived by the family, partly to emphasise their ancient origins and partly to impress other gentry families and neighbours. There were certainly enough charters in the Vavasours' possession for them to be familiar with the earlier use of Mauger and they would not have been slow to see its significance.

Soon after that the name was given to local boys called Baildon and Scatchard and the clear inference is that one of the Vavasours had acted as godfather. This seems a small number but when the alternative spelling Major is taken into account it is clear at once that the name was much more widely used. The variant was used in Mauger Vavasour's own lifetime by a close friend and kinsman, John Savill: he was godfather to John Vavasour and, in his will of 1589, he referred to the boy's father as Major Vavasour of Weston.[37]

There are many other examples: in 1625 Major Thackray married Mary Hill at Weston; in 1672 Mr Major Mawde and his neighbour Mr William Vavasor were taxed on their hearths in Burley; whilst Major Smith lived at Askwith and Major Waddington at Bramhope. In the seventeenth and eighteenth centuries Major occurred frequently enough over a much wider area, particularly in Leeds where it was used by the Earnshaws, Bradleys and Steads. Isolated examples were also recorded in Birstall, Emley and Sowerby, and it remained in favour in several rural parishes to the north of Otley as late as the nineteenth century, notably in the Haw and Rishforth families of Kirkby Malzeard and Hampsthwaite. Some writers compare Major as a first name with General and Captain, but the examples above are almost certainly variants of Mauger. That should not be surprising for the surname Major is thought to derive from Mauger.

It may not be the only case of its kind, for the Vavasours had close neighbours called Arthington who appear to have made a similar choice. They favoured the name Cyril from the late sixteenth century but this can be shown to have developed from Serle, another Norman favourite: it features in the family's early charters and then reappears in the sixteenth century. In this case the eventual replacement of Serle by Cyril could have been deliberate, for the Arthingtons were notable Catholic recusants and may have elected to associate themselves in this way with St Cyril. However, it is just as likely that they knew nothing at all about Serle and considered it to be a mere variation of Cyril. Typical spellings in the family's records are: Serlo (1186), Searle (1580), Cyrill (1610) and Serrill

(1672). If no more early examples of Serle are found it means that almost 400 years elapsed between its use in the twelfth century and its revival in Elizabeth's reign.

~

The names dealt with in this chapter prove that some of the old personal names did not die out in the thirteenth century but were preserved by individual families for many centuries. A small number were even more successful, first becoming locally popular within kinship groups and then spreading further afield, from one manor to another and from one county to another. The importance attached to such names in the Tudor and Stuart periods is not difficult to understand, since they implied a direct link with the Normans and reinforced a family's claims to gentility and prestige. It would not be surprising if some of them were deliberately reintroduced.

Notes

1   R. A. McKinley, *The Surnames of Lancashire* (London, 1981), p. 313. My own view is that Sagar was occupational, a local form of Sawyer. Many early examples have the article 'le', e.g. in 1423 John le Sager of Colne.
2   G. Fellows Jensen, *Scandinavian Personal Names in Lincolnshire and Yorkshire* (Copenhagen, 1968), p. 314.
3   P. H. Reaney and R. M. Wilson, *A Dictionary of English Surnames* (Oxford, 1997).
4   R. A. McKinley, *The Surnames of Lancashire* (London, 1981). The author also brought to our attention two very rare Lancashire by-names or surnames; Thurstonson, first recorded after 1500, and Thurstansman, a late fourteenth-century example.
5   In 1621 Edward Reyner of Elmsett in Suffolk had a son named Thurston.
6   Direct Lancashire connections seem likely in the case of Ramsbottom, Whitehead and Mather but other Yorkshire families to use Thurstan between 1500 and 1700 were the Bollings, Hunts, Hollingbriggs, Halls, Gladwins, Copleys, Lodges, Yeadons, Mitchells, Womersleys, Earnshaws and Mallinsons.
7   There were Thurstans in the Wordsworth family of Penistone from the late fifteenth century and then among their neighbours the Bilcliffes, Swindens, Bamforths, Mortons and Dungworths. The origin of Wordsworth has never been satisfactorily explained but a probable ancestor of the poet was Nicholas de Wordulworth of Penistone, whose surname may derive from the Lancashire place-name Wardleworth.
8   R. A. McKinley, *Lancashire*, p. 315.
9   For example, in 1482 Otteuell Portyngton of York, *Freemen of York 1272–1558*, Surtees Society XCVI (1897); in 1488 Otuel Oter of Pendleton, Lancashire, *Pudsay Deeds*, Yorkshire Archaeological Society, Record Series LVI, (1916), p. 39; in 1524 Otuel Hill of Tuxford, Nottinghamshire, *Wills in the York Registry*, YAS XI (1891).
10 A. H. Smith, *The Place-names of the West Riding of Yorkshire*, Part II (Cambridge, 1961), p. 280.
11 The Ryder/Rider information was sent to me by Marion Moverley of Richmond.
12 For example there were Ottiwell Whitworths in Rochdale (1642) and in

Almondbury (1682). There were Ottiwell Broadbents in Masbrough (1597), in Almondbury (1598) and in Southowram (1672).

13 J. G. Nichols, 'The First and Second Houses of Lacy', *Yorkshire Archaeological and Topographical Journal* II (1873), pp. 171–9.

14 W. Farrer (ed.), *The Court Rolls of the Honor of Clitheroe* I (Manchester 1897), pp. 505–6.

15 For example, in 1354 Ughtred Penson of Bradford. From a court roll transcript in Bradford Library.

16 C. Spencer (ed.), *Slaidburn and Bowland Wills and Administrations* II (Preston, 2000), p. 10.

17 *Wills in the York Registry*, YAS XIX (1895), p. 79.

18 According to Withycombe in *English Christian Names* the alternative spellings represent different cases in Old French.

19 For example, Hamon Beeching, Hamon Betts. L. A Knafla, *Kent at Law 1602* (1994), pp. 54, 194.

20 Compare E. Weekley, *Surnames* (London, 1917). The author offered the same explanation for the surname, and quoted Shakespeare in support: 'An anchor's cheer in prison be my scope' (Hamlet, iii.2).

21 For example, in 1390 Anker Frecheville and Anker de Brimyngton witnessed a Nottinghamshire land grant. T. W. Hall, *The Jackson Collection* (Sheffield, 1914).

22 For example, in 1359 Anker Frecheville, lord of Staveley, Derbyshire, T. W. Hall, *op. cit.* and in 1532 Ankarus Fretchewell (Keeton), *Yorkshire Fines*, YAS II (1887), p. 63.

23 I am grateful to Peter McClure for this information and for his suggestion that the Stansalls' use of the name may owe something to the Frechevilles' tenure of manors in north-east Derbyshire. He also notes that Anker was used by the Fabian family of Bunny (Notts.).

24 B. Seltén, *The Anglo-Saxon Heritage in Middle English Personal Names: East Anglia 1100–1399* (Lund, 1979).

25 W. Brown (ed.), *Yorkshire Deeds 2*, YAS L (1914), p. 104.

26 *Ibid.* p. 105.

27 F. S. Coleman, *A History of Barwick in Elmet*, Thoresby XVII (Leeds, 1908), pp. 129–77.

28 If this sounds confusing it should be remembered that Almondbury consisted of numerous townships, like many northern parishes.

29 T. W. Hall (ed.), *A Descriptive Catalogue of Land Charters and Court Rolls from the Bosville and Lindsay Collections* (Sheffield, 1930), p. 26.

30 There is no evidence that Godfrey was a Bosville family name before the sixteenth century, hence the need to understand how they too came to use it. The Foljambe connection is a promising line of enquiry and it might help to explain a second 'cluster' of Godfreys in south Yorkshire.

31 W. P. Baildon and J. W. Clay (eds), *Yorkshire Inquisitions, Henry IV and Henry V*, YAS LIX (1918), p. 20.

32 H. B. McCall (ed.), *Star Chamber Proceedings 2* YAS XLV (1911), p. 177.

33 Kirklees Archives, West Yorkshire Archive Service, Whitley Beaumont Papers, WBL/107.

34 Amer was unusual enough in the past to be confused with both Edmond and the biblical name Amos: the spelling Amor, found in nineteenth-century Holmfirth trade directories, may point to further confusion with Old Testament Hamor.

35 C. T. Clay, *Early Yorkshire Families*, YAS CXXXV (1973).

36 C. T. Clay (ed.), *Yorkshire Deeds 4*, YAS LXV (1924), p. 15.

37 W. Brown (ed.), *Yorkshire Deeds 3*, YAS LXIII (1922), p. 114.

CHAPTER SIX

Names from Abroad

W*e are familiar with the idea that names from the Continent were brought here as* *a result of the Norman Conquest. However, the extent to which first names from parts* *of northern Europe may have influenced English naming practices after 1350 should* *not be underestimated, for England's history, in trade, politics and religion, has been* *closely tied up with that of her neighbours for centuries. Many towns and cities, espe-* *cially those in the east and south east of the country, attracted numerous immigrants* *over long periods: they came from the Low Countries, the Baltic, France, Normandy* *and Brittany, and they brought their skills with them. The numbers increased from the* *second half of the sixteenth century as Protestants fled from religious persecution and* *skilled workers were encouraged to set up work here. The Huguenots in particular made* *an enormous contribution to English society. It is usual for historians to take account* *of such population movement, but little has been said about the immigrants' first* *names.*

The Low Countries and France, 1377–81

Edward III had encouraged Flemish weavers to settle in England and we might therefore expect to find their names in the poll tax returns. Certainly 'Fleming' is a frequent and well-distributed by-name in 1377–81 and the probability is that many of these individuals were relatively recent arrivals. Of course both Fleming and Flanders were also hereditary surnames at that time, evidence of an earlier wave of immigration, but the proof is sometimes in first names that have no obvious English connection, such as Hamm, Arthebuk, and the diminutive Kyndekyn. Others like Constant were uncommon among Englishmen at that time and Constancius Fleming who lived at Redenhall in Norfolk in 1379 was probably a countryman of Constancius Webstere of Houghton in the same county. The by-name here confirms that the latter was a weaver.

Occasionally such names occur in a context that points to a small colony of men from the Low Countries. 'Egidius' or Giles Flemyng was taxed in Reading in 1381 and just below him in the list were William Reynald, John Braban and John Thedrich. Thedrich is a form of the common Dutch name Theodoric or Derek, and Reynald is the first name of men elsewhere called Fleming, Brabant and Brabiner. John Braban was almost certainly from the old Duchy of Brabant, an area now divided between Belgium and the Netherlands. Many of these became hereditary and Reaney and Wilson list no fewer than ten variants under the sur-name 'Braban' and several more under Brabazon and Brabiner, including the Scottish Bremner.[1] In 1377–81 we find these names in Norfolk, as we might expect, as far west as Liverpool, and in Hallaton in Leicestershire, where Heyne Braban was a weaver; Thomas Heyne was probably his son.

In fact many of these men from Brabant had first names with English equiva-lents that could be readily latinised. There was a 'Robertus' Brabant in Kings Lynn and another John Braban who was a weaver in Stow on the Wold. A few had first names with no English parallel, e.g. Tyso Braban in Derbyshire, and in other cases the English name was uncommon, such as Augustine, Godfrey, Ranulph and especially Lambert with its diminutive Lambkin. In all these examples it was the by-name that confirmed the man as a native of Brabant. The origin is clear also in the case of Henry and John Douchman of Kings Lynn but sometimes we suspect a Low Countries origin and all we have to go on is the unusual first name and an occupational by-name associated with immigrants, e.g. Otte Goldsmyth of Boston (Lincs.), Henyng Webb of Kings Lynn and Colemayn Webster of Melchbourne (Beds.). Webb and Webster come from different parts of the coun-try but they both mean 'weaver' and they can point to a possible foreign origin, for example, Baldewynus Webbe of Preston in Somerset.[2] In fact a man's occupa-tion was often a clue to his homeland. In York in the thirteenth and fourteenth centuries the earliest armourers were nearly all Germans, whilst goldsmiths and brewers frequently came from the Low Countries.[3]

Because so many of the most popular English names were brought here by the Normans and were French in origin, it is even more difficult to identify immigrants from France by their first names alone. However, Janyn, a diminu-tive of John, must often have been French in 1377–81 and it occurs in many counties, usually combined with a by-name that confirms the identification. In Lancashire, for example, we find 'Janyn de Fraunce' of Westby, 'Janyn le Frenchemon' of Rixton and 'Janyn le Frenche' of Lowton. Other versions of the by-name are Frankysman, recorded in Yorkshire, and Fraunces, e.g. Janyn Fraunces of Ayston in Rutland. No doubt some of the numerous Janyns with less distinctive by-names were also Frenchmen, e.g. Janyn Holder of Gosfield in Essex and Janyn Pulter of Singleton in Sussex. This French form of John gave us the widely-distributed surname Jennings which Guppy in *Homes of Family Names* says was particularly common by the nineteenth century in Surrey, Hertfordshire and Warwickshire.

The various by-names that pointed explicitly to a French origin were not of course confined to men with the first name Janyn. We find 'Hamyns Frencheman' in Billesdon (Leics.); 'Gylowe le Frenchemon' in Rixton (Lancs.) and 'Gerardus Frencheman' in Ringstead (Northants). On the whole though first names are of limited use in identifying French immigrants in this period, less useful than the various by-names meaning 'French'. It is worth noting that some of them, even as hereditary names, could be used interchangeably well into the sixteenth century.[4]

Further immigration in the fifteenth century

The commercial links and immigration continued through the fifteenth century. For example the overseas trade of Hull clearly brought many of the townsmen into daily contact with continental Europe. More than 400 foreign merchants are listed in the customs accounts for the period 1453–90, and some of their ships made frequent crossings. They came from ports all round the North Sea, from the Low Countries and from France, even occasionally from distant Spain. Hull seamen were engaged on all these routes and also crossed frequently to Iceland. I have no idea of the size and constitution of the ships' crews but the clear inference is that Hull played host to many foreigners, some of whom undoubtedly settled in the town.[5]

Very often their first names would have been easily recognised and assimilated, even allowing for differences in pronunciation, e.g. Simon, Stephen, Martin and Peter, whereas other foreigners had names that are familiar to us now but were rare in England at that time, e.g. Paul, Everard, Matheus and Tobyas. In fact the most common names in the lists were Hans and Claus, pet forms of John and Nicholas, but there were also numerous unfamiliar names, including Isebrand, Tydemann and Alard. Even among the list of so-called English merchants there were some obvious newcomers from the Low Countries, notably Cornelius Lambson and Brand Adreanson, both named in 1489. The will of Brand Adryanson of Hull, 'berebrewer', was registered at York in 1503. His unfamiliar first name was the short form of Isebrand, mentioned above, as references to Izebrand or Brand Hannykyn of Hull make clear in 1528.[6] The Hull evidence further suggests that it may have been rare in the Low Countries for father and son to have the same given name, for there is no instance in which a man's first name was identical with his patronymic by-name.

David Postles has shown how the names given to foreigners in Devon were responsible for two new types of by-name in this period, those ending in –maker and those ending in –son. Among aliens taxed there in the fifteenth and

1 The Norman font of St Peter's Church, Thorpe Salvin, south Yorkshire. The carvings depict the four seasons and a baptismal (courtesy of R. H. Bird).

2 This ornate gravestone in Braithwell commemorates the wife and children of Silvanus Slater of Doncaster. Silvanus was one of the companions of St Paul and the name is found occasionally in the early twelfth century. It was revived in the late fifteenth century in Nottinghamshire by Gervase Clifton and remained in use in south Yorkshire into modern times.

3 A monument in Dent, Cumbria, to Adam Sedgwick, the great geologist. Adam was an extremely popular name in north-west England in the fourteenth century and never fell entirely out of use.

4 The great hall at Woodsome, west Yorkshire. The names of Arthur Kay (1498–1574) and his wife Beatrix are carved on the massive stone lintel of the fireplace.

5 The names and ages of Arthur Kaye's descendants are given on this painted panel. It formerly hung in the hall at Woodsome and would have been painted soon after Arthur's death in 1574. P. H. Thornborrow, courtesy of West Yorkshire Archaeology Service (copyright reserved). By kind permission of Tolson Memorial Museum, Huddersfield.

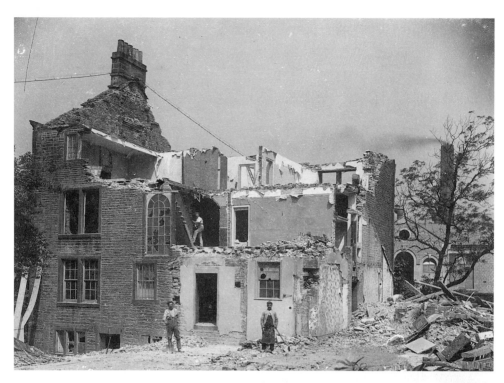

6 The demolition of the
house known as Ottiwells at
Marsden, near Huddersfield.
It owed its name to a local
man called Ottiwell Marsden
who died in 1589. The owner
in 1812 was William
Horsfall, a manufacturer
who was shot by the
Luddites.

7 A fifteenth-century room in
Bolling Hall, near Bradford.
It was the home of Robert
Bolling, who gave the names
Tristram, Rainbrown and
Troilus to three of his sons.
He died in 1487.

8 A statue in Bury St Edmunds of Edmund, king of East Anglia and martyr. When Edmund's body was discovered to be incorrupt in c. 915 it was transferred to Bedricsworth which then came to be known as St Edmundsbury and finally as Bury St Edmunds.

9 The effigy of Robert Curthose (c. 1054–1134) in Gloucester Cathedral. He was the son of William the Conqueror and Duke of Normandy. Robert became one of the most popular English names and has never fallen completely out of favour.

10 Hilda, or Hildah, was a North Riding name from the early 1600s, particularly in and around Whitby. There were known recusants among those who used it and the abbey dedication seems the obvious source of inspiration. Several other North Riding parish churches were dedicated to St Hilda.

11 The church at Aberford (near Leeds), formerly on the Great North Road. The dedication to St Ricarius appears to be unique in Yorkshire.

12 A family photograph c. 1898. Benjamin and Emma Watts of Hunshelf near Penistone, south Yorkshire, had four sons and eight daughters. This picture, taken on the moors near Langsett, shows six of the girls, i.e. Mary, Hannah, Gertrude, Ada, Laura and Bertha.

13 The cortege of Sir Tristram Tempest, Bart., passes through the front entrance to Tong Hall (near Bradford) on its way to the church. The first Tristram Tempest had been given the name 400 years earlier.

14 It was commonplace for both girls and boys to have two first names in the late nineteenth century. This Redmonds family photograph is of four of my father's siblings: George Granville, Henry Oscar, Gertrude Constance and Frederick Harcourt, all born between 1882 and 1894. My father was the youngest of eleven children.

15 My grandfather, Jonas Rushworth, with his son Jonas Lawrence, in the doorway of his shop in Sunbridge Road, Bradford, in the early twentieth century. Jonas had been a traditional name in the family since the seventeenth century.

sixteenth centuries were John Hatmaker from Brabant, Peter Stolemaker from Normandy and two Dutchmen, Henry Clokmaker and Claret Shoemaker. Postles also makes the point that the element –son was rare in Devon in the fourteenth century and that its later introduction was 'closely related to the trading communities' in the east and south of the county. The same type of name prospered in Winchester, 'where surnames with the element –son appeared for the first time from c.1462' whilst similar forms 'were being introduced by Dutch merchants as early as 1439–40' into Southampton.[7] For the most part the first names of these aliens again had straightforward English equivalents and would not in themselves have identified the men as foreigners; they included John, William, Philip, Anthony, Robert and Peter.

The early sixteenth century

There is another source that offers us an insight into a quite different type of immigrant in the early sixteenth century and it makes clear what was being lost in the translation of the names. A. G. Dickens, in *Lollards and Protestants in the Diocese of York*, quotes examples of Dutchmen whose religious beliefs had brought them into conflict with the authorities. One of those brought to trial was Gyles Vanbellaer of Worksop, whose signature was Gelen Vanbellaer. Another who was referred to as Gilbert Johnson probably did not have a hereditary surname, although as it was written it cannot be distinguished from an English name. His latinised signature 'per me Ghilbertum Johannes' suggests that 'Johnson' was a scribal convenience and that he may literally have been the son of a man called John. If that was more generally true, and it appears to be so, it explains the numerous patronymics in lists of Dutch names, some of them quoted above, and also indicates that what we are reading are by-names rather than 'surnames'. No doubt it was convenient for clerks to anglicise the names in this way.

Another Dutchman from Worksop who was brought to trial described himself as 'Lambert Sparrow ooderwise callyd Lambert Hooke, dowchman borne'. His alleged offences need not concern us here but the alias indicates how unstable his name was and 'Hooke' may simply be the Hook of Holland, either his place of birth or his last home before moving to England. We can draw a similar inference from the by-name 'Dutchman' noted earlier and which sometimes became hereditary. It was commonly used for somebody from the Netherlands or even from Germany and Dickens refers to one Dutchman whose name was translated into Latin as 'natione tutonicus' (German nationality).[8]

Dickens also mentioned a Dutch family called Freez or Frees, settled in York from c.1490 to c.1530. The immigrant was Frederick Freese, a bookbinder, and other members of the family were Gerard his brother, and his sons Edward and Valentine. Theirs was a tragic story, for Valentine was burnt at Knavesmire as a heretic, but their aliases are interesting. Edward Freese was also known as

Edward Paynter, because of his occupation, and both Gerard and Frederick were referred to as 'alias Wansford', referring to a village not far from Driffield. The reason for that is not known but it may be that they held land there or that it was the birthplace of Frederick's wife. Frederick would not become part of the English name-stock until much later but it was used occasionally in the seventeenth century and more frequently in Georgian England. Gerard could be a Continental name but was also traditional in some English families.

Bretons in Cornwall

The military survey of Cornwall in 1522 lists many aliens, parish by parish, and the majority had clearly come from Brittany to work in the tin-mines.[9] It also seems that they did not have hereditary surnames, for the first name was followed in most cases by Britton or Bretton as a by-name. At least one of the first names was French, i.e. Janyn, whilst others were Breton but indistinguishable from their English counterparts, none of which were popular in Cornwall at that time, i.e. Arthur, Alan and Yve. A high percentage had Breton names unknown over here, e.g. Homan, Noel, Ewryn or Urin, Udin and Vivian. There were also several called Hervey which suggests that some of the Herveys in the earlier poll tax might also have been immigrants. This name was rare in most parts of England in 1377–81 but occurred in good numbers in the south west and East Anglia. Typical examples where the surnames have a distinctly un-English look about them are 'Herveius Chef', 'Herveius Croche' and 'Herveius Gres'. Wareham in Dorset was one town where several Herveys were recorded.

Immigration in the sixteenth and seventeenth centuries

As the sixteenth century progressed more immigrants arrived, miners, glass-makers, haberdashers and tapestry makers. Some settled down in one community, while others were ready to move on, taking their skills to new rural areas and introducing new crafts into the towns. In 1565, for example, Daniel Houghsetter and several other Germans were granted a licence to 'open mines of gold, silver, copper and quicksilver' in Cumberland, Westmorland and Cornwall, or indeed in any of a half a dozen other counties in England and Wales. Thirty 'dutchmen' who were all master workmen were granted permission to live in Norwich so that they might make 'bayes, arras, sayes, tapestrye, mockadoes, stamens, carsay and such other outlandysshe commodities', products that were not then being made in England. With their families and servants this community numbered 300 immigrants in all. Soon afterwards a large group of so-called Spanish citizens sought denization but their names tell us that they were really from the Spanish Netherlands. Derick Williamson, Cornelius Vandor and Melchor Barnarde are names that stand out in the group but Gervase Cornelis and Regnald Harryson were also clearly from the Low Countries. John Lambert, 'born a Spanish subject', was 'to pay customs as an alien and not to live in Berwick without special licence'.[10]

In towns such as Colchester and Norwich the Dutchmen were numerous enough to have their own churches, and the Dutch church in London has registers dating from 1559. It was in the records of Colchester's Dutch church that John Titford was able to solve the origin of the apparently English surname Stonhold, taking it back to a seventeenth-century immigrant from the Low Countries via spellings such as Stoneholt and Van Steenholen. Among the first names used by this family were Adrian, Oliver and Isebrand, vital clues in his search.[11]

An immigrant French family moved from London and the Sussex Weald to Shropshire, Manchester and south Yorkshire. They were glass-makers, taking their skills to the sources of fuel for their furnaces.[12] Their surname was Pilmay, spelt a dozen different ways in the registers, and they used distinctive first names such as Jasper and Adam, both very unusual in England at that time. Frenchmen and other aliens were apparently employed in the ironworks of the Sussex Weald as early as the fifteenth century, and some of them eventually found their way in the 1640s to New England.[13] In a number of regions immigrants were at the forefront of marshland reclamation and the exploitation of peat reserves, and the names of several hundred are preserved in the seventeenth-century registers of Sandtoft in Lincolnshire. A dozen German churches were founded in London alone, starting in the seventeenth century.[14]

French Protestants

Most genealogists have read about the influence of the French language on our English surnames in the centuries after the Norman Conquest and they know also that large numbers of Frenchmen arrived here in the sixteenth and seventeenth centuries as a result of religious persecution. Yet they are not always aware of the numbers involved. For example, it has been estimated that from 40,000 to 50,000 French refugees settled in England between 1680 and 1720 and they were gradually assimilated into British society.[15] Their distinctive surnames, Roget, Bosanquet, Olivier and Courtauld, to name but a few, are thoroughly familiar to us but the first names of the original settlers have often been forgotten.

In the Sandtoft register, with entries from 1643, some of the most popular names were from the Bible.[16] For boys, in order of frequency, they were Pierre, Abraham, Isaac, David, Jacob, Jan or Jean and Jaques: the girls' names were Marie, Susanne, Ann, Elizabeth, Esther and Sarah. Among the least common were Adrian, Isenbar, Noe and Oser. The Huguenots' first church was established in London's Threadneedle Street in 1550 and it served the community for nearly a century. However, it could not cope with the continuing flood of immigrants and by 1700 there were some 28 churches in the area we now describe as Greater London.

The influence of foreign names

It is difficult to say what direct influence the names of foreigners may have had on Englishmen. 'Johannes alias Hance' Plompton of Hull was certainly English, the son of a Yorkshire merchant 'dying at Antwerp' in 1545.[17] He is likely to have been known as Hans when the family lived in Antwerp but once he was back in this country he probably had to settle for John, as clerks over here were evidently aware that 'Johannes' or John was the English equivalent. The first name Renatus or Rene, used by the Sinkinsons of Almondbury in 1628, was almost certainly French, testimony perhaps to their relationship with Rene Trippier, a French refugee who married an Almondbury girl about the same time. Later though Rene Trippier was named in a quarter sessions case as Reynold Trippier, which suggests that the clerk had confused his first name with the English diminutive of Reynold, cf. Rayney or Reonald Dinsdall of Rothwell (1642–9). The long-term influence is more apparent when we look closely at the histories of individual names.

Arnold

Arnold has a Germanic origin and it was introduced into this country by the Normans. Reaney gives it as the source of more than a dozen surnames including the spelling variants Arnaud, Arnatt, Arnall and Harnett, and his examples of the personal name and by-name cover the period 1066–1279. There are few references to Arnold after that and it was 'practically forgotten'[18] until its modest and quite recent revival. As that has been more obvious in North America than in England, it may owe something to influences from other European countries.

I have two early Yorkshire references to Arnold, one in 1234 and the other in an undated manorial survey from the reign of Henry III, probably c.1250.[19] This man, 'Arnald mercator', was probably a merchant, but on such flimsy evidence it would not be possible to say whether he was an Englishman or not. However, almost all the Yorkshire references between 1250 and 1500 are clearly to men from the Continent. In the period up to 1350 they include 'Arnaldus de Almaigne', no doubt a German, 'Arnaldus de Lakensnither' and 'Arnaldus de Lovayne'. I have not identified Lakensnither but the last of these is probably Louvain or Leuven, a market town in north Brabant. All three men were trading in York between 1327 and 1359.[20] In the period 1453–1490 Arnald featured several times in a list of shipmasters using the port of Hull and also in lists of foreign merchants.

Occasional examples of Arnold as a first name are recorded in Yorkshire after that and one at least is linked with a Yorkshire by-name, e.g. 'Arnaldus de Ayreton' of Airton (1379). However it is better remembered as a frequent choice in the Reresby family whose substantial estates were in the Rotherham area. The first of whom I have any record is Arnald Rerisby of Thrybergh who died in 1485 and he is likely to have been given the name in the first half of the century. Others are recorded in 1543 and 1631 but the name was rare elsewhere. A Beverley family was called Arnoldson in the late sixteenth century and their ancestor may have been 'Godfrey Arnaldson, Ducheman', who was a freeman of York in 1466.

In 1377–81 Arnold was a rare first name and most of those recorded were in the south and south east. One exception was Arnaldus Webbe who lived in Coventry and was probably a weaver. There were isolated examples in Essex, Kent and Sussex and one man in Berkshire listed as 'Arnaldus servant of Arnald'. The only really significant cluster was in Surrey, notably in the village of Shalford where four men had the name, spelt with an 'o' rather than an 'a'. None of them had an obviously foreign name or occupation and the same is true of two other Arnolds in Albury and Bramley. The only example that points to an immigrant is Arnald Goldesmyth of Southwark, whose by-name was one often associated with Dutchmen.[21]

Derek

The dictionaries are in broad agreement about the early history of Derek. Withycombe suggested in *English Christian Names* that it first appeared 'in England in the fifteenth century, borrowed, no doubt, from the Low Countries', and Hanks and Hodges (*First Names*) stated more categorically that it had been 'introduced to Britain during the Middle Ages by Flemish settlers connected with the cloth trade'. Although no examples of the name are recorded in 1377–81 there are several in the York Freemen's Rolls from that period, including 'Dericus Bogholl van Wosell, mercator' (merchant) in 1377, Diryk Johnson, goldsmith (1423), and Diryk Ivee, skinner (1447).[22] Such individuals usually remain undocumented but in 1528 a man called Dyrek Lussynk was at the centre of a fascinating Star Chamber case, in which he blamed the weather for his failure to deliver corn from Zeeland to Hull on time.[23]

Other references are found in the Hull records of 1453–90. One of them was a Hanseatic shipmaster from Danzig called Deryk Scaght, listed elsewhere as 'Theodoricus', a Latin version of his name which makes the origin quite clear; Deryk Clauson and Deryk Peterson were from Schiedam and Middelburg in the Low Countries. Even if the home of an immigrant or merchant is not given it is often quite clear that he was not English. Dyrrick Hollander was drowned 'in the creke of Rye' in 1578 when he went for a swim[24] and Derricke Mappin of Sheffield had a son called Otto. This boy was baptised in 1594 and subsequently known as Otto Mappin otherwise Dedwicke, the alias demonstrating how his neighbours had come to terms with the pronunciation of Derricke.

The name of Reginald Dedykson in the Hull documents makes the same point, suggesting perhaps a pronunciation somewhere between Theodoric and Derrick. A German armourer who moved from Aachen to Greenwich and died there in 1525 was called Robert Derrick, but his descendants had their name anglicised as Dethick, a similar transition.[25] The choice of English surname is fascinating, for Dethick usually derives from the place-name Dethick in Derbyshire and typical spellings in the sixteenth century are Dedyke (1524) and Deddik (1577). The first baptisms I have found of what appear to be English boys called Derek or Derrick date from 1700, for example, Derrick Topman of Leeds.

Cornelius

Cornelius is a name with both biblical and classical connotations, which Withycombe claimed was first found in England in the sixteenth century, 'brought back by returning sectaries who had taken refuge in the Netherlands'. Its popularity there is attributed to the fact that the relics of a third-century martyred pope called Cornelius had ended up in Flanders. In fact the name has a much longer history in this country and may sometimes have an English origin, e.g. Cornelius Wyrley, esquire, taxed at Fenny Drayton in Leicestershire in 1381. Many of those who bore the name in the fifteenth century were probably from the Low Countries, including Cornelius Michelson who traded in Hull in the 1460s and Cornelius Nicholas who was resident in York in 1475. Among the wills registered at York are those of Cornelius Arteson of Scarborough (1493) and Cornelius Johnson of Hull (1502), both beer brewers.

The enduring trade links with the Continent ensured that Cornelius was a name known to some Englishmen independently of the Bible. Examples abound in the parish registers of Thorne in the seventeenth century, where surnames such as Rothenborough and van Gorgon clearly refer to immigrants. Some other surnames are less obviously Dutch, such as Lambe, Pattinson, Leonard, Steer and Prole, and no doubt one or two of these were native-born Englishmen. Nevertheless the relative popularity of the name in that parish may be attributable in part to Cornelius Vermuyden, the Dutch engineer who was responsible for draining the levels. One of the men named above, Cornelius Prole, was certainly a Dutchman and when his daughter was born in 1654 she was given Cornelia as a name, the first example I have found of its use for a girl.

No doubt some of the parents who chose Cornelius as a name in the sixteenth and seventeenth centuries did so because it was in the Bible. That seems likely in the cases of Cornellius Kidd of Swine (1595) and Cornelius Wolstenholm of Heptonstall (1614), adult males who came from areas where biblical names were popular in the sixteenth century. There are numerous other seventeenth-century examples in parishes well away from obvious Low Countries' influence and in these cases also the surnames are clearly those of Englishmen, e.g. Stansfield, Batty, Stringer, Berry and Bickerdike. In a few families the name became traditional. The Recorder of Hull, from 1725, was Cornelius Caley who came originally from York; both his father and his second son had the same christian name. Ironically he published an account in the 1770s of a tour he had made through the Low Countries.

Herman

Herman or Harman is another overseas name which seems to have taken root in England. It had a Germanic origin and was brought here by the Normans, surviving long enough to give rise to the surnames Herman and Harman. However, there is no suggestion by either Withycombe or Hanks and Hodges that it remained in use in this country and both their dictionaries describe it as a German name, with the implication that it was revived in the nineteenth century. In 1377–81 it was recorded in Lincolnshire and Norfolk, and Herman Baldewen of Great Hautbois seems certain to have been a recent arrival from the Low Countries. In York there are regular examples of immigrants with the name from about the same period: Herman de Orskott (1376), a weaver, and Herman de Gulk (1403), a goldsmith, and several other goldsmiths bore the name into the sixteenth century, e.g. Herman Goldsmith, goldsmith (1513). Harman Corneluson was a merchant in 1464 and Harmon Trine was one of several Dutchmen working in the Sussex steelworks in the 1560s.

From the sixteenth century Herman and Harman are recorded at regular intervals in Yorkshire, in rural districts as well as in towns. In and around Helmsley, for example, there were several Harmans in the hearth tax returns of 1672, in the Brusby, Allen and Sheffield families. We do not know yet how the name came to be used in those cases and it may be a surname rather than a personal name but, whatever the source, it sometimes became traditional and survived into the nineteenth century. That was so in the Trueman family of Bilsdale who were responsible for spreading it much further afield. In 1774 William Trueman left England for Novia Scotia where some of his descendants are still farmers. Extracts from their correspondence and journals mention Harmon Trueman in 1806, 'cousin' Harman Wedgwood of Hawnby in 1819 and 'cousin' Harman Humphrey of Nova Scotia in 1875.[26]

Adrian

Hanks and Hodges derive both Adrian and Hadrian from Hadria, the town in northern Italy that also gave its name to the Adriatic Sea. They describe the initial 'H' as very volatile but it was there in the name of the Roman emperor who reigned from AD 117–138, who is best remembered in England for the wall that he had built from the Solway to the mouth of the Tyne. It was also the name of several popes, and was adopted by the only English pope, Nicholas Brakespear, who died in 1159. He used the title Adrian IV and Withycombe notes that Adrianus occurs for the first time just 30 years later in the Curia Regis rolls. Very little is said about its use after that by either writer, although Hanks and Hodges describe it as 'particularly popular in the English-speaking world during the past thirty years' and Dunkling comments on its popularity in the 1970s.

There have also been several saints named Adrian, two of them with strong English connections. The first was Adrian of Canterbury, an African by birth, who was named as the abbot of St Augustine's and directed an important Canterbury school. He lived there for 40 years and died in January 710. An Irish missionary named Adrian was killed in 875 on the Isle of May in the Firth of Forth, and the island later attracted numerous pilgrims. However the survival of the name apparently owed little to either of these men but is said to commemorate a Roman soldier-saint whose relics reputedly came to rest in the Low Countries. Adrian was certainly in use there long before it made any impact in England.

Reaney and Wilson quote just one twelfth-century example of the first name and the implication is that it fell completely out of use in the thirteenth century. Certainly there were no Adrians recorded in 1377–81 although it would have been known to Englishmen in towns on the east coast soon after that since it was popular among foreign sea captains in the second half of the fifteenth century.[27] There are three lists of merchants in this source and Adrian occurs 10 times under the heading 'Alien merchants other than Hansards', that is a member of the German Hanse or merchants' guild. There are 338 names in this list but some individuals possibly appear more than once, e.g. 'Adreanus Person' and 'Adrianus Petri'. By contrast the list of more than 200 Hansard merchants has just one doubtful example and there are no Adrians at all in the list of 875 English merchants. It seems that familiarity with Adrian had not yet led to its adoption by Englishmen.

In Smith-Bannister's frequency lists for 1538–1700 there is just one entry for Adrian, in the decade 1550–9, but its low position tells us that very few examples were found and we don't know where. My own earliest references fall into three distinct groups, the first in Nottinghamshire in the sixteenth century, where it was used by families called Style, Hansford, Paget and Wrathe. The examples noted are from an index of wills and they relate to adult males in the period 1573–92, which suggests that their baptismal dates would be a little earlier than 1550. There must surely be an explanation for this cluster of Adrians; unfortunately they are from parishes quite far apart and the problem requires the attention of a Nottinghamshire historian.

The second group, also referring to adults, is found in the small east Yorkshire town of Howden, in the period 1547–78, and it is of particular interest because where the sex can be determined the bearers were women, i.e. Awdrian, wife of John Smart (1578) and Awdrian, daughter of Hugh Bradmer (1577). Another woman with the name was Adriana Skyers of Rotherham in south Yorkshire (1566). Its use as a girls' name is allowed for in most dictionaries but only because Shakespeare chose it for the wife of Antipholus in The Comedy of Errors and these examples are all well before that. A significantly earlier male reference is that of 'Adrianus Breme', a doctor in York in 1518, but his surname is not otherwise recorded locally and he may have been a Dutchman, from the same town as 'Johannes van Breeme' (1467). Other Adrians are recorded in Sussex in Elizabeth's reign. Adrian Pavey, an ironworker, may have been an immigrant, but Adrian Stoughton was a gentleman and justice of peace.

Jasper

Jasper has been explained as an English form of Gaspar or Caspar, the traditional name of one of the three wise men who travelled to Bethlehem with gifts for the infant Christ. The supposed remains of the wise men were finally laid to rest in Cologne and the name has enjoyed considerable popularity since then in Germany and France. Jaspar Grondmon of 'Prucia' was living in York in 1437 and there is no doubt that Prussia and the Low Countries were often the source of the name. Nevertheless its later use may have owed more to the reputation of Jasper Tudor, the Earl of Pembroke and uncle to Henry VII. As a prominent Lancastrian in the Wars of the Roses his name would have been widely known.

Jasper was never common in this country but one pocket of popularity in Halifax can be traced to a marriage between Jasper Blythman and Isabel Lacy. The couple lived in Midgley from 1558 and their son Jasper was baptised at Halifax, as were Jasper Lacy and Jasper Brighouse. These were all gentry families, but Jasper was also used by neighbours of lesser status called Drake, Hoyle, Thorpe, Gledhill and Hemingway. Occasional examples continued to occur in that area well into more recent times and when the Pillings of Wadsworth moved from Heptonstall to Kirklees corn mill in the eighteenth century it was their use of the name that helped to confirm that migration.

It is possible that Jasper had already been transferred to the Blythmans by the Bosvilles, with whom the name was also a favourite. The estates of both families were in south Yorkshire and they had close links socially; in fact their main residences, at Gunthwaite and Royston, were only some eight or nine miles apart. There is little evidence that Jasper was ever popular in that area but examples have been recorded in the Fisher and Bullas families and the latter were close neighbours of the Bosvilles. A Jasper Bosvile, gentleman, who died in 1557, was the son of Thomas Bosvile of Stainton, and this takes the history of the name back into the late fifteenth century, when the ascendancy of the Tudors might be expected to have influenced the Bosvilles' choice.

Lambert

The source of this name was often St Lambert, a seventh-century Bishop of Maastricht, and Lambert is found in English sources after the Conquest, along with its diminutive Lambkin.[28] It was not common generally in 1377–81 but one significant concentration was in Lincolnshire, notably in Spalding, and many of these were probably Englishmen. Elsewhere the continental connection is explicit in the cases of Lamkyn de Braban of Ripon, a weaver, and Lambard Brabaner of Melchbourne, and the name continued to identify Dutchmen into the eighteenth century at least. For example Lambert Vandersluys was a 'stage dancer' in Hull in 1752.[29] There is evidence though that some English families also chose the name, influenced possibly by the cult of St Lambert or one of the few church dedications to him in this country. For example there were Lamberts in the Russell family of Lythe near Whitby into the eighteenth century at least.

~

Because so many of our English first names belong to a common European stock they cannot easily be separated from their continental equivalents in the written form, and Latin spellings emphasise those similarities. It is often difficult therefore to identify foreigners in the records without additional corroborative evidence, especially if the surnames or by-names are not distinctive. Nevertheless it is evident that numerous immigrants arrived in this country over many centuries and that they had some influence on naming practices, reacquainting Englishmen with names that were temporarily out of fashion or introducing new names, some of which became part of the traditional name-stock.

Notes

1   P. H. Reaney and R. M. Wilson, *A Dictionary of English Surnames*, revised edn (Oxford, 1997).
2   For the distribution of Webb, Webber and Webster, see C. D. Rogers, *The Surname Detective* (Manchester, 1995).
3   For example, in 1327 'Arnaldus de Almaygne, furbour'; in 1331 'Ingilbright de Alman, furbour'. These men were freemen of York and 'furbour' was an occupational term associated with the furbishing or burnishing of armour.
4   G. Redmonds, *Huddersfield and District*, Yorkshire Surnames Series 2 (Huddersfield, 1992).
5   W. R. Childs (ed.), *The Customs Accounts of Hull, 1453–90*, Yorkshire Archaeological Society, Record Series CXLIV (1986).
6   R. Horrox (ed.), *Selected Rentals and Accounts of Medieval Hull, 1293–1528*, YAS CXLI (1983).
7   D. A. Postles, *The Surnames of Devon*, English Surnames Series (Oxford, 1995).
8   A. G. Dickens, *Lollards and Protestants in the Diocese of York* (London, 1982).
9   T. L. Stoate (ed.), *Cornwall Military Survey 1522* (Bristol, 1981).

10 *Calendar of the Patent Rolls, 1563–66* (London, 1960).

11 J. Titford, *Searching for Surnames* (Newbury, 2002), pp. 181–6.

12 D. Ashurst, 'The Silkstone Glasshouses', *Old West Riding, New Series* 12 (1992), pp. 15–19.

13 R. E. Bowman, 'The English and Continental Ancestry of Braintree and Saugus Ironworkers of about 1650', *The Essex Genealogist* 20, No. 1 (USA, 2000), pp. 63–77.

14 M. D. Herber, *Ancestral Trails: The Complete Guide to British Genealogy and Family History* (Stroud, 1997), p. 216.

15 T. Murdoch (ed.), *The Quiet Conquest: The Huguenots 1685 to 1985* (London, 1985).

16 C. Jackson (ed.), 'The Stovin Manuscript', *Yorkshire Archaeological Journal* VII (1882), pp. 230–8.

17 *Testamenta Eboracensia*, Surtees Society LIII (1869).

18 E. G. Withycombe, *The Oxford Dictionary of English Christian Names*, 3rd edn (Oxford, 1977).

19 W. Brown (ed.), *Yorkshire Inquisitions*, YAS XII (1892).

20 F. A. Collins (ed.), *Freemen of York 1272–1558*, Surtees XCVI (1897).

21 *Ibid.*, in 1347 'Michael de Neukirk de Flandre, aurifaber'. There are several similar examples in this source.

22 *Ibid.*

23 H. B. McCall (ed.), *Yorkshire Star Chamber Proceedings*, YAS XLV (1911).

24 R. F. Hunnisett, *Sussex Coroners' Inquests 1558–1600* (London, 1996), p. 44.

25 A. R. Wagner, *English Genealogy* (Oxford, 1960), p. 221.

26 H. Trueman, *The Chignecto Isthmus and its First Settlers* (Toronto, 1902).

27 W. R. Childs, *Customs Accounts of Hull*, YAS (1986).

28 P. H. Reaney and R. M. Wilson, *English Surnames* (Oxford, 1997).

29 J. Sykes (ed.), 'The Registers of St Mary's Hull', YAJ XII (1893), p. 473.

CHAPTER SEVEN

Names of the Saints

The saints, and the cults that grew up around them in the Middle Ages, have been a source of fascination and inspiration to people over the centuries. Stories of their lives were once compelling reading; places were named after them and churches dedicated to them; their protection was invoked by different groups of workers; and each day in the calendar was set aside by the church in memory of a particular saint. Their names were common knowledge and yet it is not at all easy to calculate what influence they had on naming practices. It is not just that few of the names are sufficiently distinctive, nor that the motivation of the name-givers is seldom explicit, but that the saintly connection is usually just one of several factors that have to be considered. The introduction of a new name into the national name-stock is one thing, its subsequent use and popularity is another.

Names of non-scriptural female saints

Withycombe stated in English Christian Names that 'with the Reformation all the names of non-scriptural saints fell into disgrace and were for the most part speedily disused', a view that was based on nothing more than supposition. It was challenged by Smith-Bannister in Names and Naming Patterns whose statistical evidence proved that 'the sixteenth and seventeenth centuries did not witness the decline of non-scriptural saints' names'. The accounts of individual names in this chapter make the same case but first we should establish whether Withycombe was right to imply that non-scriptural saints' names had been popular until the Reformation. In fact her description of Barbara and Ursula as favourite names is quite inaccurate.

Barbara, colloquially Barbary, is of Greek origin, and its etymology links it with 'barbarous' and 'barbaric', allusions that cannot have been in parents' minds when they used it as a first name. It was in occasional use in the thirteenth century and the inspiration was almost certainly the great virgin saint, whose cult was popular in the later Middle Ages, especially in France.[1] There is no evidence though that Barbara became an early favourite in England, and it is missing from the poll tax returns. Nor was it common in the fifteenth century, although it is recorded occasionally after 1450 and rather more frequently in the sixteenth century. Contrary to what Withycombe said it then gained in popularity and was among the 30 most frequent names right through the seventeenth century.

Ursula, sometimes spelt Ursuly or Usseley, derives from a Latin diminutive of 'ursa', a female bear, and St Ursula was another martyr whose name was known through a popular legend. Again it seems to have been assumed that this would have made Ursula a popular name before the Reformation, whereas it had actually fallen right out of favour by 1377–81. It was revived in the late fifteenth century and became moderately successful in the 1540s and 1580s, mostly towards the bottom end of the frequency tables. Withycombe's assumptions about both names seem likely to have been based on occasional examples found in thirteenth-century sources.

Non-scriptural male saints' names

Withycombe's observations on male names are even less accurate. The 17 names which she claimed declined as a result of the Reformation include 10 which were absent from the frequency lists of 1377–1381, i.e. Austin, Basil, Blase, Brice, Crispin, Fabian, Quentin, Theobald, Valentine and Viel. The figures for those that were recorded are: Hilary (1), Christopher (2), Gervase (3), Martin (4), Clement (6), Benedict (8) and Denis (15). Although some of these are described by Withycombe as favourites up to the Reformation only Denis would avoid being described as 'rare' if we use the classification suggested earlier. The picture is not very different if we examine the full poll tax returns but one or two names are worth closer examination.

Basil and Basilia

The male name Basil had dropped out of use by 1377–81, but there were women called Basilia in the rolls. They were living in Little Waltham (2), Tolleshunt D'Arcy, Colchester, Wickham Bishops and Theydon Bois, all in Essex and there were single examples in Carbrooke in Norfolk and Canterbury in Kent. It seems unlikely that St Basil the Great was the inspiration for the use of this name but there is no obvious female source, although Withycombe mentions a 'very obscure' St Basilla.

Reaney and Wilson in *English Surnames* derived a number of surnames from Basilia, including Baseley and Bazeley, and they quoted three early references to the first name, one of them in Norfolk in 1134. They expressed no opinion as to its frequency at that time whereas Withycombe claimed without evidence that Basilia was 'very common in England and France' in the twelfth and thirteenth centuries. Basil as a man's name seems to have been even rarer which suggests that Withycombe was mistaken about its history both before and after the Reformation.

Augustine

Augustine, or Austin, is likely to have been inspired originally by the first Archbishop of Canterbury or by St Augustine of Hippo, whose cult was widespread in the Middle Ages, but again there is no evidence that the name was common in England in 1377–81. How popular it was before that is difficult to gauge, but it occurred frequently enough to give rise to the surnames Austin and Austen, and Guppy (*Homes of Family Names*) found these in nine counties, mostly in the South and Midlands. Because the surname became common in Kent it is tempting to link it directly to St Augustine of Canterbury but there is no evidence for that either, since the surviving poll tax returns for Kent include just one family named Austin and no examples of Augustine. There are scattered references elsewhere in the country, with one significant small cluster in Norfolk, four of them in the parish of Bacton. According to McKinley Austin was a common surname in both Norfolk and Suffolk in the sixteenth century.[2]

It is clear that most of these non-scriptural names were not popular in the Middle Ages and the impact on them of the Reformation has been misjudged, so perhaps we should stop treating them as a group and examine each name individually. In the former West Riding, for example, Augustine was recorded only twice in 1379, in a total of almost 21,000 male names, after which no example has been noted for well over a century. Nevertheless it occurred sporadically in several parishes from the early sixteenth century and was subsequently adopted by the Metcalfes in Abbotside. It flourished there in a network of family and friends right through the seventeenth century,[3] used by the Lamberts, Nelsons, Parkins, Allens and Tennants.[4]

Gervase

Gervase was a rare name before the Reformation, although occasional examples were recorded in 1377–81, and it was used from before 1200 by the Cliftons, a Nottinghamshire gentry family. They may have been related to the Markhams who also used Gervase[5] for the two families are linked in wills and other documents.[6] They also bought and sold land in south Yorkshire[7] and Gervase was in evidence there too from the early sixteenth century, used by several gentry families and their neighbours. For example in the hearth tax returns of 1672 10 men named Gervase were living in and around Worsbrough, the home of Mr Jarvas Rockley. There were Catholic recusants in this family in the sixteenth and seventeenth centuries, including one called Gervase in 1590, so that may have influenced the initial choice of the name. However, its later popularity seems certain to reflect the Rockleys' influence in that locality and there is little to suggest that their neighbours were all Catholic sympathisers.[8]

In Elizabeth's reign Gervase came into prominence in Kirkburton, a parish just to the north, and the circumstances there highlight the significance of the godparent's role. The first to bear the name was Gervase Storthes of Storthes Hall, who held the lordship of Thurstonland in the 1550s. His first name was important enough for him to give it to his first son and, when he died, to a second son. Entries in the registers, which use both the formal and vernacular forms of Gervase, show that he was also responsible for its popularity among his neighbours, none of whom ranked as gentlemen:

> 1557–8, 31 January: Gervace baptised, son of John Butrode, godfather Gervace Storthes.
>
> 1558, 10 May: Jarvis baptised, son of Mr Jarvis Stores.
>
> 1559, 10 September: Jarves baptised, son of Thomas Stonn, godfather Mr Jarves Stores.

The names of godparents are not recorded after 1560, but Gervase Storthes was probably the godfather over the next few years when the Kayes, Lockwoods, Goldthorpes and others had sons named Gervase. It was a particular favourite of the Kayes and Lockwoods and survived the Lockwoods' move to Honley in the adjoining parish, passing from them to neighbours who used it occasionally through the eighteenth century. In the registers of Almondbury and Kirkburton the godparent relationship helps to confirm the migration:

> 1560, 22 December: Jarvas baptised, son of John Lockwod of Kirkburton.
>
> 1585, 7 November: Gervase baptised, son of John Bothomleye of Almondbury, godfather Gervase Lockwodde.
>
> 1588, 14 April: Gervase baptised, son of Humfrey Armitedge of Almondbury, godfather Gervase Lockwood.

It is often such migrations that highlight the potential value of distinctive names to the genealogist. For example I was once asked by an American lady if I could direct her where to search for her ancestor Gervase Kaye who had left the north of England in the late seventeenth century. The surname Kaye has several origins in the north and on its own it cannot tell us where the family came from. However, the Kayes of Kirkburton had used Gervase since 1561, and this makes the task easier. In 1672, for example, the hearth tax returns list more than 180 Kayes in Yorkshire but only two men named Gervase, both living just a few miles from Kirkburton. One of those can be identified as a Quaker who was persecuted and imprisoned in the 1670s.[9]

Brice and Blaise

Brice and Blaise are two more non-scriptural saints' names said by Withycombe to have declined as a result of the Reformation, and the evidence again suggests that they had fallen almost completely out of favour by 1377–81. Brice was particularly uncommon at that time, although isolated examples are recorded in the Norfolk villages of Colkirk and Patesley. Indeed, in Colkirk the names Brice Child and Hugh Brice point to the possible development of Brice as a surname. Reaney and Wilson found examples of it as both a first name and by-name in Lincolnshire and Yorkshire in the early thirteenth century[10] but in 1379 Bricius Forster of Bolton Percy was the only West Riding man to bear the name. No other examples have been noted there until the early seventeenth century, when Mr Brice Allott was living in Emley, near Wakefield.

He had probably been given the name during Elizabeth's reign, when the Allots had a considerable estate in and around Emley and it was almost certainly his influence that ensured the modest popularity of Brice among families in that area. These included the Archers and Bedforths of Emley, the Nortons and Sheppards of Crigglestone and the Pollards of Kirkburton, none of them classed as gentry. It was only in Emley though that Brice gained a real foothold and there the Wilkinsons kept faith with it into the nineteenth century at least.

The choice of Blaise can be traced to the martyr St Blaise, who according to tradition was beheaded after being torn by wool-combs. Canterbury claimed relics of him and miracles were recorded at his shrine, one in 1451 it is said.[11] He was the patron saint of wool-combers and the diarist Parson Woodforde described 'the Grand Procession of Bishop Blaize' in Norwich in March 1783.[12] In Yorkshire Blaise is first recorded in Bradford, famous for textiles, and wool-combing in particular, and Bishop Blaise was honoured there too. In 1825 there was a spectacular procession of textile workers in the town, with flags, bands, fancy-dress and bonfires. A great deal of beer was consumed and a report in the *Leeds Mercury* referred to 'a blaze' that had not been put out in Bradford although 'the beer-engines had been playing upon it for several days'.[13]

The first to bear the name in Bradford was Blase Leventhorpe, a gentleman's son, born towards the end of the fifteenth century; the name was then used by families called Sugden and Phillips. In fact the Leventhorpes' choice of the name is unlikely to have had anything to do with wool-combing, for Bradford was just a small village at that time with no evidence of a Bishop Blaise tradition. Once again though the name survived the Reformation and it remained in use through the sixteenth and seventeenth centuries in all three Ridings, notably in the Hull area by families called Machon, Martyn and Dibney. The original influence there may have been a gentry family called Bates. North Riding families who used it were the Greatheads, Binks, Drivers and Saunders. This may read like quite a long list, but fewer than a dozen names have been quoted in three quite distinct localities. Blaise would certainly be a useful name to find amongst one's ancestors.

The names quoted by Withycombe were intended only as examples but it is evident that many of them were unpopular even before the Reformation; they actually came into more active use afterwards, some of them surviving within local communities at least into the nineteenth century. I will now examine a few other names in this category in order to show how their expansion can sometimes be traced to individual families. One with particular significance for north-country people is the now unpopular Cuthbert.

Cuthbert

Cuthbert is the sole survivor of several Old English names that had 'cuth' as a first element. This is usually interpreted as 'known' or 'famous' and it is linked to the words 'couth' and 'uncouth', the former still used in Scotland and the latter more generally. The second element 'berht' means bright and it is familiar to us in other Germanic names such as Robert and Herbert. Similar names that have disappeared, at least as first names, are Cuthred and Cuthwin but Cuthbald survives in the Suffolk surname Cobbold.[14]

Cuthbert's survival owes much to the inspiring story of St Cuthbert, the Northumbrian shepherd boy who became a monk in the seventh century and then, in turn, a prior and bishop. He is remembered particularly for his links with Lindisfarne and was long recognised as the most popular northern saint, a popularity reflected in the special veneration accorded to his shrine. After the destruction of Lindisfarne in 875, the incorrupted remains of Cuthbert's body were carried round northern England and parts of Lowland Scotland by monks loyal to his memory; they were finally brought to rest in 995 in Durham, where the shrine survives in the cathedral.

The cult dates from soon after Cuthbert's death in 687, and it received a significant stimulus when manuscripts of his life were produced, one of them fully illustrated. It was encouraged and developed in Durham, not least for the pilgrims and wealth it attracted to the city, but Cuthbert's name was preserved over a much wider area, notably in more than 150 church dedications throughout England and Scotland. Of particular interest are Gwbert in Cardiganshire and the town of Kirkcudbright in Galloway, which means the 'church of Cuthbert'. In faraway Cornwall there is the parish of Cubert, where the church in 1269 was also dedicated to St Cuthbert, probably replacing an older Cornish name.[15]

Withycombe said that Cuthbert's popularity 'lingered on in Yorkshire and Durham, chiefly among Roman recusants, after the Reformation', but then 'went out of general use until it was revived by the Tractarians in the nineteenth century'. She may be right about its nineteenth-century revival but her statements about its earlier history do not stand up to scrutiny. Unfortunately the poll tax material for Durham and Northumberland is missing or incomplete so these sources cannot provide us with information about Cuthbert's frequency in the north east in the fourteenth century. However, it is unlikely to have been popular there for it was recorded once only in the manor rolls of the Priory of Durham (1296–1384), and that was a clerk in holy orders in 1371.[16]

The name was certainly uncommon in Lancashire and Yorkshire in 1377–81, but it was recorded once in Howdenshire in the East Riding, where Cutbert Lynton paid 40d tax and had the status of franklin. Significantly the manor of Howden actually belonged to the Bishops of Durham, and their palace, a fragment of which survives, was close to the former collegiate church. In fact the Durham link is seldom hard to find where Cuthbert is concerned.

Although it is difficult to chart the name's history through the fifteenth century the number of references in England and Scotland increased in that period,[17] and it was certainly popular in Durham in the sixteenth and seventeenth centuries. An account book for the Priory of Durham lists more than a dozen men called Cuthbert in 1530–34,[18] and there are 26 tenants called Cuthbert in a survey of property in Durham in 1647.[19] There was no similar increase further south but Cuthbert was beginning to occur more frequently in Yorkshire and Lancashire by the mid-sixteenth century, occasionally in significant 'clusters'. When these are studied more closely it is usually possible to establish a link with north-east England.

For example, Cuthbert had never been a popular name in Ribblesdale, and it was absent from population lists for Slaidburn parish as late as 1547.[20] Soon afterwards though it was used by the Hayhursts and was unusual enough to identify Hairst as a variant spelling. There were individuals in Slaidburn called Cuthbert Hayhurst from 1600 to the end of the eighteenth century[21] and in 1682 a Quaker named Cuthbert Hayhurst emigrated to North America. His descendants kept faith with the name until at least 1789 and that can have had nothing to do with Catholicism.[22]

Cuthbert was almost certainly introduced into Slaidburn by Sir Cuthbert Musgrave, a newcomer to the parish. In 1564, in a dispute over seating arrangements in the church, he testified that he had been granted the lordship of Knowlmere in Slaidburn 10 years earlier, in return for his services to Queen Mary. He was the grandson of the northern knight Sir John Musgrave, and had previously held 'the captayneshipp' of Harbottle Castle and Ridsdale in Northumberland, territories close to the border with Scotland.[23] Another branch of the family held land in Durham; they too used the name Cuthbert.[24] Significantly the Hayhursts are known to have been tenants at Knowlmere and the inference is that a son was named Cuthbert when the landlord acted as godfather. The Musgraves may have retained Catholic sympathies but Cuthbert had been their family name from before the Dissolution.

It is clear from the church seat dispute that Cuthbert Musgrave had powerful and vindictive enemies in Slaidburn, and that may help to explain why his first name never became generally popular there. It was relatively popular though in and around the Yorkshire parish of Garforth from roughly the same period, and the influence there can be traced to the Withams, another gentry family with Durham connections.

Their surname probably derives from Witham in Lincolnshire,[25] but they lived in Brettanby, close to the border with Durham, and that was the home of Mathew Witham whose son Cuthbert graduated at Cambridge in 1545. He purchased property in Garforth from Sir Edmund Mauleverer in 1568,[26] and was the first of three Cuthbert Withams to be rector at Garforth. The will of the second of these, written in 1644, illustrates two ways in which the testator influenced the expansion of his first name in that part of the West Riding.[27] First of all, there were money bequests to three grandsons called Cuthbert, two of them Withams and the other the son of Christopher Wade of Kilnsey. This Cuthbert Wade was a noted justice of peace and a captain of horse in the army of Charles I, and through him Cuthbert was to become traditional in other branches of the family. For example, in 1745 Cuthbert Wade of Preston in Lancashire bequeathed his estate in Kilnsey to 'sister Allanson and her son Cuthbert Allanson'.[28]

There was also a bequest in Cuthbert Witham's will to Cuthbert Chamber, possibly another grandchild and certainly a godson, and three separate gifts of 5s each to Cuthbert Brearcliffe, Cuthbert Pulleyne and Cuthbert Twisleton. These were all children of local families and it seems likely that they were his godchildren, although there is no direct evidence for that in the will and the early Garforth registers have not survived. The use of the name spread eventually to parishes around Garforth but it was rare elsewhere in the county as the following figures show:

Parish	Period	Male baptisms	Cuthbert
Hooton Pagnell	1684–98	78	–
Brandesburton (ER)	1684–98	89	–
Braithwell	1684–98	88	–
Lythe (NR)	1684–90	169	–
Leeds	1684–88	734	–
Garforth	1684–98	119	6

There is no evidence that Cuthbert had a history in Garforth before the arrival of the Withams, but it became relatively popular whilst they held the rectory and continued to be used there into at least the nineteenth century, remaining distinctive enough to be of help to genealogists. For example its use draws attention to different branches of the Johnson family in Garforth and Swillington between 1698 and 1755 and also serves to identify a number of surname variants. There were Cuthberts with the surnames Bargh, Barugh, Barke, and Barge in Garforth and Kippax between 1637 and 1762, and Morresby, Morsbey and Mosby in Garforth between 1745 and 1812. Clearly Cuthbert was still being used in the parish into the nineteenth century, in the families of church-going colliers and labourers, and they owed their name to family tradition not to the Tractarian revival which was the source suggested by Withycombe. The more difficult names Wilfrid and Ninian allow me to make similar points.

Wilfrid

Most writers agree that Sir Walter Scott was responsible for Wilfrid's revival in the nineteenth century and its relative popularity in the early twentieth century.[29] It is Old English in origin and usually associated with the Northumbrian bishop Wilfrid, whose support for the Roman church carried the day at Whitby in 644. The cult was centred initially on Ripon and Hexham, where the crypts of his churches survive, but it spread to other parts of the country when both Canterbury and Worcester laid claim to his relics. Even so Wilfrid was rare in the Middle Ages, although Reaney and Wilson in *English Surnames* noted examples of it as a personal name in Durham in 1055 and as a by-name in Worcestershire in c.1280. Otherwise its early history is obscure and it is missing from the poll tax returns and the frequency lists of 1538–1700.

In fact there were adults named Wilfrid in Norfolk from 1431[30] and in Yorkshire from later in the century.[31] The most notable of these was Wilfrid Holme of Huntington near York, the Protestant poet who wrote *The Fall and Evill Success of Rebellion* in 1537, a significant but little-known politico-religious poem.[32] His family were important local landowners and had gentry status and that probably accounts for the success Wilfrid had among their neighbours in the sixteenth century and early seventeenth century. These include the Pinders, Featherstones, Nelstrops, Newarks and Lazenbys. It was also in regular use around Ripon and Leeds, and survived there through the eighteenth century in such families as the Pooles and the Pyemonts. Indeed there is a Wilfrid Pymont in the register of St Mary, Castlegate as late as 1819. Confirmation of Wilfrid's revival later that century can be found in the family tree of the Tempests of Ackworth Grange, where Wilfred Francis Tempest had brothers called Wulstan, Aelred and Aeden (1846).

Ninian

Ninian was a fifth-century British saint who preached the gospel among the southern Picts, and most writers connect the name with both Scotland and Ireland. Apart from one possible example in 1258 it seems to have come into use in Yorkshire in the reign of Henry VII, when Thomas Markingfield of

Markingfield Hall called one of his sons Ninian. Soon afterwards it found favour with the Tankards whose estate was near by at Boroughbridge. Local families who used Ninian in the sixteenth century were the Pullans, Aldersons, Granges and Wrays and some of these were Catholic recusants.

This concentration of the name in the Ripon area would not explain its appearance in other parts of Yorkshire in the sixteenth century, when it was recorded in the scattered rural townships of Sharow, Kirk Deighton, Farnham, Adel and Marrick, and there were other baptisms in the major urban centres of York and Hull. A more significant cluster in that period occurred in the parish of Carlton juxta Snaith, with other examples in Snaith itself, Womersley, Drax, Pollington and Fishlake. All these were in the north and east of the county and I have no evidence that Ninian was ever in favour elsewhere in Yorkshire. Nor did that distribution change significantly in the seventeenth century, when fewer examples are recorded. That decline continued and by the eighteenth century it was probably confined to a few families; these included the Wrays in Aldborough, and the Cooks and Proctors in Hampsthwaite, as late as 1779.

For several years I was puzzled by the name Trinian, which occurred in much the same areas as Ninian. It was familiar because of the notorious St Trinian's (the girls' school in Ronald Searle's children's books) but I found no mention of it in reference works until I read in W. J. Watson's *The Celtic Place Names of Scotland* that Trinian was a Gaelic variant of Ninian.[33] The evidence shows that it was effectively an alias, implicitly so in the case of the Watsons in Swaledale and explicitly in the Smithson family of Easington, e.g. in 1616 'Trinian alias Ninian' Smithson.[34] Both names had diminutives and these are on record not long after the first reference to the full name, e.g. in 1551 Ninie Blythman of York.[35] The Warwick family's use of Ninian emphasises its value to genealogists, for it links branches of the family in Ripon, Rothwell and Kippax between 1672 and 1760. Trinny Warwick was baptised in Kippax in 1694.

Dedications to St Ninian are rare in Yorkshire, although there are examples in Stokesley in 1497 and Tickhill in 1482.[36] Probably the most interesting location is St Trinian's in Easby near Richmond, where the Robinson family lived in the seventeenth century, and the location suggests that it may have inspired the choice of Trinian by Swaledale families, including the Smurthwaites, Fawcetts, Milners, Metcalfes, Tanfields, Hutchinsons and Boulbys. It survived until at least c.1750 in the Anderson family.

These rare first names pose some problems for researchers. Trinian for Ninian is an extreme example, but Wilfrid also had an alternative spelling that is seldom mentioned, for example, in 1671 Wilfrid alias Wilfrey Harrison of Eccup.[37] In fact the saint was referred to as 'Seynt Wilfra' in a Pontefract will of 1472.[38] The names have also caused both scribes and transcribers problems, a point family historians need to keep in mind, especially when working with published material. The editor of the North Riding quarter sessions records referred to 'Triman' Smith (1609) as 'another peculiar name', but it was probably Trinian, whereas Vnion Tidswell of Adel (1617) may well have been Ninian Tidswell.

Church dedications

It has already been suggested that a family's choice of christian name may have been influenced by a local church dedication and the connection can sometimes be inferred. For example there were several dedications to St Hilda in North Yorkshire, including the abbey at Whitby, and Hilda, a name revived in the 1860s, first occurs in that part of the county in the seventeenth century. I find no evidence to suggest that it had survived there from the Old English period, as Withycombe suggests, and the only earlier example I have noted was in Lancashire, Hilda Jacwyfe of Lonsdale (1379).

What is uncertain is whether the revival of a saint's name can be traced directly to a particular church or more generally to the influence of the cult. For example, there are just two dedications to St Alkelda, an obscure 'princess' who was reputedly strangled by two Danish women in about 800. These are the churches of Middleham and Giggleswick, and the only recorded examples of Alkelda as a girl's name are in the latter parish.[39] Two other women's names in this category, Syth and Frideswide, have more obvious implications for genealogists.

Syth

This rare name is not in the standard reference works, possibly because it has not been recognised as a short form of Osyth, recorded at least once in 1379 at Buxhall in Suffolk. After the abdication of Sighere, King of the East Saxons, his wife Osyth founded a convent at Chich in Essex and was venerated as a saint after her death: her name is preserved in the village of St Osyth. In a passage on false relics the poet Wilfrid Holme referred in 1537 to the lady as 'Sainct Sithe' and it was this form of the name that was familiar to educated northerners. Her cult was widespread in the Middle Ages, and that probably explains why the name was given in the late fifteenth century to Syth Markingfield, whose family revived Ninian about the same time. Other examples, from about 1500, have been noted in York and Thirsk, and Syth later became a favourite with the Robinsons at Easby, alongside Trinian. Because it is a woman's name and not a man's, it is more difficult to demonstrate how it passed from one generation to another, but that happened in the sixteenth and seventeenth centuries in the interrelated Swaledale families of Allen, Smelt, and Robinson.[40]

Syth was never common, but it survived into the nineteenth century at least and developed one or two interesting variants, possibly because many people were unaware of its true origin. Some parish register spellings suggest that it may have been associated by clerks with the ancient region known as Scythia and its nomadic inhabitants, referred to in Colossians 3. 11. and it may even have been confused with the Old Testament name Seth.[41] When it passed from the Knaggs family to the Porrits of Lythe, in the seventeenth century, it became a regular choice for daughters and was still being used in 1801, when Sythe or Sytheon Porrit signed her name Sethe in the register.

Frideswide

There are two early examples of this name in Berkshire in 1381 and it features in most of Smith-Bannister's frequency lists up to 1600, although never as one of the more popular names. St Frideswide is said to have been the daughter of a king of Mercia and to have founded a religious house in the eighth century in Oxford, where a shrine was erected over her remains in the cathedral.[42] The Saviles' connections with Oxford may explain their early use of the name, for example, Frissold or Frideswide Savile of Grantham (c.1575).[43] In the early 1580s three girls were given the name in Hooton Pagnell, a south Yorkshire village where the Saviles had an interest. Withycombe noted that corruptions of Frideswide were common and quoted 'Fridayweed', found in Henley.

A second and apparently unconnected use of Frideswide was in the North Riding parish of Lythe, but the registers survive only from 1619 and the earliest history of the name there is not yet known. It is certain, though, that it had been used by the Hutchinsons from early in the century and that Friswell or Frizwell was the preferred local spelling. Using the registers it is possible to work out how the name passed from this family to the Taylors, Stonehouses and Fletchers in the period 1683–1781. The last references I have noted are to Friswell Fletcher of Barnby in that parish, whose children were born in the period 1783–1804.

Oswald

Three male names which owe something directly to a church dedication are Oswald, Ricary and Michael and they illustrate different aspects of the subject. The Old English name Oswald survived into the fourteenth century, since Reaney and Wilson in *English Surnames* and Seltén in *Anglo-Saxon Heritage* found examples in East Anglia, the latest in 1332, and Osewald Nundy was taxed in Finedon in Northamptonshire in 1379.[44] However, there is no evidence that it had been in continuous use in Yorkshire from the Anglo-Saxon period as Withycombe suggests, although it is on record there from the late fifteenth century. Its reappearance may therefore owe something to Oswald of Northumbria, the seventh-century king and martyr who was venerated as far south as Italy, or to another Oswald who was Archbishop of York.

At least 20 Yorkshire churches are dedicated to St Oswald and there is some evidence that these influenced name-givers. Usually this can only be inferred: for example Oswald Forster had links with St Oswald's Priory at Nostell in 1498, and in 1545 William Chamber bequeathed a lease to his brother Oswald of the rents of 'the late monasterie of sancte Oswaldes'.[45] Among the dedications to St Oswald in the Dales are churches at Castle Bolton and Askrigg which may explain how Oswald came to be used by the innumerable Metcalfes of Wensleydale. The first example was an adult living in York in 1501,[46] but others are recorded at regular intervals in the sixteenth and seventeenth centuries.

A record that particularly catches the attention is the 1673 hearth tax return for Bainbridge, an extensive territory in Askrigg parish. It contains the names of 70 men named Metcalfe and 13 named Routh, and no fewer than 5 of the Rouths were called Oswald. The will of Christopher Routh of Hardraw in 1668 illustrates the links between these families, for he made bequests to his brother Oswald and two branches of the Metcalfes, in Mossdale and Gayle. He appointed Oswald Routh of Appersett and Oswald Routh of Hawes to be tutors to his three young daughters, and the appraisers of his inventory included Augustine Metcalfe, Ninian Metcalfe and Oswald Routh. These Christian names are a clear indication of the families' spiritual affinity and possibly of their parents' Catholic sympathies, and it would be impossible, I suspect, to find them together in a document in any other part of Yorkshire, possibly in any other part of the country.

Other Yorkshire families favoured Oswald in the sixteenth and seventeenth centuries, including the Leventhorpes, Redmans and Wilstrops among the gentry, and the Bucktrouts, Schofields, Chapmans, Armisteads and Dicksons at a lower level. In Snaith no fewer than five boys were given the name between November 1567 and April 1568 out of a total of 23 baptised: and this can almost certainly be attributed to the influence of Oswald Riccard, a local gentleman, although the registers contain no information about godparents. Wills might establish a link and that is the sort of project a family historian might undertake.

Ricary

The earliest examples of Ricary occur in Aberford and they relate to a yeoman family called Bucktrout. The Great North Road once passed through the parish and the church there is dedicated to Saint Ricarius, apparently a unique dedication in Yorkshire. In 1548 Thomas Bucktrout named three brothers in his will, one called Ricarie, and in 1549 John Bucktrout left the family farm to Ricarie his son.[47] One of these Ricary Bucktrouts, if indeed there were two, had nine of his children baptised at the church between 1549 and 1565 and yet not one of his sons was named after him.

Between 1552 and 1566 Ricary was used in Aberford by families named Hole, Wilson, Smith, Akid, Becket and Backhouse, and the statistical significance of that is apparent when it is considered that only 62 boys were baptised there in the same period. Once again the godparents' names are missing but it must be suspected that Ricary Bucktrout acted as godfather in at least some of those cases, and that the families named were among his closest relatives and neighbours.

Ricary did not survive in the Bucktrout family, nor even in Aberford, and one possible explanation for its decline is that it was 'tainted' with Catholicism, especially since members of the Bucktrout and Backhouse families were named in lists of recusants. Miles Backhouse, whose son was called Ricary, was indicted for recusancy in 1571 along with his wife.[48] Even so, the decline in Aberford was not the end of the story; the Ricary Backhouse baptised in 1566 then disappeared from the Aberford registers, but he probably moved elsewhere as there is no record of his death. The following references in neighbouring parishes seem likely to refer to his descendants:

> 1678, 31 October: Elizabeth baptised, daughter of Rickory Bacchus, Leeds.
> 1682, 13 September; Rickaery baptised, son of Mathew Bachouse, Swillington.

Rickree Bacchus died in Leeds in 1723 and in his lifetime his neighbours the Masons and the Brayhams also had sons named Ricary. No later examples have yet been located but one of the problems for researchers is that the name was so unusual, especially away from Aberford, that some transcribers may have interpreted it as Richard, especially since 'Richary' was one early spelling.

Michael

We don't think of Michael as a distinctive name but we can link its expansion in Halifax in the sixteenth century to a particular church dedication. In fact statistics show that it was not a common name in England in 1377–81, although still used often enough to be the source of the surname Mitchell, noted by Guppy in more than 20 counties (*Homes of Family Names*). It occurred only seven times in the West Riding, roughly once for every 3,000 males, and later sources offer no evidence of a significant change in its fortunes. In a subsidy roll of 1545 for the Calder Valley, containing more than 2,000 names, the only Michael listed was Michael Ottes of Halifax,[49] whose name is an important link in a fascinating chain of evidence.

It is in Halifax, soon after 1545, that we first observe Michael's spectacular and very localised expansion. In 1541, for example, there were no Michaels in 119 male baptisms recorded in the parish, whereas there were 21 in 1571, out of 160 male baptisms, placing it second to John in popularity. If these Halifax statistics are compared with those for neighbouring villages it is clear that this was not part of a more general trend, for no Michaels were baptised in that year in the extensive parishes of Rothwell, Kirkburton and Birstall.

Nor was Michael popular with all the families in Halifax parish, although with a few it soon became a particular favourite. For example, between 1551 and 1568 no fewer than eight Michael Bairstows were baptised, and another seven were recorded in the 1580s, some of those inevitably named after their fathers. The following references are just a few of those which illustrate how that expansion began in the Oates family and spread to their kinsmen and friends the Broadleys:

1543, 5 November: George Ottes married Isabella Brodeley.

1545, 25 October: Mychaell baptised, son of Michael Ottes.

1549, 3 July: Michaell baptised, son of Richard Ottes.

1556, 15 November: Michaell baptised, son of Edward Brodley, godfathers George Ottes and Thomas Bairstowe.

1557/8, 6 February: Michaell baptised, son of John Ottes, godfathers Michaell Ottes and Robert Brodley.

In this way a naming custom was established in the valley which persisted in some cases into the nineteenth century at least. Eventually, of course, Michael's importance locally would be masked by a more widespread popularity, but it would be interesting to know if that increase was the result of several significant localised expansions or a more general use of the name nationally. In either case it is worth establishing what lay behind its revival in Halifax.

The circumstances in which the first Michael Ottes was given his name are not explicit, but a Halifax will of 1538 throws some light on the matter. The testator was Robert Thomson, evidently not a native of the town since he bequeathed 3s 4d 'to the churche...of Sanct Michaell in Maladaill', i.e. Kirkby Malham, a parish some 30 miles to the north where there had been Thomsons from c.1450.[50] Three additional items in the will touch on the use of Michael, of which the most important is that Robert Thomson had given the name to his son who was an assignee and executor. That choice seems likely to have been inspired by the dedication of his former parish church, which he specifically mentioned.

It is evident also that the testator had become an influential and well-integrated member of the Halifax community, for he left 4d 'unto evere chylde' to whom he had been godfather. It is unfortunate that he did not give the children's names, for that would certainly have told us more about his affinity, but as he held his lease of land in Ovenden 'of Brian Otes', and Robert Berstow witnessed his will, the links with these two families are clear.

There were, of course, other parishes where Michael was in use at that time, and there may have been similar localised ramifications, but that does not alter the fact that Michael is a useful clue in that period, helping to identify Halifax men who moved to other chapelries and parishes. Its popularity in the Bairstow family makes that point, since men called Michael Bairstow were living in Birstall in 1612 and Heptonstall in 1646. Another Michael Bairstow emigrated to New England in 1630. Michael also proves useful in identifying Bairstall as a variant of Bairstow when this spelling became normal for a time from 1568. The variation persisted for 10 years or so and survived a migration over the border into Lancashire:

1568, 27 June: Michaell baptised, son of Michael Bayrstall, Halifax.
1642: Michaell Burstall, Rochdale.[51]

~

It emerged in Chapter 3 that many of the names that rose to popularity in the fifteenth century were those of saints, for both men and women, and this was evidently part of a much wider influence that saw less well-known saints emerge as regional favourites. Local cults and dedications may have been responsible for this but the initial choices were usually made by members of the gentry, and the expansions took place within families and small communities, their success ensured by godparents and family members. This influence did not end with the Reformation and at times was almost certainly associated with recusancy but that must have played an increasingly limited role as family continuity became the most important factor in a name's survival. It was a success that saw some distinctive names move further afield, even overseas, and in some cases it lasted into the nineteenth century at least, coinciding with the revival of such names for other reasons. Once such locally significant names are identified they are obviously a valuable tool for family historians but account has to be taken of the difficulties that arise from unusual diminutives and alternatives, for these will not necessarily have found their way into our major dictionaries.

Notes

1   D. H. Farmer, *The Oxford Dictionary of Saints*, 3rd edn (Oxford, 1992).
2   R. A. McKinley, *Norfolk and Suffolk in the Middle Ages*, English Surnames Series (1975).
3   H. Thwaite (ed.), *Abstracts of Abbotside Wills, 1552–1688*, Yorkshire Archaeological Society, Record Series CXXX (1968). The author attributed its popularity in Wensleydale to the local custom of naming children after their grandfather.
4   In the hearth tax of 1673 for Bainbridge there were two Austin Metcalfes, one Austin Parkin and one Austin Allen.
5   Peter McClure notes that Gervase de Clifton was an adult in the pipe roll of 1201.
6   *Index of Wills in the York Registry, 1389–1514*, YAS VI (1889).
7   *Yorkshire Fines, 1486–1571*, YAS II (1887), p. 120.
8   H. Aveling, 'The Catholic recusants of the West Riding of Yorkshire, 1558–1790', *Proceedings of the Leeds Philosophical Society X*, Part VI (1963).
9   F. A. Collins (ed.), *The Parish Registers of Kirkburton II* (Exeter, 1902), p. 44.
10 P. H. Reaney and R. M. Wilson, *A Dictionary of English Surnames*, 3rd edn, (Oxford, 1997).
11 D. H. Farmer, *Dictionary of Saints*.
12 J. Woodforde, *The Diary of a Country Parson, 1758–1802* (Oxford, 1978).
13 I. Dewhirst, *Yorkshire through the Years* (London, 1975).
14 See Chapter 1.
15 O. J. Padel, *A Popular Dictionary of Cornish Place-Names* (Penzance, 1988).
16 J. Booth (ed.), *Durham Halmote Rolls*, Surtees Society LXXXII (1889).

17 See, for example, G. F. Black, *The Surnames of Scotland* (New York, 1946).

18 J. Raine (ed.), *Durham Household Book*, Surtees IV (1844).

19 D. A. Kirby (ed.), *Parliamentary Surveys of the Bishopric of Durham*, Surtees CLXXXIII, CLXXXV (1971, 1972).

20 W. Farrer (ed.), *The Court Rolls of the Honor of Clitheroe* I (Manchester, 1897). R. W. Hoyle (ed.), *Early Tudor Craven: Subsidies and Assessments 1510–1547*, YAS CXLV (1987).

21 C. J. Spencer and R. H. Postlethwaite (eds), *The Registers of St Andrew, Slaidburn, 1600–1770* (Preston, 1994).

22 G. E. McCracken, *The Welcome Claimants Proved, Disproved and Doubtful* (Pennsylvania, 1985).

23 J. S. Purvis, 'A Note on Pews and Stalls', *Yorkshire Archaeological Journal* XXXVII (1951), pp. 162–94.

24 W. Brown (ed.), *Yorkshire Deeds*, YAS L (1914).

25 *Testamenta Eboracensia*, Surtees XLV (1865), pp. 264–8.

26 *Yorkshire Fines, 1486–1571*, YAS II (1887), p. 361.

27 *Abstracts of Yorkshire Wills at Somerset House*, YAS IX (1890), p. 87.

28 Claremont, Leeds, West Yorkshire Archive Service, MD 247.

29 L. A. Dunkling, *First Names First* (London, 1977), p. 195.

30 *A Calendar of the Freemen of Great Yarmouth, 1429–1800* (Norwich, 1910).

31 There is an apparently isolated reference to the name in 1382, but it has not been checked. See T. W. Hall (ed.), *Land Charters and Court Rolls from the Bosville and Lindsay Collections, etc.* (Sheffield, 1930), p. 61.

32 A. G. Dickens, 'Wilfrid Holme of Huntington: Yorkshire's First Protestant Poet', YAJ XXXIX (1958), pp. 119–35.

33 W. J. Watson, *The Celtic Place Names of Scotland* (Edinburgh, 1926 and 1993).

34 Rev. J. C. Atkinson (ed.), *Quarter Sessions Records*, The North Riding Record Society (1884), p. 142.

35 H. B. McCall (ed.), *Yorkshire Star Chamber Proceedings* II, YAS XLV (1911), p. 34.

36 *Testamenta Eboracensia*, Surtees LIII (1869), p. 129; ibid., XLV (1865), p. 274.

37 'Local Muniments', YAJ III (1875), p. 73.

38 *Testamenta Eboracensia*, Surtees XLV (1865), p. 203.

39 For example, in 1578 Alkelda Browne of Giggleswick.

40 Rev. Canon Raine, 'Marske in Swaledale', YAJ VI (1881), p. 279.

41 For example, 1640 Seeth Bayle, a girl, baptised, Emley; 1701, Scythia Lye, adult, Hampsthwaite; 1711 Seythian Cock baptised, Lythe.

42 D. Attwater, *The Penguin Dictionary of Saints* (2nd edn, 1983).

43 J. W. Clay, 'The Savile Family', YAJ XXV (1920), p. 37.

44 Peter McClure makes the point that Chaucer named his Norfolk reeve Oswald (c.1390), but the name is missing from the county's poll tax returns.

45 G. D. Lumb (ed.), *Testamenta Leodiensia*, Thoresby Society XIX (1913), p. 120.

46 *Register of the Freemen of the City of York, 1272–1558*, Surtees XCVI (1896).

47 G. D. Lumb, (ed.), *Testamenta Leodiensia*.

48 H. Aveling (ed.), 'Catholic Recusants', p. 286.

49 'Lay Subsidy of Aggbrigg and Morley, 1545', *Thoresby* XI (1904), p. 122.

50 J. T. Fowler (ed.), *Memorials of the Abbey of St Mary of Fountains*, Surtees CXXX (1918), p. 242. R. W. Hoyle (ed.), *Early Tudor Craven Subsidies*, p. 29.

51 H. Fishwick, *History of the Parish of Rochdale* (1889).

CHAPTER EIGHT

Names from Legend and Literature

The fifteenth century saw some names revived and others added to the country's name-stock; we have seen that the saints were one source of inspiration, with the gentry at the forefront of changing fashions. Literature was another source they could draw on, with choices ranging from names in the Arthurian cycle of legends and such medieval poems as Chaucer's Troilus and Criseyde, to the works of the great classical authors. Many of these names were linked with heroic and romantic characters and, at a time when honour and pride in the family name were of increasing importance, it is hardly surprising that gentlemen sought to associate themselves with such great figures. From the gentry these names then passed to their immediate kith and kin, helping to cement the alliances that were at the core of fifteenth and sixteenth-century communities.

The medieval romances

A few names from the medieval romances were already in use by 1377–81, but they were rare, almost exclusively male, and often of uncertain derivation. Examples drawn from the Arthurian cycle were Percival, Gawain and Tristram, with Oliver and Roland from the legends associated with Charlemagne. The popularity of the female name Isolde, Tristram's tragic mistress, makes it an exception. Little has been written about where and when these names were first revived.

Perceval or Percival is of interest because it is said to have been invented by Crestien de Troyes for the hero of his poem of that name, towards the end of the twelfth century. Withycombe quotes an example in 1375 (English Christian Names) and it occurs once or twice also in 1377–81, e.g. Persival Plowman of Wymondham in Leicestershire and Percyvall Pensax of Beckwithshaw in Lower

Wharfedale. It was used more frequently after that but is absent from the frequency lists of 1538–1700 and none of the dictionaries throws much light on its early history.

The Beckwithshaw reference is interesting, for the Lindleys held land there and they used Percival consistently from the fifteenth century. Towards the end of the century it was also becoming popular among their neighbours and was recorded in a muster roll of 1535 in the families of Wade, Duffield, Jenkinson, Foster and Hawksworth. Other examples can be found in parishes nearby and it was still well represented there in the hearth tax returns of 1672. It was even given occasionally to girls, for Parsabella Whaites was baptised in Leeds in 1692.

Lower Wharfedale was not the only area where Percival was locally popular but tight-knit concentrations of this kind are easily missed in selective name counts over a wider area. For that reason family historians should always be prepared to carry out their own investigation into a name's popularity, and they will be surprised at how localised some naming patterns once were. However it is important for them also to be able to identify the name they are interested in, since less-common christian names, like surnames, caused the clerks problems. Typical variant spellings of Percival include Persefowle, Parsibell and Percever.

One of the most successful of all the Arthurian names is undoubtedly Gawain which achieved considerable popularity as Gavin in the 1970s, having spread into this country from Scotland. Once again though the dictionaries say little about its earlier history, although Withycombe thought that it was 'fairly common in the Middle Ages' and quoted examples from seventeenth-century Lancashire wills. Apparently she found no references between 1379 and 1530, and there is no evidence that Gawain was ever common generally in England. Nevertheless dozens of examples have been recorded in the northern counties from c.1300, including Gawen Parcivell of Thornaby (1672). The varied spellings include Galvan (1304), Gawin (1476), Gawane (1574), Gawinge (1592) and Gowin (1719).

Like most Arthurian names Lancelot has a disputed etymology, and it also suffers because it was never popular nationally. It has been considered sufficient in the past to comment on its use in the north of England and its more general revival in the early nineteenth century, avoiding questions about where and when it became popular. Sadly its absence from the poll tax returns and most of Smith-Bannister's lists does nothing to enlighten us, and for most people it remains somewhat obscure. Perhaps things would have been different if Lancelot Brown, the great Northumberland landscape gardener, had not earned the nickname 'Capability'.

I am uncertain which family actually revived Lancelot but the Neviles and the Percys were among the first to use it and several men who bore the name in the late fifteenth century were natives of the north west, today's county of Cumbria. Their surnames are the clue, for they derive from Cumbrian place-names, e.g. Lancelot Thrilkeld (1485), Launslet Lowther (1487), Lancelett Hoton (1490) and

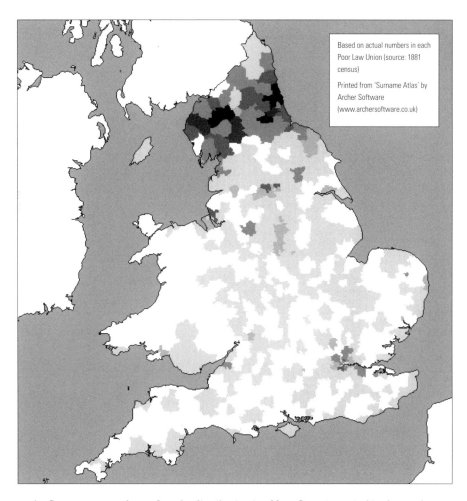

Based on actual numbers in each Poor Law Union (source: 1881 census)

Printed from 'Surname Atlas' by Archer Software (www.archersoftware.co.uk)

5 **The first name Lancelot (1289)** The distribution in 1881 reflects its revival in the north, probably in the 1400s, and its enduring popularity there.

Lancelot Wharton (1511). No fewer than six Lancelots are listed in a rental of 1541 for Ravenstonedale in Westmorland, and it was clearly popular there by that time.

One or two wills from that period illustrate how the expansion was taking place and how Lancelot was beginning to move further afield. The first of these is the will of Henry Percy, Earl of Northumberland, written in 1485.[1] In it he confirmed a grant to Lancelot Thrilkeld, esquire, probably the man described by Lancelett Hoton of Hutton in Cumberland as his 'gossip' in 1490. Lancelote Stapilton of Wath, whose mother Jane was the daughter of Lancelot Threlkeld, apparently died childless in 1538, but he bequeathed 40s to his godson Lancelote Conyers, 'so that his father put the saide 40s in a stoke to go forwarde to thuse of the saide childe'.[2] In his wife's will of 1545 there were bequests to Lancelote Fox,

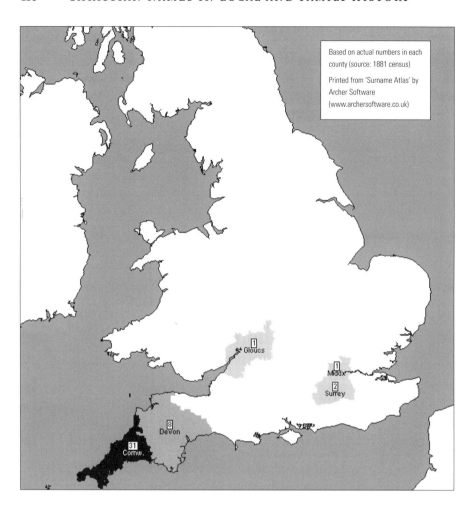

Based on actual numbers in each county (source: 1881 census)

Printed from 'Surname Atlas' by Archer Software (www.archersoftware.co.uk)

6 The first name Digory (43). Degarre or Degare was the son of a Breton princess, and his search for his lost mother is the theme of a medieval romance. The name has been found principally in Cornwall and Devon. The spelling Diggory occurred only five times in 1881.

Lancelote Browne and Lancelott Knapton.[3] This group of gentry families, with their godchildren and neighbours, is what I would describe as a typical affinity.

In south-west England the name Degory or Digory was in use from the six-teenth century and unusual enough to help identify the origins of Degory Priest, the *Mayflower* emigrant. Bardsley surely exaggerated when he said that it was 'on everybody's lips when Henry VIII was king',[4] but he recorded several sixteenth-century examples and there are others in both Devon and Cornwall from that period, e.g. Digory Bligh of Launceston (1564)[5] and Degory Shepherd of Hartland (1642).[6] It can be traced to a fourteenth-century metrical romance in which the hero is Degare, the son of a princess of Brittany.

Charles

Charles is the most prestigious of the names in the Charlemagne cycle for it has repeatedly been associated with kings. Even so aspects of its history are obscure and the direct source of its inspiration here has not always been recognised. At least its etymology poses no problems since it derives from a Germanic word meaning 'freeman'. It was linked therefore with 'carl' or 'housecarl', the word used before the Norman Conquest for the royal bodyguards or household troops. Our modern 'churlish', the adjective from 'churl', has the same origin but has come to mean 'ungracious' or 'grudging', an intriguing semantic development comparable with 'surly'.

The best known bearer of the name was Charlemagne or Charles the Great, the Holy Roman Emperor who died in 814. Other Frankish leaders had borne the name, including his grandfather Charles Martel or Charles the Hammer, but it is Charlemagne who is credited with establishing the name's popularity on the Continent, where it was borne by a succession of emperors and kings. Although it was never a favourite with the Normans, scattered examples can be found in early English records and Reaney and Wilson noted several in East Anglia before 1300, early enough to give rise to a surname. For example Charles of Yarmouth held land in both Norfolk and Suffolk early in the thirteenth century and was succeeded by his son and grandson, William Charles and Edward Charles.[7] The surname had stabilised in those three generations.

It is true nonetheless that Charles was unpopular in the fourteenth century and no example was noted in 1377–81. Hanks and Hodges claimed that Mary Queen of Scots (1542–87) re-introduced it to Britain but that cannot be true, although her son Charles James (1566–1625) probably contributed to its later popularity. As James VI of Scotland, and James I of England from 1603, he was father and grandfather to two English kings called Charles and that must have played a significant part in its wider acceptance, certainly amongst royalists. However, the evidence shows that northern gentry families were using the name long before that, the Mortons of Bawtry as early as 1425 and the Pilkingtons of Lancashire by the middle of the century. What influence their choice of Charles may have had more generally is difficult to judge but Sir John Pilkington's will of 1478 offers one or two clues.[8]

The Pilkingtons had estates in both Lancashire and Yorkshire and when Sir John fell ill at Skipton he asked to be buried in his own chantry in Wakefield. He bequeathed property in the Huddersfield area to his brother Charles Pilkington, who must therefore have been given his name in the middle years of the century. A second Charles Pilkington was a minister and prebendary in that part of the county by 1482. Their gentleman neighbour Charles Storthes (1472)[9] was almost certainly responsible for the wider popularity the name then enjoyed in Kirkburton parish, where it was used by the Copleys, Stones, Woodheads,

Eastwoods, Mitchells and Whittakers. Most of these men had no gentry connections, and the probability is that they were godchildren of Charles Storthes.

It is impossible to say at this stage what influence these two gentry families may have had on the use of Charles further afield, but the wills make it clear that the Pilkingtons had links with Oxford University and with London. The first Charles died in Worksop in 1485 and Sir John Pilkington's national status is probably implicit in his appointment of the Earl of Gloucester and the Lord Chamberlain as executors. Charles was probably being revived in other parts of the country but what cannot be doubted is that it was an established christian name long before Mary Queen of Scots was born.

Oliver

Two other names from this cycle that came into general use were Roland and Oliver, linked for all time in the twelfth-century *Chanson de Roland*, a legendary account of a rearguard action by Charlemagne's army in the Pyrenees. Both names were brought here by the Normans and there is early evidence for their use as by-names and surnames. In fact Guppy in *Homes of Family Names* found the surname Oliver well represented in more than a dozen counties, whereas Rowland(s) was less widespread, being more common in Wales than anywhere else.

Roland was not a popular first name in 1377–81 but it occurred in several parts of the country, notably in Cornwall alongside Oliver. Withycombe described Oliver as a moderately common name in the Middle Ages and into the seventeenth century, which went completely out of fashion after the Restoration. She attributed this to its association with Oliver Cromwell, but typically offered no evidence to support her claim. In fact Oliver was never a favourite in England, although in 1377–81 it was recorded over a wide area from Oxfordshire to Westmorland, and it was distinctive enough in Weston in Rutland to identify a servant with no by-name. However, not all the Olivers listed in the poll tax returns were Englishmen and at least two came from overseas, one from Flanders and one from the Baltic. The name obviously had a wide appeal but it remained an unusual choice in England and was absent from Smith-Bannister's tables for 1538–1700.

In Yorkshire Oliver has been recorded consistently from the twelfth century and its early history there throws light on naming practices which may have been typical elsewhere. In 1379 there were just five examples in the West Riding but it occurred regularly throughout the fifteenth century and by 1545 was the twenty-ninth most common name in the Calder Valley, just outside the category which qualified as 'quite popular'.[10] It was rather more common there than it was in England generally but declined through Elizabeth's reign and the seventeenth century, without ever disappearing completely. In fact it continued to be used by several families into the eighteenth century, including the Tathams and Ripleys of Leeds.

That modest expansion by 1545 can be traced to a group of inter-connected families in the Wakefield area, where Oliver had been recorded once in 1379. It started in Woolley with the Woodruffes and Franks, both substantial land-owning families whose records show they had common interests.[11] The first Oliver Woderove died in 1430, the same year as Oliver Franke of Spofforth, but he is mentioned in 1416 and must have been born in the previous century.[12] A second Oliver Frank died in the Nottinghamshire village of North Collingham in 1484 but that potential area of expansion has not yet been researched.

Several neighbouring families used the name between 1430 and 1470, includ-ing the Mirfields, Pickburns and Haighs, and it is tempting to see them as belonging to the same affinity. Genealogical work might eventually show exactly how they were all related, but at the moment we have little more to go on than their common choice of Oliver as a first name and references in the Woodruffes' land charters.[13] For example, an indenture 'for the settlement of variances and debates' in 1456 described one party in the dispute as comprising 'Oliver Mirfeld, William Haigh, John Lokwode and other kin and friends'.[14] This confirms the link between Woodruffe, Mirfield and Haigh and introduces the Lockwoods, an important family with branches in several parishes close to Wakefield. The fol-lowing references illustrate how their use of Oliver spread from Kirkburton to Almondbury, Halifax and Swillington:

> 1468: Oliver Lokwodd, named in an affray in Kirkburton.[15]
> 1498: Sir Oliver Lokwod, priest, tenant of land in Thurstonland.[16]
> 1518: Oliver Lokwode, purchaser of a house in Skircoat, Halifax.[17]
> 1543, 20 May: Janet baptised, daughter of Oliver Lockwood, Swillington.
> 1545: 21 April: Olyver baptised, son of John Lokewode of Skircoat, Halifax.
> 1578, 23 February: Oliver baptised, son of Henry Lockwod of Hallbower, godfather Oliver Lockwodde, Almondbury.

These indicate how Oliver ramified in one family, and the godparents' role is evident, both explicitly and implicitly. Its influence on families with a different surname is more difficult to prove, particularly before there were parish regis-ters, but once again there are documents that point to a connection between the Lockwoods and some of their neighbours, notably the powerful Waterhouse family of Skircoat and Warley:

> 1523: Richard Brygg of Warley, Halifax, surrendered land in Southowram to Robert and Sibyl Waterhouse, witnessed by Oliver Lokwode.[18]
> 1524: Oliver Waterhouse and Oliver Sykes of Slaithwaite.[19]
> 1537: John Waterhous, Richard Brige and Oliver Lokwode, jurors at Halifax manor court.[20]
> 1543: Oliver Hurste of Slaithwaite.[21]

Tristram

Three twelfth-century versions of the medieval romance of *Tristan and Isolde* are known to survive and the story has been a source of inspiration to artists, musicians and writers ever since, ensuring that the names of the tragic lovers have been continually before us. Tristram, said to have been influenced by the French word 'triste', is the usual Anglo-Norman version of a Celtic personal name, on record in England from 1189. Surnames were derived from it in the thirteenth century but it never achieved popularity and was rare in 1377–81. However, one notable by-name is that of a young lady called Isolda Trestrem, taxed in Appletreewick in 1379, and this surely confirms the source of inspiration. Just above Isolda in the list was 'Cecilia ux' Trystrem' ('ux' short for 'uxor' or wife), a widow and, as her deceased husband had no second name, the inference is that his first name was distinctive enough for him not to need one. Tristram remained in occasional use and its history in the Bradford area is illuminating.

It was used there by the Bollings of Bolling Hall, and one account of their origins mentions a Tristram de Boling as early as c.1200. I have not seen that reference and cannot vouch for its accuracy, but there were certainly other Tristrams in the family in the fifteenth and sixteenth centuries. The first of these was 'Tristram, son and heir apparent to...Robert Bollyng, squyer', mentioned in a deed of settlement dated 1446.[22] The terms governing Tristram's marriage to Beatrice Calverley make it clear that he was just a boy at the time, probably no more than 10 years old, so he must have been given his name about 1436. Later in the century, after a reversal in the family's fortunes, Bolling Hall passed into the possession of the Tempests, and the Bollings were obliged to move away. However, they kept faith with the family name and two further Tristram Bollings are known to have lived in Heaton, taking the name's history into the seventeenth century.

By that time other gentry families who employed it were the Burdetts, in Sandal and Birstall, the Middletons of Middleton and, not surprisingly, the Tempests who had inherited Bolling Hall. However, the family responsible for Tristram's wider use in the sixteenth and seventeenth centuries were the Ledgards, whose main home was Mirfield but who probably came into contact with the Bollings after acquiring land in the Horton area of Bradford in the fourteenth century. There is indirect evidence of that relationship in 1516 in the will of Tristran Ledyerd who was just one of several members of the family to bear the name.

Others were the Tristram Ledgeard who was baptised in Mirfield in 1568 and a Tristram Ledgard who was named in a Bradford deed of 1670 relating to tithes.[23] The will of a fourth Tristram Ledgard, who was a merchant in Bawtry in south Yorkshire, was proved in August 1648. Yet another Tristram Ledgard was living in Calverley parish in the mid-sixteenth century and it was there that

Tristram became moderately popular, used by the Lillys, Kitsons, Kitchens and Hares among others. It was Beatrice Calverley who had married Robert Bollyng back in 1446.

I have no proof yet that the Bollings were kinsmen of the other families who used Tristram in that part of Yorkshire but there are items of circumstantial evidence which indicate that they were connected. For example, Tristram Horton was a Wakefield priest who wrote his will in 1548. In it he made several bequests, including 40s to Tristram Bolling, gentleman, and 40s to the widow of Tristram Ledgeard of Horton.[24] The value of such an unusual name for the genealogist is that it draws attention to scattered branches of a family and here it clearly identifies the testator's links with Bradford.

However, this history of Tristram cannot be completed without reference to two of Tristram Bolling's brothers, for their distinctive christian names identify Robert Bolling the father as one of the most important innovators in the county. Of the two Troilus has the more obvious source, known to us through medieval poetry as the lover of Cressida and through classical literature as the son of Priam and Hecuba. There is no entry for Troilus in any of the major dictionaries, which may suggest that the Bollings were one of a very few English families with whom it found favour. It is so unusual that we are tempted, even without evidence, to see a connection between the Bollings and two other local men, Trollis Brodley of Huddersfield (1524) and Trowlis Rayner of Batley (1535).

The Townend family also used Troilus and a connection here seems more probable since they lived in Methley where the Bollings had an interest during the fifteenth and sixteenth centuries.[25] For example, Troles Townnend was taxed in Methley in 1545 and Troles Tounsend was buried in the neighbouring parish of Kippax in 1594, apparently the last to bear the name. However, Troilus was so distinctive that it was used colloquially as an alias of the family's surname, made explicit only when one of them was buried, e.g. Thomas 'Townend alias Trollis' in 1623 and John 'Townsend alias Trollis' in 1680. When Mary died, in 1661, she was described as the wife of 'William Townend vulgo Trollis' (commonly called Trollis) and this seems to confirm that Trollis was used by neighbours to distinguish these Townends from other families with the same surname.

In the neighbouring parishes of Swillington and Rothwell the alias was not explicit but it is clear nonetheless that the by-name could sometimes replace the surname, for example, Lancelot Trolisse of Swillington (1650).[26] The use of the distinctive christian name Lancelot, alongside both Townend and Trollis, is a key part of that identification.

The name of the younger brother, Rainbrown or Rainbrow, is even more obscure, but he is referred to in several documents. The most interesting of these is a licence, granted in 1491 to the vicar of Brotherton, which allowed him to 'solemnize the marriage between Raynebrowne Bolling and Alice Philip of Methley without banns, they having lived long as man and wife and wishing to avoid the scandal consequent upon the publication of banns'.[27] There appears to be no precedent for this name but it seems to combine two Germanic elements and it is possible that Robert Bolling had found it on one of the family's early charters, along with Tristram.

Although it is unlikely that Rainbrown Bolling lived in the Bradford township of Allerton cum Wilsden, the evidence suggests that he came into possession of some of his father's lands there, for several families in that part of Bradford used his christian name in the sixteenth and seventeenth centuries. The most notable of these were the Wilmans or Willmans, who seem to have persisted with Rainbrown long after any other family, probably for something like 150 years. The first to be recorded was Raynbrowne Willman of Wilsden, listed in a muster roll of 1539, and the last is Rainsbroughe Willman of Wibsey, a tenant at Royds Hall in 1651. Other Wilsden families with the name were the Milners, Wrights, Hills and Binnses and the inference once again is that they probably belonged to the same affinity. In fact there is confirmation of a link between the Bollings and the Wrights in a deed of 1564, in which Robert Bolling of Wybsay granted to Thomas Bolling, his son, 'a messuage and lands in Wibsay, in the occupation of Raynebrowne Wryght'.[28]

This was such a rare first name and occurred in such a restricted geographic area that it is tempting to believe that all the 'Rainbrowns' were in some way connected. There is no evidence yet though to link either the Bollings, or any of the Wilsden families, to two men from Lower Wharfedale, Ranbrowne Snawden of Collingham (1545) and Raynebrowne Tomson of Otley (1599).

The three Bolling brothers were given their unusual names in the period 1435–50, and the choices raise intriguing questions about Robert Bolling's motives, especially as Tristram may have been a deliberate revival.[29] His reasons must surely have had something to do with his status as a gentleman and the names would certainly have drawn attention to his family right through the neighbourhood. He is likely to have seen Tristram in particular as adding lustre to the Bolling surname, bringing reflected glory to the family through its associations with a romance that was older even than the story of Lancelot and Guinevere. Its prestige would have helped to authenticate the Bollings' claim to a long and distinguished pedigree, and there is evidence that other families chose Arthur for similar reasons.

Arthur

The documentary evidence takes Arthur back to 596 but once again the etymology is uncertain. Those who support the idea that it has a Celtic origin say that it derives from 'artos', the word for a bear, although an alternative word meaning 'stone' has also been suggested. There are others who associate it with the Roman family or 'clan' name 'Artorius' and there are even supporters for a derivation from Old Norse Arnthor. These disputes are probably best left to the linguists but they emphasise the name's obscurity and help to confirm its antiquity.

No matter what its origin Arthur certainly owes its prestige to the legendary exploits of King Arthur, first mentioned by name in 796 but supposedly active in the fifth and sixth centuries, after the departure of the Romans. Other examples of the name are recorded in 1086 and it occurs as a by-name as late as 1246, sufficiently late for it to have given rise to a surname. Arthur must also have been used in several different regions, for Guppy noted in *Homes of Family Names* the frequency of the surname in places as far apart as Cornwall and Devon in the south west, Monmouth on the Welsh border and Northumberland in the far north, territories where British kingdoms had survived the Anglo-Saxon settlement.

There is no agreement about how Arthur fared after the thirteenth century, although it is known to have fallen out of favour. It was certainly extremely rare in 1377–81 and one theory is that it became unpopular because of the untimely fate of Arthur, Duke of Brittany, allegedly done to death in 1203 by his drunken uncle King John. Most dictionaries leave the story there, concentrating on the name's revival in the eighteenth century and its success in Victorian England, when it was one of the most popular names in the English-speaking world. That popularity is attributed partly to the fame of Arthur Wellesley, Duke of Wellington, and partly to a reborn interest in the Arthurian legend. Its decline dates only from the 1970s.

This forgotten period from c.1250 to c.1850 is the most fascinating in the name's history and writers are wrong to dismiss it as unpopular throughout those centuries. We need only examine Smith-Bannister's tables in *Names and Naming Patterns* to see that it occurred regularly from 1538 to 1639 and actually enjoyed a measure of popularity in the decade 1550–59. This modest revival actually began before the sixteenth century and it corresponds roughly with the accession to the throne of Henry VII who named his first son Arthur. This choice was commented on by Professor Dickens when he wrote about the influence of Geoffrey of Monmouth on the Tudor age:

> Indeed, the succession of a Welsh monarch to the throne had greatly augmented this influence, since it fulfilled Geoffrey's account of the promise made to Cadwallader, last King of Britain, that his people should once again possess the land of their fathers. And Henry VII, naming his heir Arthur, had not failed to capitalise upon the legend.[30]

This christening, heavy with symbolism, had taken place at Winchester in 1486, when the infant prince was named in honour of the British race from which the Tudors sprang. There was certainly widespread rejoicing over the birth which appeared to unite the red and white roses: on the face of it, the relative popularity of the name in the early sixteenth century might seem to be a result of Henry's diplomacy. The general evidence appears to favour that interpretation but local information again throws a quite different light on the matter.

The Yorkshire evidence

Arthur was recorded in Great Waltham in Essex in 1381 but I have found no other examples of the name in the poll tax returns. There is certainly no evidence for its use in Yorkshire then or in the early fifteenth century, so to that extent Arthur's history in the county is typical of its history more generally. Nevertheless, by the 1540s it was enjoying the modest popularity profiled at the national level by Smith-Bannister, and significant new evidence shows that the crucial 50 years are those in the middle part of the fifteenth century. References to adults named Arthur in the 1460s indicate that it was in use in Yorkshire long before Prince Arthur's baptism.

The first of these was a merchant called 'Arthurus' Talbut who in 1463 was shipping quantities of 'stokfish' out of Hull on a vessel called the *Antony*. We cannot be certain that he was an Englishman, even though his surname may suggest that he was, for Hull was a port with a long history of influence from the Low Countries and Arthur was a name used by foreigners. In 1521, for example, Arthurus Boyer, 'doucheman', was resident in York.

The second bearer of the name was Arthur Wentworth of Wrangbrook, a prominent gentleman in the county, who was mentioned in a deed of 1468 when he was already an adult.[31] He received 40s in the will of Sir John Pilkington in 1478, an interesting bequest which may point to a link with Arthur Pilkington, baptised in 1482. Their fellow gentry locally included Arthur Lacy and Arthur Wood of Longley in Almondbury, and none of these could have owed their name to the king's later decision. Indeed, Arthur Wentworth would have been born c.1440. In fact this was not the only 'cluster' of Arthurs in the county, for the name has also been noted in the Ripon area before 1486 and there were doubtless similar groups elsewhere in England. The king had merely capitalised on Geoffrey of Monmouth's account of a legend that had been widely known for some time, and Arthur was just one of several names inspired by a renewed interest in the Arthurian legends.

Arthur Kaye of Woodsome

In the will that linked the Pilkingtons and the Wentworths, mentioned above, there were bequests to several members of the Kaye family who possessed estates in Lancashire and Yorkshire and were linked to the Wentworths in a sequence of complicated marriage settlements. A pedigree of the family states that the Kayes were 'of great antiquity...and descended from Sir Kay, an Ancient Briton, reputed one of King Arthur's Knights of the Round Table'. We are left to wonder if this was a fiction of the person who compiled the pedigree or a piece of wishful thinking on the part of Arthur's father.[32] I am inclined to discount both possibilities, although Arthur himself may have approved of the link with Sir Kay. The truth is that when Arthur was baptised, in 1502, he was not the heir to the estate and came into possession of it only because his cousin Nicholas died prematurely. In view of the agreements drawn up in the marriage settlements it is much more likely that Arthur Wentworth was the boy's godfather.

Whether or not that is true there is no doubt that Arthur Kaye was the architect of the family's fortunes and that his first name became a model among his kith and kin. It survived in the main branch of the family until the line at Woodsome became extinct in 1726, and was an almost obligatory choice for other Kaye families throughout the neighbourhood. The parish registers provide evidence of that and of the way it passed to generations of their neighbours:

> 1539: Arthur Kay, bastard son of John, Fulstone.[33]
> 1563, 11 July: Arthur baptised, son of John Lockwodde, godfather Arthur Kaye.
> 1572, 8 March: Arthur baptised, son of Arthur Kaye of Holme.
> 1577, 3 March: Arthur baptised, son of Robert Chaple of Holme, godfather Arthur Kaye.
> 1681, 13 October: Arthur baptised, son of Thomas Kay of Thorpe.
> 1742: Arthur Kaye of Choppards, Holmfirth.[34]

Names from the medieval romances were used throughout post-Conquest England, but the source proved more attractive to the gentry in the fifteenth century as they attached increasing importance to their alliances and status. They chose distinctive names that associated them with heroes from an illustrious past and with their own ancestors where possible, linking scattered branches of the family and neighbours within their affinity. In some cases the innovators and influential godfathers can be identified and from them the names spread to other social classes, creating distinctive naming patterns in the fifteenth and sixteenth centuries. A few of them, Arthur and Charles for example, established themselves successfully in the national name-stock but others fell out of use or were kept alive locally and at a lower level of popularity through family tradition.

Classical names

It has been claimed that the names of classical antiquity made little impression in England and the rare appearance of Greek and Roman names in the poll tax returns supports that view. This was not necessarily true if the name was also borne by an early saint, and the noble Roman maiden St Sabina was probably the inspiration behind Sabina's limited popularity in Essex in 1381. The by-name occurred there and also in Berkshire, where Sabina Sabyn was taxed at Long Wittenham. Guppy found the surname Sabin almost confined to Oxfordshire and McKinley in his book on Oxfordshire surnames noted it there in the form Damesabine. He thought the source might have been a lady called Sabine del Frith who held land of Eynsham Abbey in the thirteenth century.

Cassandra is another woman's name with a classical origin. She was the Trojan princess who possessed the power of prophecy but could find nobody to believe her, and she eventually died at the hands of Clytemnestra. Her name was never as popular in the Middle Ages as the dictionaries claim and very few examples occur in the poll tax returns, but it seems likely nevertheless to have been responsible for the surnames Cass and Casson. It became rather more popular in the sixteenth century and Cassandra Swynnerton's will illustrates how that might have happened. This Staffordshire lady made bequests in 1565 to four goddaughters, all called Cassandra, whose surnames were Gyfforde, Congreve, Westonne and Berdmore.[35]

Penelope was the name of the faithful wife of Ulysses, king of Ithaca. She is said to have been approached by numerous suitors during her husband's absence and to have kept them waiting by declaring that she was busy making a large robe for her aged father-in-law, Laertes. She successfully avoided her suitors' attentions by working on it during the day and then unpicking the stitches at night. Penelope Devereux, the daughter of the Earl of Essex, is reputed to have been the first to bear this name and she was baptised in 1562. It was used in 1579 by the Waterhouse family of Braithwell where Penelope Waterhouse had siblings called Pettinger, Gervis and Cressie.

Rather more successful than Penelope was Phyllis, which may date from c.1500 since Philicia was the name of a nun at the time of the Dissolution (1539). It was then in regular use until the middle of the seventeenth century. Its derivation from the Greek word for 'foliage' may have encouraged the myth that grew up around the name. The story is that Phyllis, the daughter of the king of Thrace, was betrothed to the son of Theseus who then went to Attica to settle his affairs. However, he was slow to return and Phyllis, feeling herself betrayed, ended her life and was transformed into a tree. It is difficult though to separate Phyllis from the more familiar Felis or Felicia and the two names were confused in the sixteenth century.[36] The same confusion can be seen in the surname Phylliskirk which derives from Felixkirk in the North Riding. Phillida, an alternative form of Phyllis, is also recorded from the sixteenth century.

A few male classical names were rare enough to identify individuals. For example there was an Achilles Bosevile in the late fourteenth century, a Ulysses Fox in 1593, and a Jason Redman in 1594. Hannibal Swales, baptised in Thornton in Lonsdale in 1734, must surely be the Hannibal Swale who was described as a 'traveller' over 40 years later in Hampsthwaite, a parish 40 miles to the south east. The surname Swales is not uncommon in that area and it is difficult to see how the identification could be made without the help of his distinctive first name.

Parmenio finds no mention in our dictionaries but it was the name of a distinguished Macedonian general in the service of Alexander the Great, and a Mr Beckwith of Snaith chose it for his son in 1592. He may have been less influenced by its credentials than by the fact that it began with the letter 'P', for he already had children called Prudence, Priscilla, Polene and Peregrine. These names help us to trace the family's move from Leeds and they appear to point to the father's religious leanings, since Prudence and Priscilla are associated with the Puritans. Peregrine might be for St Peregrine, as Withycombe suggests, but the name means 'pilgrim' and was also used by Puritans. The choice of Polene is puzzling since the sex of the child is not given but it may be a diminutive of Paul. Mr Beckwith fathered an illegitimate daughter in Leeds in 1583, possibly a reason for his move eastwards; she was christened Katherine.

The unusual name Archelaus has several possible sources of inspiration in antiquity and it also occurs in the New Testament. Among the few examples that I have found are several which refer to an Archelaus Hoyland who was living in Wath on Dearne in 1685. In this case it is a valuable clue to the mobility of the Hoyland family, for a title deed of 1767 links Anthony Hoyland of County Kildare and James Hoyland of Burniston in the North Riding with another Archelaus Hoyland who lived in Great Yarmouth. Some spellings leave us in doubt as to which classical name was intended. For example, Archilaus Waddington appears to be identical with Achilles Waddington of Bramhope (1597–1632).

Arkillis and Harcollis might seem to belong with Archelaus but they were actually variant spellings of Hercules, which occurs more frequently in the sixteenth and seventeenth centuries than either Achilles or Archelaus, and was favoured by families called Buck and Plasterer. Marcus Playsterer of Snaith named his son Harcules in 1614, inspired perhaps by his own first name, but the first name and surname are distinctive enough for us to identify this child as the Hercules Plasterer who was buried later that year in Rothwell, nearly 20 miles to the west. The first name is unusual enough for me to wonder if Hercules Buck and Hercules Bucktrowte (c.1600) were the same person: it was after all quite usual for surnames to be abbreviated in that way.

The only Aurelius I have recorded was a Batley man, Awrelius Clerk, named perhaps after the martyr Aurelius or the Roman emperor Marcus Aurelius. The fate of the unfortunate man was as unlikely as his name, for a witness in an assizes case of 1689 claimed that 'Sarah ordered them to bury him in the midden, which they did, with all his clothes on'.[37] Other classical names that I have recorded once or twice only include Nestor, Plato, Mercury, Aristarchus, Clytemnestra and Dido in the seventeenth century, and Theseus, Terence, Paris, Artaxerxes and Agrippa in the eighteenth century.

The genealogical value of such names can be easily demonstrated. Callisthenes is remembered as a pupil of Aristotle who accompanied Alexander the Great into Asia and wrote a ten-volume history of Greece. For a time I had several apparently unconnected references to this name in my indexes, but genealogical research showed that they were all related, starting with a gentleman called Callesthenes Brooke in 1638. From the Brookes the name passed to the Anbys or Hanbys and from them to the Eltons. When John Elton married Margaret Anby in 1714 they called their first son Callisthenes.

Julius was a favourite with a few families such as the Mortimers of Rothwell but unusual enough generally to help us identify Mortiman as a variant spelling of their surname. Withycombe said Julius was brought to this country by Cesare Adelmare, a Venetian physician to Queen Elizabeth who dropped his second name and became Julius Cesare. It is an almost irresistible combination and it tempts us to see a link between Julius Jackson of Thornton in Lonsdale and Cesar Jackson of Kirkheaton.

Caesar is also a rare first name but Reaney and Wilson recorded it in 1185 and it is in the York poll tax returns of 1377. I also have a dozen references on file from c.1600, almost all of them recorded in townships to the west and south west of Wakefield, i.e. Thornhill, Emley, Flockton, Lepton, Kirkheaton and Horbury. A glance at the map will show that these lie close together in the middle reaches of the Calder Valley and in every case the surname is Jackson. I have had no occasion to look into the history of families named Jackson in that area but this distinctive first name seems certain to be a link between them. Slightly further away, just to the north of Leeds, I have also found Caesar Jackson of Aberford (1741) and Cesar Jackson of Killinghall near Harrogate (1793).

Of particular interest is the inclusion of Cesar Heaton in the list of residents in the Protestation Return for Mirfield of 1642, for he is not mentioned in the parish register. Mirfield and Heaton (i.e. Kirkheaton) share a common boundary, with hamlets such as Helm having land in both parishes. The inference is that Cesar Heaton was in fact Cesar Jackson of Heaton, whose name first appears as a witness on a will of 1636. 'Heaton' might therefore be a scribal error or possibly a by-name.

It has probably already become obvious that two major sources account for many of the distinctive classical names in northern parish registers, the story of Troy and the exploits of Alexander the Great. From the same sources we have Hieronymus, thought to have accompanied Alexander into Asia, whose name was used by the Markhams of Nottinghamshire in the sixteenth century, and Hector, the champion of Troy, slain by Achilles. Hector was rarely recorded in England but occurred more frequently in Scotland, initially in honour of the hero, but then as an anglicised form of a Gaelic name when these were frowned on by the authorities. Most of the Yorkshire references are linked with the surname Atkinson, in parishes as far apart as Leeds, Birstall and Giggleswick.

Aeneas was another Trojan hero whose name came into occasional use, once as early as c.1250 near Ilkley. In a series of title deeds for Stubholme and Middleton there are references to Eneas, son of Hugh, Eneas de Stubum and

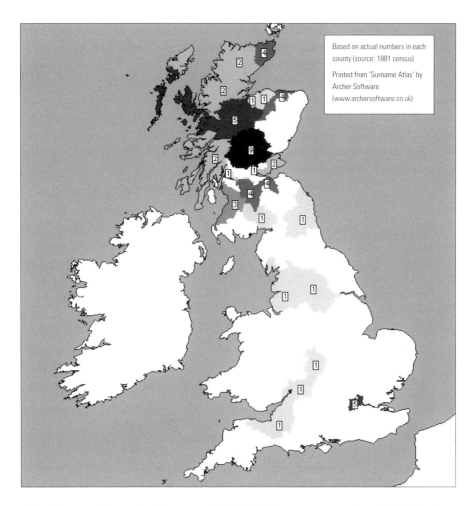

Based on actual numbers in each
county (source: 1881 census)

Printed from 'Surname Atlas' by
Archer Software
(www.archersoftware.co.uk)

7 The first name Aeneas (59) The name of the Trojan hero occurs occasionally in England
from the thirteenth century but it found favour in Scotland where it is associated with the
Gaelic *Aonghas* (Angus).

Eneas de Midelton, but these are probably by-names not surnames and it is likely
that one man only was involved.[38] The only significant later references are to the
Bottomleys of Slaithwaite and their neighbours the Walkers, families who
favoured the name for at least two hundred years, starting in the mid-seventeenth
century. The first name was so unusual in that period that it helps to identify a
branch of the Bottomley family in Leeds and another over the Pennines in
Saddleworth. The varied spellings include Aeneas, Eneas and Oneas.

~

Classical names were rare but they were used intermittently in the Middle Ages and more frequently from the sixteenth century, as the rise of humanism introduced educated gentry families to the classical heroes. The humanists were Renaissance scholars who studied, and in some cases rediscovered, Latin and Greek classics. These names were probably drawn from the printed sources that became more readily available from the late fifteenth century. Although they never achieved the popularity enjoyed by names from the romances, their use throws some light on the influence of humanism and they merit a mention because of their potential value to family historians.

Notes

1   *Testamenta Eboracensia*, Surtees Society XLV (1865), p. 308.
2   *Testamenta Eboracensia*, Surtees CVI (1902), p. 85.
3   *Ibid.*, pp. 232–3
4   C. W. Bardsley, *Curiosities of Puritan Nomenclature* (1880, reprinted 1996).
5   *Calendar of Patent Rolls 1563–66* (London, 1960).
6   T. L. Stoate (ed.), *Devon Taxes, 1581–1660* (Bristol, 1988).
7   R. A. McKinley, *Norfolk and Suffolk Surnames in the Middle Ages*, English Surnames Series (London, 1975), p. 9.
8   *Testamenta Eboracensia*, Surtees XLV (1865).
9   Claremont, Leeds, West Yorkshire Archive Service, Wakefield Court Rolls, MD 225.
10 'Lay Subsidies of the Wapentakes of Aggbrigg and Morley', *Thoresby Society* IX, XI (1899, 1904).
11 *Index of Wills in the York Registry, 1389–1514*, Yorkshire Archaeological Society, Record Series VI (1889), p. 65.
12 W. Brown (ed.), *Yorkshire Deeds*, YAS L (1914), p. 150.
13 C. T. Clay (ed.), *Yorkshire Deeds*, YAS LXXXIII (1932), p. 102.
14 A. S. Ellis (ed.), 'Yorkshire Deeds', *Yorkshire Archaeological Journal* XIII (1895), p. 77.
15 Claremont, Leeds, West Yorkshire Archive Service, Wakefield Court Rolls, MD 225.
16 A. S. Ellis (ed.), 'Yorkshire Deeds', *YAJ* XII (1893), p. 304.
17 *Yorkshire Fines 1571–83*, YAS V (1888), p. 32.
18 W. Brown (ed.), *Yorkshire Deeds*, YAS LXIII (1922), pp. 129, 131.
19 Kirklees Archives, West Yorkshire Archive Service, Slaithwaite Court Rolls, DD/R/M.
20 A. Weikel (ed.), *The Court Rolls of the Manor of Wakefield, 1537–40*, Wakefield Court Rolls Series IX (1993), pp. 72, 88.
21 Kirklees Archives, WYAS, Slaithwaite Court Rolls, DD/R/M.
22 S. Margerison (ed.), *The Calverley Charters*, Thoresby VI (1904).
23 *Wills in the York Registry, 1636–52*, YAS IV (1888), p. 164. *West Yorkshire Deeds*, Bradford Historical and Antiquarian Society, Local Record Series II, (1931–6), p. 11.
24 Bradford Antiquarian Society, New Series III (1912).
25 H. S. Darbyshire and G. D. Lumb, *The History of Methley*, Thoresby XXXV (1937).
26 For a detailed account of this unusual alias see G. Redmonds, *Surnames and Genealogy* (1997), pp. 90–92.
27 E. E. Barker (ed.), *The Register of Thomas Rotherham, Archbishop of York 1480–1500*, (Canterbury and York Society, 1976).

28 *West Yorkshire Deeds*, p. 63.

29 Robert Bolling is said to have had six sons in all and of these the choice of William is unremarkable. James and Humphrey had both been uncommon in 1377–81 but later increased in popularity, James more obviously than Humphrey.

30 A. G. Dickens, 'Wilfrid Holme of Huntington: Yorkshire's First Protestant Poet', YAJ XXXIX (1958).

31 J. W. Walker (ed.), *Abstracts of the Chartularies of the Priory of Monk Bretton*, YAS LXVI (1924).

32 C. A. Hulbert, *Annals of the Church and Parish of Almondbury* (London, 1882), p. 190.

33 A. Weikel, *Wakefield Court Rolls*.

34 C. E. Whiting (ed.), *Two Yorkshire Diaries*, YAS CXVII (1952).

35 I am grateful to Pauline Litton for this information.

36 C.f. Fayles Staniforthe (1572), Sheffield Parish Register.

37 *Depositions from York Castle*, Surtees XL (1861).

38 C. T. Clay (ed.), *Yorkshire Deeds*, YAS LXIX (1926).

CHAPTER NINE

Names from Surnames

The gentry's insistence upon rank and status in the sixteenth century was expressed in a variety of ways, including a preoccupation with coats of arms, ancestry and family surnames, so it is hardly surprising that surnames came to be used as first names in that period.[1] The innovation was commented on favourably by the antiquary and historian Camden (1605), who saw it both as an expression of affection and good will, and a legitimate desire by families to ensure the survival of their name. The custom established itself in the second half of the sixteenth century and then spread to every class of society, influencing naming habits permanently.

Aristocratic names

In this chapter names from different categories will be looked at more closely, with the aim of identifying some of the innovators, their motives, and the influence their choices had, either nationally or locally. The first three examples are drawn from the aristocracy.

Sidney

On the afternoon of January 26, in the year 1788, a fleet of 11 ships entered the harbour of Port Jackson, carrying more than 1,000 male and female convicts. This was the arrival of the famous 'First Fleet', a landmark event in Australian history, and the modest harbour would soon be renamed Sydney, after Thomas Townshend, Lord Sydney, who had replaced Lord North as Home and Colonial Secretary at the end of 1783. It was a further twist in the history of Sidney, which had started out as a place-name, given rise to a surname and then been used as a first name. The wheel had turned full circle.

The origin of Sidney is disputed and doubt has been thrown on the theory that it derives from 'St Denis' in Normandy, although similar developments are not uncommon, for example Sinclair from St Clair and Sample from St Paul. The French origin is theoretically possible for there is a record in Norfolk of a man called Roger 'de Sancto Dionisio' in the early thirteenth century (the Latin equivalent of St Denis) and also of a fourteenth-century John Seyndenys. Withycombe expressed no doubt about it, saying that 'the Sidney family was founded in England by William Sidney or Sydney, the Chamberlain of Henry II who came from Anjou'.

Reaney thought that this was inconclusive and his alternative explanation owed much to the research of C. L. Kingsford, who derived Sidney from a small locality in the Surrey parish of Alfold, quoting in evidence John ate Sydenye, from a Surrey roll of 1332.[2] The recently published poll tax returns for that county support the idea that this became a hereditary surname, with Nicholas atte Sydeneye located in Shalford in 1381. The English place-name source is therefore a plausible alternative, and Kingsford's suggestion was that it derives from two Old English words meaning 'extensive, well-watered land'.

Dictionaries trace the emergence of Sidney as a first name to the eighteenth century but I have examples in the seventeenth century and no doubt even earlier references will be discovered. For example Sidney Constable of Scarborough was a child in 1641 and Sidney Lutton of Knapton, a 'Citizen of London', was born that same year.[3] Although the surname is always acknowledged to be the inspiration, and there was a direct family connection in some cases, the motives behind its use may be complicated. Sidney Herbert, Lord Herbert of Lea, who was born in 1810, was said to have been named after his ancestor Mary Sidney, whilst others are thought to have been named in memory of Algernon Sidney (1622–83), the republican and writer who was idolised by the Whigs.[4] The name's popularity in the nineteenth century peaked between 1875 and 1925,[5] and was attributed by Hanks and Hodges to the influence of Sidney Carton, the hero of Dickens's novel A Tale of Two Cities (1859).[6] However, the essayist and wit Sydney Smith must also have contributed to its rise in status and I noticed two Sidney Smiths recently on the war memorial in Thetford church. Now it is a first name in its own right, although temporarily out of fashion.

There are girls called Sidney in the records from the eighteenth century, but that is seldom mentioned although they occur frequently enough. For example Sidney Machan of Sheffield, baptised in 1733, was the daughter of Joseph Machan, and Sidney Sunderland was a spinster in Rothwell in 1784. The clue may lie in baptisms such as that of Sidonia Bulmer (1748), where the spelling clearly points to the alternative girls' name Sidony. Hanks and Hodges claimed that this was comparatively popular in the later Middle Ages, but I have no evidence of that and Withycombe found 'no early example of the name'.

Neville

This was a rare name until the 1860s when it came into more regular use. It was never especially popular even then but started to be more widely used in the 1920s and 'reached a minor peak' of popularity in the mid-1950s.[7] It is always said to derive from the surname of the great Neville family, prominent for so long at a national level, and there is plenty of evidence to confirm that origin. In 1637 Mary Nevill married Sir Richard Tankard of Whixley and they called their son Nevill. A Nevill Kay who died in 1623 owed his name to his mother, Beatrix Nevill of Ragnall in Nottinghamshire, who had married Edward Kay c.1580. In such cases, of course, the ultimate source is the place in Normandy which gave rise to the aristocratic surname.

The Neville family was so powerful in the sixteenth century, and had such extensive interests, that examples of the first name are not confined to the north which was their major power base. In distant Sussex, for example, Nevel Chisman was a juror at Rotherfield in 1592, a very early reference. He may have been connected with Henry Nevell, Lord Abergavenny, who had lands in Rodmell, or with Francis Nevell, a justice of peace in the county. Not surprisingly there are occasional examples in the seventeenth and eighteenth centuries in the north where the evidence of a direct link with the great Neville family has not been established. These include Nevil Moor of Rothwell (1669), Nevil Simmons of Sheffield (1724) and Nevill Hedley of Hull (1727), and they may be evidence that Neville was becoming more established as a genuine first name. Much earlier than that, in 1524, a man with the name Nevell Morrens was taxed in York, probably the 'Newellus Morres, staconer', who had been made a freeman in 1519.[8] Significantly he was described as a Frenchman, so there may have been an alternative source across the Channel.

Percy

If we look for the first name Percy in our dictionaries we shall see that it is said to have its origin in the surname of the great Percy family, whose ancestor William de Perci arrived in England with the Conqueror, in which case its etymology would depend on the village in Normandy from which they took their surname. In fact Withycombe went so far as to say that Percy was at first 'confined to persons connected with that family' and quoted Lord Percy Seymour who died in 1721 as the first example of its use. The Percy connection in that case was through his mother Lady Elizabeth Percy, an heiress who married the Duke of Somerset. Another example that is often quoted is the poet Percy Bysshe Shelley, born in 1792, although the Percy connection in this case was remote. Nevertheless it is the poet who is sometimes said to have contributed to the more general popularity of the name in the nineteenth century.

There is no doubt that Percy sometimes derives from the surname but it has a quite separate origin which never seems to be mentioned, and that is as a diminutive of Peter or Piers. The direct evidence for the diminutive goes back to the year 1600 when 'Percy alias Peter' Stanley of Womersley died:[9] a later example is 'Percy or Pearce' Tempest of Tong in 1653.[10] In other cases the evidence is not explicit. For example Percy Watson of Newholme in Lythe (1657) was almost certainly the Peter Watson baptised in 1635. A much later example is the baptism in 1730 of Parcy, the son of Thomas Beadel of Drypool. Ironically, 'Perce' has been commented on as a short form of Percy.[11]

A will for John Percy of Scarborough, a rich merchant who died in 1500, is worth quoting in this context.[12] His family had a long connection with the town, at least back to the reign of Edward III when Peter Percy was the Scarborough MP. A footnote to the will traces several generations of Percys, ending with another Peter Percy of Scarborough who was buried in 1517. The references to these individuals are interesting. For example, in his will John Percy referred to his brother Peter three times, once as 'Peyrs Peyrse', once as 'Perse Percy' and finally as 'the whiche Peyrse': his own son and grandson were both named as 'Petyr Percy'. It is difficult to know what to say about this except that it identifies Petyr and Peyrs as alternative forms of the first name, but it seems also to confirm that Peter and the surname Percy were connected in the mind of the testator. If that were true it would suggest that the use of Percy as a diminutive of Peter may go back earlier than the examples I have quoted.

Percy was also used as a girls' christian name, and the first example I have noted is the baptism in 1598 of Percye, the daughter of Henry Farrer of Beverley. Mr Christopher Farrer had a son Peter baptised in 1611, but a branch of the Percy family lived in the town from 1597 and this is a more likely explanation of how a girl came to have the name. On the other hand there is evidence in Hampsthwaite parish register to suggest that Percy as a girls' name may also have been a familiar form of Percival. The burial register there contains the names of Piercie Holm, widow (1728) and Percival Holm, spinster (1743). It was in this part of Lower Wharfedale that Percival as a boys' name was quite popular in the sixteenth century.

Gentry surnames

The origins of names in this category can pose a problem for there are cases where a transferred surname might be confused with the first name from which it derives. For example the usual source of Gregory was St Gregory but Gregory Armytage of Keresforth Hill was so named after his mother, Emma Gregory of Hull, who married John Armytage of Kirklees c.1568. Both families were enjoying new-found prosperity in the wake of the Dissolution and the choice of Gregory in this case was probably intended to commemorate and consolidate a notable union.

A parallel case is Vincent, again usually a saint's name, but derived from the surname when used by the Waterhouses. In 1573 Thomas Waterhouse of Halifax married Dorothy Vincent of Braithwell, an heiress who descended from John Vincent, receiver to Richard, Duke of York, slain at the Battle of Towton. The Vincent Waterhouse baptised in 1574 was doubtless named in honour of his mother's family, and the many Vincents baptised in Braithwell from 1579 probably owed their name indirectly to the same family.

A name in this category, about which different views have been expressed, is Ingram, another Norman personal name. Withycombe thought that recent examples were likely to be adaptations of the surname, but also said that the personal name could still be found 'as a christian name as late as the seventeenth century'; in Hanks and Hodges it is simply said to be a 'transferred use of the surname'. It was never popular as a first name in Yorkshire, but is recorded there regularly from the twelfth century to the seventeenth, by which time it was traditional in one or two families. In 1678, for example, Ingram Holmes of Leeds was baptised, the son of Ingram Holmes. Its survival may owe something to Sir Ingelram Percy (1538). The name occurs occasionally after that, but it would require painstaking genealogical work to establish whether it was a transferred surname or a genuine survival from the Middle Ages, like Thurstan, Amer and others.

It is clear that where names in this category are concerned, statements about their origins, and about when and where they were first used, should be treated with caution, for we are far from having a complete picture of their development. The popularity of Stanley, for example, dates from the end of the nineteenth century and it is usual to attribute that to the exploits of Henry Stanley the explorer. Withycombe certainly considered it to be a recent development and yet there are much earlier examples, e.g. Standly Gore of Sheffield (1633) and Stanley Shaw of Cudworth (1672). The 'Stanley' link here may be the family name of the Earls of Derby.

Similar views have been expressed about Clifford which till relatively recently enjoyed considerable popularity. Not surprisingly, it was used in the seventeenth century by the Tempests of Bracewell who were connected to the Cliffords by marriage. The Cliffords were the Earls of Cumberland and important landholders in the north, and the history of Clifford as a first name in that area has not yet been thoroughly researched. Certainly there were several Cliffords baptised in Leeds from about 1700, in families of quite modest status, e.g. in 1699 Clifford Pate and in 1719 Clifford Thirlby. These may be examples of a very local custom, which would make them especially valuable to family historians, a point that will be developed in the following brief histories.

Early transferred surnames

It is scarcely surprising that one of the first people to help establish the new fashion in the north was Henry Savile Esq., of Lupset and Barrowby. He was a well-established member of the northern gentry, an MP for Yorkshire, High Sheriff of the county, and Surveyor of the Crown for the Northern Provinces. In his will, dated 5 January 1569, he bequeathed an estate in Nottinghamshire first to his wife 'during her life' and then to his third son, Cordell Savile. The boy had been named in honour of his godfather Sir William Cordell, Master of the Rolls, and he, in turn, called his first-born son Cordell.[13] I have no evidence that Cordell ever enjoyed any widespread or long-lasting popularity but from the late sixteenth century it was used by a few families in parts of Nottinghamshire and south Yorkshire. These included the Shaws, Rogers and Storrs.

Cordell's history appears to be fairly typical and, in the years up to the Restoration, there are numerous examples of transferred gentry surnames that were recorded a few times only. These include Wilstrop (c.1570), Lister (1575), Radcliffe (1582), Askwith (1593), Copley (1594), Sheffield (1598), Foljambe (c.1600), Mallory (1604), Maleverer (1608), Beeston (1608), Fairfax (1612), Calverley (1618), Pigot (1618), Ashton (1625) and Stanhope (1646). A closer look at Lister will show how names of this kind sometimes offer a lead when more conventional genealogical methods are not producing results.

Lister

Litster or Lister is a very common and widely distributed surname in Yorkshire and, even in the sixteenth century, it was present in a number of parishes in all three Ridings. Nevertheless it was rarely used as a first name, and the remarkable fact is that all the examples I have collected, between 1575 and 1700, are linked with the surname Simonson, which has no obvious origin in the county. The first of these was a Lytster Symondson who was baptised in Braithwell in 1575, when Lister was not a surname known in the parish. His father Christopher Symondson was last mentioned in Braithwell three years later: his more popular first name would continue to occur alongside Lister throughout its history.

In 1609 there was a man named Lister Symonson who served as a park keeper for the Clifford family of Skipton, with responsibility for his lordship's deer at Birk House near Buckden.[14] This parish was over 70 miles to the north west of Braithwell, in a mountainous part of the county, and the two places appear to have very little in common. The move north would certainly not be an expected migration, but the combination of first name and surname, both of them unusual, suggests that it took place.

The next reference may be to this man's son: it was a licence in 1623 for Lister Symondson and Alice Calvert of Starbotton to marry in Kettlewell, the parish which adjoins Buckden. Perhaps he was the Lister Simonson whose daughter Sara was born in 1641 in Giggleswick, a parish some 12 miles south east of Buckden. He was a contemporary there of Christopher Simonson of Stockdale, but again the parish register contains only a single entry. After that date all the information I have collected relates to the family in Kettlewell: a Lister Simonson made his will there in 1660, and the hearth tax return for that village in 1672 list two men with the name, Lister Simonson, senior, and Lister Symondson, junior, the latter a blacksmith. In 1674 and 1687 Christopher and Lister Simondson of Kettlewell are mentioned in quarter sessions records.

It is a tantalising sequence of references, all part of an unfinished story, and we can still only speculate about the choice of Lister as a first name. As a surname it was prominent in Halifax so perhaps the first Lister Simonson in Braithwell owed his first name to a connection between his family and the Listers and Waterhouses of Halifax. We have already seen that Thomas Waterhouse married a Braithwell heiress in 1573. Of course not all transferred surnames were so family specific and two with a wider history are Cotton and Tempest, both brought into use when the godparents were still important name-givers.

Cotton

The pedigree of the Gargrave family shows that Sir Cotton Gargrave of Kinsley near Hemsworth, who died in 1588, owed his unusual first name to a connection by marriage, and it remained a favourite in the family well into the eighteenth century at least.[15] For example a Mr Cotton Gargrave was the vicar of Kippax from about 1653 until his death in March 1682 and another Cotton Gargrave was baptised there in 1696, possibly the Cotton Gargrave 'clerk of this parish' who was buried in 1777. During that period the use of Cotton as a christian name was spread by other local families far beyond Kinsley.

As early as 1562 Sir Thomas Gargrave conveyed lands in Felkirk to Richard Horne, whose son, named Cotton, later acted as the bailiff at Hemsworth to Sir Cotton Gargrave. In the next generation Richard Horne's grandson, also named Cotton, became Steward of the Honour of Pontefract, and he is remembered as the donor of almshouses at Wakefield; he died in 1656 and was buried at Mexborough.[16] A younger brother called Francis moved eventually to Almondbury, over 20 miles to the north west, and this branch of the family also favoured Cotton as a first name.

At least half a dozen other south Yorkshire families made the same choice in that period and, although it is not yet possible to prove a direct connection with the Gargraves in every case, there is usually some evidence that points to the family's local influence. For example the Scholeys had been a Hemsworth family for centuries, and in 1601 a certain Cotton Scholey held land in the adjoining township of Havercroft. This man died in 1637 but he may have been related to, or indeed identical with, the Cotton Scholey who held part of a messuage in Sowerby near Halifax in 1585.[17] A third Cotton Scholey was involved in a land transaction in Crigglestone in 1651.[18] Other local men to bear the name were Cotton Abson (1597) who lived in Frickley, a township where the Gargraves were landholders, Cotton Juit (1580), Cotton Hartley (1598), Cotton Gill (1618) and Cotton Wombwell (1637). The name was increasingly being used by south Yorkshire families who were not of gentry status: Cotton Ferram, for example, was a Sheffield cutler in 1656.

Tempest

Possibly the most successful of these new gentry names, at least for a time, was Tempest, the surname of a landholding family with interests in the Skipton and Bradford areas. In 1574 Tempest Thornton was baptised in Calverley near Bradford, the son of William Thornton and Beatrice Tempest, and their use of the name established a family tradition that had an impact on both kinsmen and neighbours, lasting into the nineteenth century. For example, in the seventeenth century Tempest was used as a first name by numerous families in and around Calverley, among them the Crabtrees, Goodalls, Lees, Cordingleys and Pollards, many of them with the status of husbandman or yeoman. Beatrice's sister Anne married Robert Nicholl of London and they too called their son Tempest.

In fact the use of this distinctive name can serve to link relatively scattered branches of such families, for there were Tempest Pollards between 1630 and 1809 in Calverley and some distance away in Horbury. This is not the only example: one Tempest Goodall was living in Tong in 1642 and a second in Snaith in 1653, some 30 miles to the east. When such a rare first name is used, we also have the opportunity to identify variant spellings of the accompanying surname, in this case Cordley and Cordingley. These two surnames often occur side by side in the records but without evidence to confirm a common origin. The problem is simplified when Tempest Coardley and Tempest Cordingley occur in the same parish from 1680 to 1709.

Other references to Tempest Cordingley occur in the quarter sessions, the latest I have noted being in Bradford in 1741. An earlier instance, in a deposition of 1711, is worth quoting at length since it evokes a long-forgotten but picturesque incident in rural life. In his testimony the plaintiff, Francis Thornton, claimed to have seen 'two of the daughters of Joseph Robinson drive a cowe...into a cloase belongeing to Tempest Cordingley, where Ann, the mother, was sett downe neare to a well with a kitt' (a wooden pail). When he called to the woman 'she rune awaye and dipping her kitt in the well made all the water white'. Ann Robinson was brought before the magistrates and accused of stealing milk, but she proclaimed her innocence, saying that it was soap suds that Thornton had seen.

The above examples of Tempest as a first name can be traced to links with the Bolling branch of the Tempests but similar evidence can be found in Lower Ribblesdale, the area close to Skipton where the family had another estate. They also had tenants with the distinctive surname Slinger.[19] One Tempest Slinger, a gentleman, was living in Slaidburn in 1632 and other Tempest Slingers are recorded at regular intervals for over 200 years. The father of one baptised in 1829 was apparently a plasterer, a clear indication that by then the tradition was not confined to the gentry. Nor indeed to boys, for when Henry Coulthurst of Gargrave, also a gentleman, married Margaret Slinger prior to 1717, he chose to name his only daughter Tempest. When she died in 1767, still unmarried, she was buried at Gargrave. However, his son, also called Henry, established himself as a merchant in Barbados and named one of his sons Tempest, taking the tradition into the nineteenth century.[20]

Others with the name in that district were Tempest Towers of Waddington (1600) and Tempest Willson of Skipton (1705), apparently isolated examples, whereas the Oddys of Gisburn, who were near neighbours of the Slingers, kept the name in the family for something like 200 years. Almost certainly related to them were the Tempest Oddy baptised in Halifax in 1727 and another Tempest Oddy who was living in Leeds in 1832. In the nineteenth century Tempest continued to occur sporadically as a first name in different parts of west Yorkshire but the links with the Tempest family, if indeed they still existed, are far from obvious. In fact some of them are quite likely to be part of the more general use of transferred surnames, for this custom was by then firmly entrenched locally at all levels of society. Fretchfield and Bingley will illustrate different aspects of this later development.

Fretchfield

The Frecheville family of Staveley in Derbyshire had close connections with gentry families in the Almondbury area from the sixteenth century at least. In 1574 Sir Peter Fretchvile married the widowed daughter of Arthur Kaye of Woodsome and, as Margaret Fretchwell, she was godmother to John Caye, the son of Robert. Sir Peter's daughter, also called Margaret, then married John Ramsden of Longley; their grandson, Fretchevile Ramsden, was baptised in 1656. He was the first of several Ramsdens to bear the name, the last being Sir John Frecheville Ramsden, the sixth baronet. He sold the family estates to Huddersfield Corporation in 1920 and died in 1958, bearing a first name that was part of a tradition going back almost 400 years.

In the latter part of that period the name was also used among their tenants, possibly for no better reason than the evidence it provided of a 'relationship' between them and the lord of the manor. Although the Ramsdens held the lordships of Huddersfield and Almondbury in the eighteenth and nineteenth centuries, their home was at Byram near Castleford, over 20 miles away. They were infrequent visitors to the area but that did not prevent tenant families from choosing to have sons named Fretchfield, using the colloquial form of Frecheville. The most splendid combination occurred in the name of Fretchfield Furbisher, a militiaman in Lockwood in 1790. His ancestors had arrived in the area some 70 years earlier, a branch of the much more prestigious Frobishers, and they kept faith with Fretchfield as a christian name for several generations. A personal diary of Fretchfield Frobisher of Brighouse, for the years 1896–1928, was recently discovered by his grandson and made the subject of a feature in the local newspaper.

Bingley

If family considerations and tenant loyalty contributed to the use of surnames as first names, it was almost certainly the influence initially of the godparents which helped such names to expand, resulting in the sort of limited popularity that Cotton, Tempest and others enjoyed. However, the importance of the spiritual relationship declined as the years passed and in general the motives behind name-giving were to become more complex. One notable exception to that is shown in the rather unusual will of Henry Bingley, an eccentric and prominent gentleman who retired from life in London to the mining village of Bolton on Dearne in south Yorkshire. He lived there without a servant, on a diet of water, gruel and celery, except that during harvest time he had sparrow pies made from fledglings, caught for him by some of the less well-off local inhabitants. He rewarded them for the service, increasing the rate on feast days and on those hiring days known as 'the statutes'. Extracts from his will, dated 1789, illustrate the way in which the surname Bingley came to be used as a first name in parts of Nottinghamshire and south Yorkshire:

> I further Give unto John Bingley Humplebee aged about 21 years who now lives with his father at Bolton upon Dearne, One Hundred Pounds.

> I likewise Give to my Godson Bingley Watson aged about fourteen years who now lives with the Reverend Mr Butter, Minister at Ackworth, One Hundred Pounds.

> I likewise Give to my Godson Bingley Swallow who lives with his father in Bolton upon Dearne, One Hundred Pounds.

> I Give to my Godson Bingley Birks who lives with his father, an Engine maker at Mansfield in Nottinghamshire, and is now about the age of sixteen years, One Hundred Pounds.

> I Give to my Godson Bingley Nightingale whose father is a Butcher there at Rotherham and keeps a public House the Sign of the Plough the infant being now about two years of age, One Hundred Pounds.[21]

A widening of the custom

From the eighteenth century the use of transferred surnames became more popular and spread to all levels of society. They were still in a minority, but the reasons for their use were more diverse, and one aspect of that was the desire by the mother of an illegitimate child to identify the father. At first the child was simply baptised with the father's surname but eventually it was linked with a more conventional first name. This aspect of the custom was soon so widely established that it invites us to speculate about the possible father even when his name is not given. The following baptismal entries in the registers illustrate the trend:

> 1602: Cunnell, base child of Catherine Browne, by James Cunnell, Leeds.
> 1707: Hepworth, the base-born son of Robert Hepworth and Anne Judgson, Methley.
> 1707: Wormwell, son of Hannah Allen, base begot, Rothwell.
> 1740: Wroe, a bastard child, the son of John Wroe and Anne Crossland, Hooton Pagnell.
> 1769: Levit John, son of Ann Hurst, putative father John Levitt, Rothwell.
> 1773: Hannah Brook, daughter of Margaret Dickinson, putative father Richard Brook, Rothwell.
> 1773: Sarah Graveley Stoney, daughter of Sarah Graveley, bass born, Rothwell.

By the end of the nineteenth century there were some communities in which it had become relatively commonplace for a child to be named after a relative, particularly the maternal grandfather. The more manageable combinations, such as Ramsden Mallinson, Lawton Varley, Illingworth Saville, Beaumont Dyson, helped to create a distinctive genre, typical of the northern industrial towns, and several regional novelists exploited the custom, in order to give local colour to their work. It was a passing phase and, although one or two such names achieved a certain popularity, notably Dyson, it soon became customary to give a child two names, the transferred surname following a more traditional Joseph or James. In close-knit communities it occasionally happened that the parents had the same surname and it must be suspected that this lies behind such unfortunate names as Heyworth Heyworth or Sykes Sykes.

In other cases a child might be named after a local personality or a nationally important figure and this, rather than just respect for kith and kin, may explain the choice of certain names. It is certainly possible that it played a part from an early date in the popularity of Sidney, Howard and Clifford, and occasionally we have what appears to be direct evidence of that. In 1623, for example, Favour Brearcliffe of Halifax was baptised just after his father had been made Parish Clerk by Dr Favour, the local vicar. It is tempting to see a political motive behind the naming of Cromwell Kingsley of Hull, an adult in 1717.

The present high level of interest in family history seems destined to produce more information on this particular aspect of name-giving, and recent

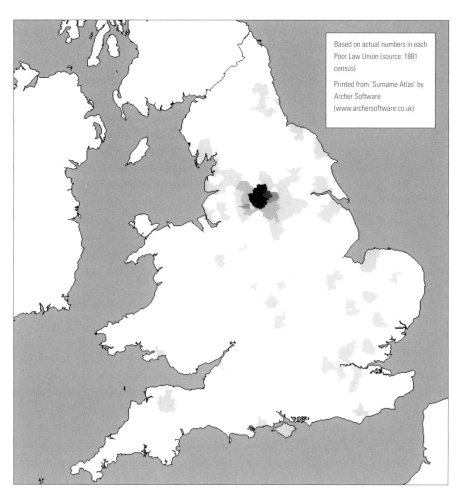

Based on actual numbers in each Poor Law Union (source: 1881 census)

Printed from 'Surname Atlas' by Archer Software (www.archersoftware.co.uk)

8 The first name Dyson (483) The progenitor of the Dyson family was Dionisia of Linthwaite and that township was still at the heart of the surname's distribution in 1881. As a first name it was most popular in the West Riding, particularly in Huddersfield (160).

correspondence persuades me that there are fascinating lines of inquiry here for genealogists and local historians. For example Marion Moverley of Richmond came across a certain Sandford Hardcastle, who had something to do with the tithes of Coverham, and then noted that Hardcastles around Leeds, Wakefield and Methley used the same christian name. Research by Margaret Barwick of Honiton in Devon concerned nineteenth-century Lumbs who lived in Scammonden, a territory between Elland and Huddersfield. Her interest was aroused when she discovered that Michael Lumb of Deanhead had called one of his sons Addison in 1833, even though there was no obvious family connection.

Other branches of the Lumb family then also used the name, and her research shows that it survived migration to Australia.

She also commented to me on the use of Addison by neighbouring families not known to be connected to the Lumbs. In 1851, for example, Martha Sykes of West Carr in Scammonden had a young child called Addison, and there was an Addison Holroyd, aged 26, in nearby Ripponden, a slightly earlier example than the first Addison Lumb. A contact in New Zealand told Margaret Barwick of an Addison Crabtree of Southowram in Halifax, born probably in 1839. The youngest of this man's eight children was also called Addison and two of the others later gave the same name to their first-born sons. Clearly this particular search could continue fruitfully for some time and it may be that it will eventually reveal how Addison came to be chosen as a christian name in the first place. The surname is not characteristic of that part of Yorkshire, so one possibility is that it was originally inspired by the famous writer, Joseph Addison, or even, as Margaret Barwick suggests, that it was given in honour of Thomas Addison, the physician who first recognised the disease now named after him.

~

The use of surnames as first names started as a gentry practice in the middle years of the sixteenth century and then spread to other levels of society, first of all perhaps within spiritual affinities, and then via family tradition and tenant loyalty. Even in the seventeenth century some mothers took advantage of the custom as a convenient way of identifying the father of an illegitimate child and it eventually became widespread, particularly in some working-class communities towards the end of the nineteenth century. Although most of these names had only a short existence a few found their way into the permanent name-stock, predominantly those with an aristocratic origin.

Notes

1   This was described as 'a principle deep-grounded in the social philosophy of the age'. M. Campbell, The English Yeoman, (London, 1942, reprinted 1983). For example, in a church seat dispute in 1571 the philosophy found practical expression: 'It is...ordered that the gentlemen and gentlewomen being nowe by this order removed from the Ladye quere [choir] shalbe convenientlie placed neare the quere and the husbande men removed and set lower, and that no stalles be sett in the Ladie Chapell hereafter, onles yt be formes in the lower parte thereof for servantes.'
2   P. H. Reaney, The Origin of English Surnames (London, 1967), p. 9.
3   J. W. Clay, Dugdale's Visitation of Yorkshire, with additions, Part X (Exeter, 1912), p. 231.
4   E. G. Withycombe, The Oxford Dictionary of English Christian Names, 3rd edn (Oxford 1977).
5   L. A. Dunkling, First Names First (London, 1977), p. 195.

6   P. Hanks and F. Hodges, *A Dictionary of First Names* (Oxford, 1990), p. 302.

7   L. Dunkling and W. Gosling, *Everyman's Dictionary of First Names* (London, 1983).

8   *Register of the Freemen of the City of York, 1272–1558*, Surtees Society XCVI (1897).

9   *Wills in the York Registry, 1594–1602*, Yorkshire Archaeological Society, Record Series XXIV (1898).

10 J. W. Clay, *Dugdale's Visitation of Yorkshire*, Part I (Exeter, 1894), p. 45.

11 L. Sleigh and C. Johnson, *The Pan Book of Boys' Names* (1965).

12 *Testamenta Eboracensia*, Surtees LIII (1869).

13 J. W. Clay, 'The Savile Family', *Yorkshire Archaeological Journal* XXV (1920), pp. 1–47.

14 T. D. Whitaker, *The History and Antiquities of Craven* (1812), p. 319.

15 J. W. Walker, *Wakefield: its History and People* (2nd edn, 1939).

16 J. F. Horne, 'The Hornes of Mexborough', *YAJ* XIX (1907), pp. 417–34.

17 A. Weikel (ed.), *The Court Rolls of the Manor of Wakefield, 1583–85*, The Wakefield Court Rolls Series IV (1984), p. 106.

18 Claremont, Leeds, West Yorkshire Archive Service, MD 99.

19 R. W. Hoyle (ed.), *Early Tudor Craven: Subsidies and Assessments 1510–1547*, YAS CXLV (1987), p. 23.

20 T. D. Whitaker, *History of Craven*, p. 184.

21 I am grateful to Walter Norris for drawing my attention to this will.

CHAPTER TEN

After the Reformation

In 1377–81 the Bible had been a more important source of names for men than for women but that changed in the sixteenth century when it became a regular source for both sexes. Many of these were from the Old Testament, some of them being used for the first time, and they added significantly to the national name-stock. The Puritans were responsible for other important innovations and, although most of these were less successful, the new choices marked a fundamental change in naming practices, with influential name-givers emerging from the clergy and lower ranks of society.

Local statistics

It should not be presumed that Smith-Bannister's national tables in *Names and Naming Patterns* always reflect what was happening at the local level, even though they were based on material drawn from forty parishes in different parts of England and a sample size of 122,710. Such statistics are impressive but they can also mislead us by masking the subtle differences that existed between one region and another, sometimes even between neighbouring parishes. These differences can be valuable to local historians and genealogists and they were occasionally obvious enough to be observed by contemporary writers, as the following comment on Halifax makes clear:

> A tincture of early puritanism yet continues to appear in the manners and in the Christian names of the people; and perhaps there is not a parish in the Kingdom where old testament names have so nearly superseded those of the new.[1]

Those words were written in 1816, much later than the period we are concerned with here, but the custom commented on by the writer undoubtedly had its origins in the naming practices of Elizabethan Halifax. To demonstrate that point a comparison is drawn below between the two former West Riding parishes of

Leeds and Halifax, just 15 miles apart. Leeds was then a busy commercial centre on low-lying land to the east of the Pennines; Halifax was in the hills, a populous parish thriving on the production of woollen cloth. The two communities belonged to different cultures, and that difference found expression in the sixteenth century in christian name choices, particularly those from the Old Testament.

The tables below have been prepared from 300 male baptisms and 300 female baptisms from the registers of Halifax and Leeds, starting in 1590. These show the names in rank order and the number of baptisms for each name in brackets. For purposes of comparison they are flanked by columns on the left showing the rank order of names nationally in 1379 and on the right by Smith-Bannister's frequency table for baptisms nationally in 1590–99.[2]

One half of the Halifax names in 1590–92 represented long-standing, traditional choices, i.e. John, William, Richard, Henry, Thomas and Robert. Almost one sixth were names that had risen to prominence in the fifteenth century, i.e. James, Edward, Anthony, George, Francis and Christopher. However, apart from James these did not perform as well locally as they did nationally, and there were noticeable differences in the cases of George, Francis and Christopher. In Halifax Michael was in third place with 20 baptisms, in sharp contrast to Leeds with just one baptism and to the national table where it was in sixteenth position. That popularity in Halifax reflects Michael's distinctive local history, a phenomenon discussed in Chapter 7. However, the number of Old Testament names among the top twenty in the Halifax table is even more obvious, i.e. Samuel, Jonas, Abraham, Isaac, Daniel, Nathan and Jacob. That is also in marked contrast to Leeds, and to parishes right across the country, where only Samuel figured in the top 20.

One or two of the Old Testament names that were popular in Halifax had been in occasional use nationally in the Middle Ages, Abraham and Isaac for example, but there is no evidence that they had survived in Halifax through the fifteenth century, and a comparison with the frequency table for 1379 emphasises how radical these choices were. Jonas in particular must have sounded almost revolutionary to people from outside the region at that time, and the same could be said of Old Testament names further down the list, such as Jeremiah, Jonathan, Reuben, Tobias, Joshua and Samson. These names had not been introduced at the expense of John, which remained pre-eminent, but many other traditional names had fared badly and several were missing altogether, e.g. Ralph, Nicholas, Roger, Peter and Walter.

In Leeds, on the other hand, Old Testament names had still made no great impact by 1590, which makes the presence of twins called Aser and Asahell even more surprising. They were the children of Randall Tench, a newcomer to the parish and possibly from outside the county, although little is known about him beyond his obvious status in the community. The names Paul, Gabriel and Titus

MALE NAMES

	1379	Baptisms in Halifax 1590–92		Baptisms in Leeds 1590–93		Baptisms nationwide 1590–99	
1	John	John	(74)	William	(54)	John	1
2	William	William	(24)	Thomas	(44)	William	2
3	Thomas	Michael	(20)	John	(35)	Thomas	3
4	Richard	Richard	(18)	Robert	(24)	Robert	4
5	Robert	James	(15)	George	(21)	Richard	5
6	Henry	Samuel	(15)	Richard	(18)	Edward	6
7	Roger	Henry	(14)	Christopher	(12)	Henry	7
8	Walter	Thomas	(12)	Francis	(11)	George	8
9	Adam	Jonas	(11)	James	(10)	James	9
10	Nicholas	Abraham	(10)	Henry	(10)	Nicholas	10
11	Hugh	Edward	(9)	Matthew	(7)	Francis	11
12	Geoffrey	Robert	(8)	Brian	(5)	Anthony	12
13	Simon	Anthony	(8)	Edward	(4)	Christopher	13
14	Ralph	Isaac	(7)	Peter	(4)	Roger	14
15	Peter	Joseph	(5)	Ralph	(4)	Ralph	15
16	Stephen	Daniel	(5)	Samuel	(3)	Michael	16
17	Gilbert	George	(5)	Alexander	(2)	Matthew	17
18	Philip	Matthew	(4)	Edmund	(2)	Peter	18
19	Reginald	Nathan	(3)	Lancelot	(2)	Samuel	19
20	David	Jacob	(3)	Nicholas	(2)	Walter	20
21	Laurence	Ambrose	(3)	Roger	(2)	Stephen	21
22	James	Francis	(3)	Ambrose	(1)	Andrew	22
23	Edmund	Jeremiah	(2)	Andrew	(1)	Daniel	23
24	Alan	Jonathan	(2)	Arthur	(1)	Edmund	24
25	Denis	Martin	(2)	Asahell	(1)	Nathaniel	25
26	Michael	Joshua	(2)	Aser	(1)	Joseph	26
27	Alexander	Reuben	(2)	Charles	(1)	Philip	27
28	Matthew	Gilbert	(2)	Cuthbert	(1)	Charles	28
29	Andrew	Austin	(1)	Ellis/Elias	(1)	Humphrey	29
30	Edus	Benjamin	(1)	Gabriel	(1)	Simon	30
31	Giles	Christopher	(1)	Gilbert	(1)	Hugh	31
32	Benedict	Edmund	(1)	Gregory	(1)	Valentine	32
33	Edward	Elias/Ellis	(1)	Leonard	(1)	Mark	33
34	Luke	Humphrey	(1)	Mark	(1)	Roland	34
35	George	Lewis	(1)	Martin	(1)	Isaac	35
36	Gregory	Luke	(1)	Michael	(1)	Miles	36
37	Clement	Peter	(1)	Miles	(1)	Gregory	37
38	Elias	Samson	(1)	Paul	(1)	Martin	38
39	Bartholomew	Stephen	(1)	Philip	(1)	Reynold	39
40	Martin	Tobias	(1)	Simon	(1)	Abraham	40
41	Jena			Titus	(1)	Adam	41
42	Nigel			Wilfrid	(1)	Benjamin	42
43				Pigott	(1)	Cuthbert	43
44				Freeman	(1)	Lawrence	44
45				Sheffield	(1)		45

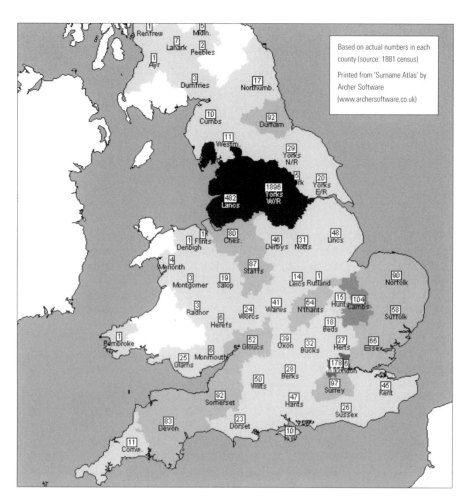

Based on actual numbers in each county (source: 1881 census)

Printed from 'Surname Atlas' by Archer Software (www.archersoftware.co.uk)

9 The first name Jonas (4289) Jonas was in widespread use in 1881 but its distribution still reflects the early history of the name in the Haworth area. It came into use there in 1562 and was popular by 1672. In Thornton, where 100 males were taxed, it was the second most frequent name (12), more popular than William (7), Thomas (4), Richard (4) and Robert (3). It was not one of Smith-Bannister's top fifty names in 1670–79.

are also worth noting, but each occurred once only and it must be said that most biblical names in Leeds were those with a high national profile, for example Matthew, Andrew, Mark, Philip and Simon. In fact the parish was very conservative compared with Halifax, and the names correspond quite closely to those in the national table for the same period. Only Brian, with a total of five, provides evidence of a significant local custom, and the influence there was almost certainly Brian Beeston, a prominent local gentleman. Just a few of the less common names in the list have interesting histories in Yorkshire, for example Lancelot, Ambrose and Wilfrid, and the three surnames, Pigott, Sheffield and

FEMALE NAMES

	1379	Baptisms in Halifax 1590–91		Baptisms in Leeds 1590–92		Baptisms nationwide 1590–99	
1	Alice	Mary	(64)	Elizabeth	(43)	Elizabeth	1
2	Agnes	Susanna	(55)	Anne	(38)	Margaret	2
3	Joan	Grace	(42)	Alice	(33)	Mary	3
4	Matilda	Anne	(22)	Mary	(32)	Anne	4
5	Isabel	Sarah	(20)	Grace	(26)	Agnes	5
6	Margaret	Elizabeth	(12)	Isabel	(22)	Joan	6
7	Emme	Esther	(11)	Jane	(16)	Alice	7
8	Marg'	Martha	(9)	Margaret	(14)	Jane	8
9	Margery	Isabel	(7)	Agnes	(13)	Catherine	9
10	Ellen	Eden	(6)	Jennet	(11)	Isabel	10
11	Julian	Alice	(6)	Dorothy	(7)	Susanna	11
12	Cecile	Judith	(6)	Helen	(6)	Dorothy	12
13	Christine	Jane	(5)	Sybil	(4)	Elinor	13
14	Katherine	Sybil	(5)	Effan (Euphemia)	(3)	Sarah	14
15	Edith	Margaret	(4)	Mercy	(3)	Margery	15
16	Amice	Bridget	(3)	Judith	(3)	Ellen	16
17	Elizabeth	Dorothy	(3)	Katherine	(2)	Frances	17
18	Beatrice	Rebecca	(3)	Cecile	(2)	Grace	18
19	Magot	Agnes	(3)	Susanna	(2)	Martha	19
20	Sarah	Effan (Euphemia)	(2)	Phyllis	(2)	Helen	20
21	Sybil	Ruth	(2)	Lettice	(2)	Janet	21
22	Felice	Priscilla	(1)	Agatha	(1)	Bridget	22
23	Christian	Julian	(1)	Christian	(1)	Judith	23
24	Avice	Leah	(1)	Dowsabel	(1)	Joyce	24
25	Denise	Frances	(1)	Esther	(1)	Edith	25
26	Is'	Lettice	(1)	Eden	(1)	Thomasin	26
27	Isolde	Joyce	(1)	Edith	(1)	Barbara	27
28	Lucy	Patience	(1)	Frances	(1)	Lucy	28
29	Petronille	Prudence	(1)	Fortune	(1)	Mabel	29
30	Rose	Tabitha	(1)	Idan (Idony?)	(1)	Rebecca	30
31	Mariot	Thebe (sic)	(1)	Idaw (Idony?)	(1)	Cecily	31
32	Mabel			Margery	(1)	Emma	32
33	Lettice			Rebecca	(1)	Phyllis	33
34	Custance			Rosamund	(1)	Rachel	34
35	Anne			Sarah	(1)	Amy	35
36	Idony			Thomasin	(1)	Emmat	36
37	Eve			Ursula	(1)	Millicent	37

Freeman bear witness to a gentry innovation not shown in the Halifax sample.

Girls' names from the Bible were also prominent in Halifax in this period, almost two-thirds of the total, but the biggest influence was undoubtedly the New Testament, with Mary, Susanna, Elizabeth and Martha in the first eight.

Elizabeth and Mary were also very popular in Leeds but there were only two Susannas there and no Marthas. The difference between the two parishes is further emphasised when we take Old Testament names into account for these were numerically important in Halifax, e.g. Sarah (20), Esther (11), Eden (6),[3] and Judith (6), but relatively unimportant in Leeds where only Judith (3) appeared more than once. In Halifax the names Rebecca, Ruth, Leah and Tabitha, lower down the order, further emphasise the new choices being made, whereas the Leeds names, apart from Grace which is dealt with later, are very similar to those nationally.

Susanna and Martha stand out in the Halifax list. The success of Susanna by the 1590s was remarkable for it had been rare everywhere in the county until the sixteenth century. It was first used in Halifax in 1546 and then occasionally through the 1550s, finally becoming the most popular choice in 1571, marginally ahead of Mary and Grace. It accounted for more baptisms in 1590–91 than all the Old Testament names together and was far more prominent in Halifax than it was nationally. The inspiration is likely to have been the New Testament reference in Luke but the apocryphal tale of Susanna and the Elders may also have been an influence. In this story Susanna was the beautiful wife of Joachim, falsely accused of adultery and saved from execution by the intervention of Daniel. The Susanna window in the cathedral church of Bury St Edmunds is thought to date from the early sixteenth century, just before the name became more popular generally.

Martha was the sister of Mary and Lazarus and her care of Jesus gave her the reputation of an industrious and thoughtful person, making her the patroness of those who tended the sick and needy. Her name derives from an Aramaic word meaning 'lady', and it occurs in Canterbury in 1377–81. However, in Halifax it was used for the first time in 1556, in the Oates family, and soon became quite popular.

Halifax name-givers, 1538–70

The use of non-traditional biblical names was well established in Halifax by 1590, earlier than in most Yorkshire parishes. It is important, I believe, to establish exactly when and where the custom started as well as to identify the names and status of the innovators wherever possible. There had been innovations before, of course, but the lead then had come from the gentry and aristocracy. If ministers from non-gentry families and people of quite ordinary rank were now making their own choices, that was a momentous change and it seems even more significant if it was true of one parish and not of another.

Fortunately the registers for Halifax are remarkably complete from 1538 and they contain the names of the godparents for several hundred baptisms in the 1550s, making it possible to say which families introduced the new biblical names and when they became more popular generally. The first signs of change can be seen in the period 1542–53, which covers the last part of Henry's reign and all that of his son Edward. The break with tradition was gradual, and eight 'new' biblical names were introduced in those years, several of them from the New Testament, i.e. Paul, Luke, Dorcas, Susanna and Mark, each recorded once only. In 1546, though, Thomas Ambler of Southowram called one of his sons Abraham, a deliberate choice from the Old Testament, and one that now appears especially significant. Four more Abrahams had been baptised by 1553 and a new tradition established. The two remaining names were Joseph and Gabriel, used by the Saviles who were the only family in the group with known gentry connections.

Although these 12 names capture our attention, they represent a very small percentage of the total number of baptisms in the parish – a tentative start to a new naming practice, but one that gathered momentum even when Mary was on the throne. In her reign Abraham became a regular choice and Samuel well established; other Old Testament names introduced were Judith, Sarah and Isaac. From the New Testament both Luke and Mark remained in use and Susanna began its steady rise to extreme popularity, soon to be followed by Martha. The one really unusual girls' name in those years was Heyden or Edan, referred to earlier.

In the next 12 years the tradition became even more firmly established, and the range of Old Testament names increased for both boys and girls, as the following list indicates: Joshua and Esau (1559); Esther (1560); Abel, Samson, Caleb, Ruth and Tobias (1561); Daniel (1562); Jonas, Simeon and Dinah (1563); Rebecca and Solomon (1564); David, Nathan and Nathaniel (1565); Jeremiah and Amos (1567); Reuben, Zacchaeus and Leah (1569); Aaron (1570). Other significant choices in that period were Raphael, the archangel, and Eunice from the New Testament. These children were not named after parents or godparents and there is no real evidence that the innovations were gentry inspired, although the Saviles, Waterhouses and Oateses were influential families who played some part in the new practice. There were three vicars in this period: Robert Holdsworth, John Harrison and Christopher Ashburn.

Most reference works comment on the use of Old Testament names in the seventeenth century and not on their introduction in the mid-sixteenth century, and yet the practice was not confined to Halifax. Doubtless they became popular in other parts of the country, if not always quite so dramatically as in Halifax. In the seventeenth and eighteenth centuries the giving of such names became an accepted practice generally; even the longest and most unwieldy Old Testament names were brought into use. The importance of Halifax is that it was one of the first parishes to break with tradition, and names were chosen that did not repeat those of the parents or godparents.

Old Testament names in the fourteenth century

Withycombe referred briefly to the use of biblical names before the Reformation, listing the names of the apostles and those traditionally used in the Mystery plays, most of them from the Old Testament. In the latter category were just 18 names, 12 of them male: Abraham, Absalom, Adam, Daniel, David, Isaac, Jacob, Jonah, Joseph, Noah, Samson and Tobias, and 6 of them female: Anna, Eve, Hester (Esther), Judith, Sarah and Susanna. Withycombe made no serious attempt to determine what the history of these names was in the fifteenth century, although there is evidence to show that several of them remained in occasional use throughout that period, e.g. Adam, Joseph and Abraham, and that others came with immigrants from the Low Countries. A study of two or three biblical names emphasises how individual their local histories can be.

Seth

Seth was the third son of Adam, born after the death of Abel, and the name is said to mean 'compensation' or 'substitute' – literally 'another seed in place of Abel'. Writers have largely ignored its early history and we are invited to believe that it was one of the Old Testament names brought into use after the Reformation. Withycombe expressed that view when she referred to Seth Holywell, a Huntingdonshire clergyman who died in 1557, as 'the earliest example noted'. The reality is that Seth is on record, in good numbers, a century before most Old Testament names were at all popular. It is difficult to say exactly when it was first used, as the earliest recorded bearers were adults.

The first use though must have been c.1450 at the latest, for a man called Seth Gillow was made clerk of Bishop Booth's markets in Durham in 1476. This family had its origins in Lancashire and had migrated into Yorkshire and Durham along with Archbishop Booth. Seth Gillow's kinsman Henry Gillow held several offices in Yorkshire; he was a sub-dean of York in 1477–8, had a prebend at Fridaythorpe and was granted the rectory of Gilling in 1480. Robert Gillow, vicar choral, was admitted to the chantry at St Stephen's altar in York Minster in 1473.[4]

The Gillows would almost certainly have known William Snawsell, the goldsmith and alderman of York whose son and heir Seth was admitted to the Guild of Corpus Christi in 1483, and it is tempting to think that they were kinsmen. Seth Snawsell became a freeman of the city four years later and the family's recently restored town house in York gives us some idea of their status and wealth. They were also lords of the manor of Bilton, with property at Huntington near by and in Sawley near Ripon. Their position as wealthy members of the local gentry is confirmed by the role they played in a dispute brought before the Court of Star Chamber in the 1490s.[5]

Seth Snawsell was not the only bearer of the name in that part of Yorkshire, for Seth Hogeson was also taxed in Bilton in 1524, and another neighbour, Seth Holme, was the son of Snawsell's kinsman Wilfrid Holme. This was the man whose anti-clericalism was mentioned earlier and who also possessed an estate in Huntington. The wider use of Seth in and around Bilton is probably evidence of the Snawsells' network of kith and kin, but it does not explain why such an unusual name was given in the first place. Perhaps it was chosen by well-educated individuals who were aware of its meaning and symbolism, or perhaps both Seth and Wilfrid were attempts by these families to emphasise their gentility or anti-clericalism. Alternatively those who made the choice may have encountered the name in the text of the *Cursor Mundi*, or one of the source works from which it derived.[6] Seth figured prominently in that section of the book which dealt with the story of the cross, and the author was a northerner whose poem is thought by some to have been written near Durham. Sadly we cannot be certain what motivated the original name-giver, but his choice was a remarkable innovation for that period.

York, and the area around the city known as the Ainsty, was not the only district in which Seth occurred in the late fifteenth century and early sixteenth century. It was traditional also in the Holland family of Nottinghamshire, and one Seth Holand purchased property in Tickhill in 1500.[7] He was probably the Seth Holland of Bothamsall whose will was proved in 1517, but a second Seth Holland died at Treswell in the same county in 1529, almost certainly a kinsman.[8]

A third group was located in Halifax parish: Seth Moldson was taxed in Stainland in 1524,[9] and the Halifax registers record the names of adults such as Seth Tattlaw and Seth Haldeworth in 1539–40. More interestingly a Halifax will of 1508 was witnessed by a minister called Seth Cawod, whose surname might link him with York or Lancashire rather than Halifax.[10] It might be thought therefore that Seth would have come into more general use in Halifax when Old Testament names became popular, but it belonged to a different tradition and was not recorded among the baptisms during Elizabeth's reign.

Seth continued to be relatively popular, as late as the 1670s, among families living in the area north of Huntington and Bilton. These included the Judsons, Lazenbys, Skeltons, Agars, Stotts, Amersons and Hodgsons, the last of these suggesting a direct connection with the Snawsells and the Holmes mentioned above. In fact the later use of Seth can often be traced to this source. When the Leeds historian Ralph Thoresby published his *Ducatus Leodiensis* in 1714, it contained a pedigree of the Skeltons of Osmondthorpe, compiled from 'writings' passed to the author by the heir Seth Skelton. This man's grandfather, also named Seth Skelton, had been born in 1650, the son of the mayor of Leeds, whose mother Jane was the daughter of Seth Holme of Huntington. His sister Elizabeth was the mother of Seth Soothill, who was baptised in Leeds in March 1635 and later became Governor of Carolina.

Although Seth was never popular it remained in regular use well into the eighteenth century at least. Seth Kirkby of York, for instance, who was buried in 1714, had three sons, William, Henry and Seth: they were mariners and watermen, and all three ensured that Seth passed into the next generation. The Seth Kirkby who died in 1751 was described in the register as 'an old mariner out of the hospital'. By then of course his first name had a history in the city that went back at least 300 years.

Paul

There is no evidence that Paul was a popular name in the thirteenth century, and it was also missing from most counties in 1377–81. In the West Riding it was recorded just three times in 1379 and scarcely at all in the fifteenth century, and one of those examples was Paulus Fresshe, a German immigrant in 1414.[11] After the Reformation, when names from the Bible became more popular, Paul was again used occasionally, and scattered examples have been noted over a wide area from c.1540. However, it remained a generally uncommon name as late as c.1800.

One remarkable exception to that is highlighted in the hearth tax returns of 1672. Paul was still a rare choice in most parts of Yorkshire at that time, but it was one of the most frequent names in Morley Wapentake, with a total there of 20, almost all of them recorded in the upland chapelry of Heptonstall. This was the western section of the ancient parish of Halifax, and there were no Pauls recorded in the eastern section. Even more remarkably the Morley total of 20 included no fewer than 10 men with the name Paul Greenwood. The popularity of this combination is even more apparent in the Heptonstall register, for 37 Paul Greenwoods were baptised in the period 1599–1659, most of them after 1630. There were just six in the earlier part of the period and four of those were in the township of Wadsworth, some of them in the locality known as Old Town.

The Greenwoods were already an exceptionally numerous family in the chapelry, and Paul was clearly one of their favourite names in the seventeenth century. As the earlier registers have not survived, we do not know who first bore the name, but it may have been a Wadsworth clothier called Paul Greenwood who died in 1609.[12] He was almost certainly born no later than 1570, for there are other records which show that he purchased land locally in the 1590s.[13] His name was linked occasionally with that of his kinsman Ambrose Greenwood, and the potential significance of that connection will emerge later.

No fewer than 24 other families in the chapelry used Paul in the same period but, with two exceptions, these were all after 1624. Unfortunately the marriage register is defective for some of those years and the names of the godparents are not given in the baptismal register, so it is impossible to determine how much of Paul's popularity resulted from links that the Greenwoods had with these families. The likelihood is, though, that most of them were kinsmen or friends, and it is worth noting that several prominent local families never used Paul. We can sometimes find circumstantial evidence of those links if we examine the names and surnames of the families concerned. The following references point to possible ties between the Greenwoods and their neighbours the Ackroyds, Townends and Widdops:

1595: Paul Grenwode purchased from Henry Ackroide '4 messuages, a water mill and a fulling mill in Wadsworth'.[14]
1604, 18 March: Paul baptised, son of Ambrose Grenwod.
1619, 25 July: Paul baptised, son of Simion Greenwood.
1628, 14 December: Paul baptised, son of Henry Aycroide of Wadsworth.
1641, 4 July: Paull baptised, son of Ambrose Widdopp.
1648, 9 July: Paul baptised, son of Symeon Townend.

Because the Greenwoods were numerically so important in Heptonstall it is tempting to presume that they were responsible for introducing Paul into the chapelry. It should be noted though that two of the earliest Pauls baptised were in the Kay and Widdop families and it is possible that the name passed to the Greenwoods from one of them. Paul Wedopp, for example, was the father of a girl baptised in 1601 and a contemporary of the Old Town clothier Paul Greenwood. The court rolls for the late sixteenth century might throw more light on that point.

The Greenwoods continued to use Paul into the nineteenth century at least, throughout a period when it enjoyed little general popularity and because of that the name seems to point back to sixteenth-century Wadsworth whenever and wherever it occurs in the records:

1667: Paul Greenwood, scole master, Methley parish register.
1672: Paul Greenwood, Stanbury hearth tax.
1725, 18 November: Paul Greenwood married Grace Land, Leeds.
1731: Paul Greenwood of Wycoller in Lancashire.[15]
1845: Paul Greenwood, farmer, Stansfield, Heptonstall trade directory.

Gamaliel

This Hebrew name is found in both the Old and New Testaments, but is most familiar to us as the name of a teacher of Saul of Tarsus. It is said to mean 'benefit of God' and the earliest dictionary reference is Withycombe's Gamaliel Chase, the rector of Wambrook in Somerset (1621). There are earlier examples, and Gamaliel's history has two points of interest for first name researchers.

The first concerns Sir Gervase Clifton, of Clifton in Nottinghamshire, who died in 1491 leaving at least seven sons. Four of them had the names Gervase, Gamaliel, Silvan and Ezechie, choices that mark the father out as an innovative name-giver, almost on a par with his contemporary Robert Bolling of Bolling Hall.[16] The fact that his first son was named Gervase is not surprising, for it was a traditional name for the eldest son in the family from the twelfth century. However the biblical names of his three brothers were certainly unusual and would have attracted immediate attention.

We cannot know why such names were chosen nor the full extent of their influence, but they certainly make it easier to follow the brothers' migrations. The Cliftons had widespread land interests and none of the three sons remained in Nottinghamshire. Silvan eventually moved to Winchester, and Ezechie or Ezekiel to Holderness in the East Riding, where Ezekiel was almost immediately taken up as a name by families in and around the parish of Preston.[17] Gamaliel was the most mobile of them all and spent time, or held offices, in Yorkshire, Herefordshire and Berkshire, as well as in his native Nottinghamshire. He was a distinguished and well-educated lawyer, closely concerned with the divorces of Henry VIII. It is possible that his family was indirectly connected with another Gamaliel, whose story allows me to make the second point.

By the late sixteenth century there were Gamaliels in several Yorkshire parishes. These included Gamaliel Drax, a Catholic recusant in Ilkley in 1578, and Gamaliel Wilson of Southowram in Halifax, whose brother was called Erasmus (1577). However the best-known bearer of the name was Gamaliel Whittaker, the vicar of Kirkburton from 1615. His father was the rector of Thornhill and closely involved in the fortunes of the great Wentworth family, who possessed extensive estates in Nottinghamshire and south Yorkshire. His wife Hester was sister to Mrs Wentworth of Elmsall and his sister Dorothy married Matthew Wentworth of Cawthorne. As a young man Gamaliel had been a contemporary, at St John's College in Cambridge, of Charles Greenwood of Heptonstall, who later became the tutor of Thomas Wentworth, the great Earl of Strafford, and eventually succeeded Gamaliel's father at Thornhill.

Gamaliel Whittaker was a committed Royalist, one of a very few local ministers who refused to sign the oath of Protestation in 1642, and he was ejected from Kirkburton soon afterwards. The church register records that his wife died in January 1644, 'slain the twelfth day att night' in suspicious circumstances and Gamaliel himself died in captivity later the same year, it is said 'of ill usage' at the hands of his Parliamentarian captors.[18] It is clear from earlier quarter sessions records that he was at odds with many of his parishioners from about 1637 until his death, and he was held responsible by many of them for a raid on the town of Holmfirth by the Earl of Newcastle's troops.

Kirkburton was an extensive parish consisting of eight or nine townships, and said to be staunch in its support for Parliament, although it is unlikely that the population was all of one mind. Between 1637 and his untimely death in 1644 Gamaliel became involved in accusations of assault and theft in the parish, and he was at loggerheads with his churchwardens. Nevertheless Gamaliel was a frequent choice in the parish from that time, used by families called Battye, Moseley, Brooke, Kaye, Booth, Roberts and Marsh, and it remained in favour long after the minister's death. The first Gamaliel Battye was baptised in 1669 and others followed at intervals; Gamaliel Battye of Hollingreave was married in December 1817. Perhaps the original choices tell us where certain individuals stood in the political and religious disputes that divided the parish in the seventeenth century.

Puritan names

It has been argued that the word 'puritan' was originally a term of abuse, and that it remained so for decades, directed at those who set themselves apart from their fellows by 'conspicuous religiosity'.[19] The Puritans' striving after virtue manifested itself in their love of sermons and psalms, in their readings from the Bible, and, of course, in their first name choices, notably those from the Old Testament. They are credited also with having introduced the so-called virtue names and phrase-names. The virtue names were usually given to girls and were coined from nouns which highlighted certain virtues or desirable qualities, such as Prudence, Obedience, Honesty and Faith. It is true that some Puritans favoured names of this type but they may have been part of a longer tradition. Bardsley called them 'grace' names and described Grace itself as one of the first to find favour in the Elizabethan period. In fact it has a much longer history.

Grace

It has recently been said that Grace was first used by the Puritans in the seventeenth century,[20] even though both Bardsley in *Curiosities of Puritan Nomenclature* and Withycombe (*English Christian Names*) had already noted sixteenth-century examples. Indeed we have seen that it was the third most popular girls' name in Halifax in the 1590s and in Smith-Bannister's tables it is regularly represented from 1538. Other Yorkshire references occur in 1417, 1464, 1472 and 1497, and, in the poll tax returns of 1377–81, it is found in Essex, Norfolk and Sussex. In fact Reaney and Wilson have several examples of Gracia or Gratia in the early thirteenth century and of Grecia from a generation before that. We may therefore be dealing with more than one name and, as Grecia has been recorded in eleventh-century France, the etymological questions are complex and probably best left to the linguists.[21]

Despite that, the history of Grace in Halifax is worth looking at in more detail for the name was certainly more popular there than it was nationally; there are more than 30 examples in the baptismal register before 1545, long before the Puritan influence on first names was apparent. The Broadleys were one family with whom it found favour: Robert Broadley (1517) and John Broadley (1537) made wills in which they referred to daughters called Grace, and Edward Broadley had a daughter named Grace in 1540. It was popular also with one branch of the powerful Savile family, and their influence almost certainly played a part in its more widespread use. For example Thomas Sayvell of Copley died in 1533, leaving £40 to his daughter Grace 'for hir hoole childes porcione'.[22] The witnesses were John Waterhouse, Richard Saltonstall, William Burnlaye and Richard Longbothome and every one of these families had a daughter named Grace between 1540 and 1558. They lived in Warley and Northowram, two townships which seem to have been at the heart of these developments.

It is not difficult to see why Grace proved attractive to the Puritans even though they did not invent the name, for they would certainly have associated it with divine influence and salvation. It is more than likely also that it helped other abstract nouns to become acceptable as names, some time before the Puritans found them attractive. Smith-Bannister has Charity in the 1540s and Bardsley found Patience being used in Cornwall in 1549; in the same year Fayth, the wife of Richard Smith, was buried at Howden in east Yorkshire. In Nottinghamshire Godfrey Foljambe had a wife named Troth in 1560,[23] and the name was afterwards used by other branches of the family and by gentry neighbours such as the Eyres of Derbyshire.

From the 1560s the use of such names increased, at least in some parishes, and some of these are likely to have been Puritan innovations. In 1567 John Waterhouse of Northowram named his daughter Prudence and his lead was followed by the Maudes, Fearnsides, Wilkinsons and others. It was a frequent choice for girls in that neighbourhood and similar names soon followed. One of the trend-setters was Richard Hall who had four daughters between 1578 and 1583; they were called Prudence, Fortune, Grace and Mercy. In most parishes though such names remained occasional choices and only Grace was at all popular generally. Charity, Patience and Fortune figure regularly in the frequency tables but always in the lower half.

Once the precedent had been set many more names of the same type came into use, for example Hope, Silence, Peace, Comfort and Unity, but as these in their turn became accepted, more adventurous choices were made, including Repentance, Temperance, Reconciliation and Discretion. The majority of these were given to girls of course, and they appear to have been most popular with Puritans, but it has been noted that Grace was also used occasionally for men and among Catholics, so assumptions are dangerous and the evidence needs to be studied carefully in each case. Patience, for example, could be used for either boys or girls.

Patience

Withycombe said of Patience that it came into use as a christian name in the seventeenth century and it is true that it first enters Smith-Bannister's frequency lists in 1610–19. However, there is one much earlier example in Halifax. Thomas Seed was the minister at Ripponden, a chapel of ease near Elland, and when he died in 1577 administration was granted to his daughter Patience, who therefore seems likely to have been named no later than the 1550s. Patience never became a popular name in Yorkshire, but examples occur over a wide area well into the eighteenth century, and there is at least one well-known case of it being given to a boy.

Sir Patience Ward, the Lord Mayor of London in 1680, was the son of Thomas Ward of Tanshelf in Pontefract, born in 1629. In his memoirs he wrote that his father 'having had six sons and one daughter...did frequently say if he had another he would call him Patience, which he accordingly did'. The Wards had held the manor of Tanshelf from the Crown since 1507 and were said to be a Puritan family active in enforcing the 'orders of Parliament against the Church'.[24] They also claimed descent from the St Andrew family of Gotham in Nottinghamshire, and the register of Hooton Pagnell reveals how they used Patience and Saint Andrew as first names well into the eighteenth century. A later Patience Ward was buried there in 1786 and Saint Andrew Ward named his son Saint Andrew in 1780.

Puritan phrase-names

There were among the sternest Puritans a few who were not satisfied with choosing Old Testament names or 'virtue' names, although both categories enjoyed some prominence from the second half of the sixteenth century. So, in an attempt to avoid what a contemporary called 'heathenish names', they invented eccentric compounds such as Praise-God and Hate-Evil, often described as phrase-names. It was a custom that Thomas Adams commented on critically in *Meditations upon the Creed* (1629), saying that William and Richard were just as gracious as Safe-Deliverance or Fight-the-Good-Fight-of-Faith. His view must have been widely held for the new fashion met with only limited success.

Nevertheless it was a striking innovation and C. W. Bardsley discusses it at some length in *Curiosities of Puritan Nomenclature*. He considers the names to be a phenomenon of the period c.1580 to 1640 and largely confined to the southern counties, particularly Sussex and Kent. Phrase-names were certainly rare in the north although Gods-Gift Kerby was living in Wakefield in 1676[25] and James Chadwick of the same parish had children called Seekepeace, Mary, Mortifie and Reforme (1665).[26] In Birstall, in 1680, Simeon Brooke and Marie Hardie called their bastard son Seekepeace, a name that invites sympathetic speculation.

It was of course in the early seventeenth century that many religious enthusiasts found their way to New England, and William Brewster of *Mayflower* fame had children called Love, Wrestling and Fear. Other names to cross the Atlantic were Hopestill, Search-the-Scriptures, Standfast and Freegrace, and the records suggest that the new fashion may have found stronger support in the New World than it did in England. That was certainly the case with Puritan favourites from the Old Testament.

Bardsley attributes the custom to a few extremely zealous clergymen who in turn influenced their parishioners. Two of the examples he quotes are from Sussex parishes, the first at Salehurst where Mr William Hopkinson was the minister. He named his sons Stedfast (1587) and Safe-on-High (1591), whilst his daughters were Persis (1579) and Renewed (1588). In the same period the Warbleton minister Thomas Heley called his sons Much-Mercye (1585) and Fear-Not (1589) and his daughters Increased (1587) and Sin-Denie (1588). Bardsley found more than 100 similar examples of 'eccentric Puritanism' in the Warbleton register in the 15 years after that. The fact that zealots were responsible for this practice diminishes the role of the individuals concerned but alerts us to the more general, if less noticeable, influence that ministers could have.

Because phrase-names and the exotic virtue names were such a colourful break with tradition they inevitably find their way into most books on the subject, but the interest they arouse is probably out of proportion to the influence they had, and there were many parishes where such names were completely unknown. Moreover, they are always dealt with as a phenomenon that was characteristic of a fairly limited period, an expression of extremism, and there is little in our dictionaries about their history or the individuals concerned. The story of one Yorkshire example, initially the choice of a minister, may therefore be of interest.

Whatgodwill

George Crosland was the minister at Almondbury from 1598 to 1636, and he betrayed Puritan sympathies when he gave the names Phineas and Theodore to two of his sons, and followed that up by calling a third son Whatgodwill, a name apparently of his own invention. Theodore became a senior fellow of Trinity College, Cambridge, and he referred in his will, in 1665, to his brother and his brother's son, both named 'What-God-Will'.[27] When George Crosland died he was succeeded as vicar of Almondbury by another son who had the more conventional name John; it was during his years of office, after 1636, that Whatgodwill was used more frequently. That may have owed something to family ties and something to shared religious views, but when the Hirsts, Blackburns, Ellistones and Whitakers called their sons Whatgodwill it was all the more noticeable because there was no other name of this kind in the parish. There was a

Deodatus in Rochdale, just over the Lancashire border, but even Halifax, for all its strong Puritan tradition, had nothing comparable.

If many of our ancestors have slipped quietly into obscurity, it may be because so many of them had commonplace names. Whatgodwill does not permit anonymity, but serves rather to focus attention on its bearer and on otherwise unremarkable events. For example, Whatgodwill Crosland, junior, was indicted at the quarter sessions in 1685 for illegally shooting at pigeons 'with a hand gun loaded with gunpowder and hail-shott'. It was a run-of-the-mill misdemeanour but the offender's name draws our attention to it.

The name was altogether too heavy a burden for Whatgodwill Hirst. In 1676 witnesses testified to this man's depravity, recounting how he had thrown stones through neighbours' windows, broken down Martha Kaye's door and assaulted her, threatening to 'have her life' – all this it seems 'in the afternoon in tyme of devine service'. Surprisingly Whatgodwill's plea of insanity was accepted and he was not imprisoned. On the grounds that he was not responsible for his actions, he was 'sent home to his own habitation without any punishment', so perhaps his name had influenced the magistrates more than they realised.

If the diarist Oliver Heywood is to be believed the name alone was enough to stir up prejudice, particularly once Charles II had been restored to the throne. He said that a jury empanelled at the assizes in 1672 was objected to and dismissed solely because the foreman was named as Whatgodwill Crosland. It is therefore remarkable that it should have remained in use long after similar names are said to have been discarded. Its colloquial form was Godwill, used by George Crosland in his will in 1636, and occasionally in the registers. In the neighbouring township of Lepton there was a Godwill Berry as late as 1787 and the coppice wood near his home was known as Godwill Spring. This colloquial spelling contrasts sharply with 'Quod-vult-deus' in the seventeenth-century registers.

~

Phrase-names enjoyed only temporary and local success but the Puritans had a more permanent influence on naming practices from the sixteenth century, coining new virtue names or drawing their names from the Bible. In one respect that influence may be less decisive than is sometimes claimed, for there is evidence that changes had already affected both classes of name in the fifteenth century, inspired by the gentry in their traditional role. The contribution here of families like the Gillows, Snawsells and Cliftons was particularly important. The real significance of the Puritan influence was that it was exercised by ministers and people below the rank of gentleman, initially in isolated parishes and then more generally.

Notes

1 T. D. Whitaker, *Loidis and Elmete* (Leeds, 1816), pp. 370–1.

2 The statistics for 1379 are from the poll tax returns and appear more fully in Appendix I. Those for 1590–99 are from Scott Smith-Bannister, *Names and Naming Practices 1538–1700* (Oxford, 1997), pp. 192–3 and 197–8.

3 Eden could be an alternative for Edith, e.g. 1631–2 Eden or Edeth, daughter of Lanclet Spetch of Briggate, Leeds parish register. In Halifax, where Edith was rare, it may have been inspired by the Old Testament place-name. Spellings varied, e.g. Heyden, Eydon, Edan.

4 *Testamenta Eboracensia*, Surtees Society XLV (1865), p. 282.

5 W. Brown (ed.), *Yorkshire Star Chamber Proceedings*, Yorkshire Archaeological Society, Record Series XLI (1909).

6 This poem dates from about 1300 and covers the spiritual history of mankind up to the Last Judgement. It has been described as 'a very successful, readable piece of popular instruction'.

7 *Yorkshire Fines, 1486–1571*, YAS II (1887), p. 15.

8 F. A. Collins (ed.), *Wills in the York Registry, 1514–53*, YAS XI (1891), p. 90.

9 'Subsidy Roll for Aggbrigg and Morley', *Yorkshire Archaeological and Topographical Journal II* (1873), p. 56.

10 J. W. Clay (ed.), *Halifax Wills* (Privately printed, n.d.).

11 *Register of the Freemen of the City of York, 1272–1558*, Surtees XCVI (1896).

12 *Wills in the York Registry, 1603–11*, YAS XXVI (1899).

13 *Yorkshire Fines,1594–1603*, YAS VIII (1890), p. 12.

14 *Ibid.*, p. 48.

15 Wakefield Registry of Deeds, West Yorkshire Archive Service, Quarter Sessions Rolls, QS1/71/2.

16 *Testamenta Eboracensia*, Surtees LIII (1869), pp. 64–71.

17 The evidence suggests that there was confusion there between Ezekias and Ezekiel. The name was used in the sixteenth century by the Southwicks, Johnsons, Atkinsons and Prestwoods.

18 H. J. Morehouse, *The History and Topography of Kirkburton and the Graveship of Holme* (Huddersfield, 1861), pp. 21–5.

19 P. Collinson, 'English Puritanism', *General Series* 106, The Historical Association (1983).

20 P. Hanks and F. Hodges, *A Dictionary of First Names* (Oxford, 1990).

21 I am grateful to Peter McClure for his help with the earliest history of Grace.

22 J. W. Clay, *Halifax Wills*, p. 97.

23 *Yorkshire Fines, 1486–1571*, YAS II (1887), p. 236.

24 C. E. Whiting, 'Sir Patience Ward of Tanshelf', YAS XXXIV (1939), pp. 245–72.

25 J. Horsfall Turner (ed.), *The Rev. Oliver Heywood, 1630–1702* III (Bingley, 1883), p. 174.

26 *Wills in the York Registry, 1660–65*, YAS XLIX (1913), p. 112.

27 C. W. Bardsley, *Curiosities of Puritan Nomenclature* (1880, reprinted 1996), p. 135.

Changing Customs

English parents are free now to choose whatever name they like for their children:
no restrictions are placed on them and there are literally thousands of possibilities to
be considered, most of them finding a place in our standard dictionaries. Old names
seldom disappear altogether and new names are constantly being revived, borrowed
or coined, so our name-stock continues to grow. The influences are world wide and
they include sports people, actors, writers, pop stars, characters in novels and films
or any famous person, and it is difficult to imagine the process of innovation being
reversed. This is not a freedom enjoyed in all countries and it was not a freedom
enjoyed by all our ancestors in the sixteenth and seventeenth centuries. However, it
was in that period that significant changes began to take place and this final chapter
looks at later innovative customs and the increasingly important role played by
individuals.

Two christian names

Before the seventeenth century it was most unusual for a child to be given more
than one christian name, but occasional examples have been recorded as early as
the fourteenth century and precedents were set by aristocratic and royal families.
The custom was established in some European countries before it was in
England and would have been familiar to educated and well-travelled people
here. Not surprisingly therefore some of the examples found in the seventeenth
century are in families from abroad and in the landed gentry: it is easy to see how
the habit would develop class connotations.

In 1645, for example, William Wentworth, Earl of Strafford, married Henrietta
Mary Stanley, the daughter of the Earl of Derby. It is likely that she had been
named in honour of Queen Henriette Marie, the French wife of Charles I, and

soon after the Restoration this double name became more popular, especially in gentry families. For example Henrietta Maria Norcliffe was baptised in Oswaldkirk in 1664. However, the baptism of Heneritta (sic) Maria Kelshaw in Leeds, in 1704, was one of several examples about that time among families lower down the social scale. A fascinating piece of genealogical work by Marion Moverley traces this name, in the female line, through five generations in Coverdale from 1739, the surname changing from Hardcastle to Watson, Wright and Calvert. In some cases the Maria was dropped but Henrietta Maria Watson married Matthew Mawer in 1860.[1]

Interestingly the combination Anna Maria, which also had a continental origin, was used in Leeds in 1659 by a family of ordinary status, possibly an extravagance that anticipated the freedoms of the Restoration. At almost the same time a merchant called Metcalfe gave both his sons two names, calling them Thomas Hennerick (1659) and John Charles (1661). The first of these seems to show the influence of continental versions of Henry, but Charles as a second name was probably a celebration of Charles II's return to the throne. In a similar gesture Mr Thomas Holden named his son Carolus Benedictus Andreus in June 1660, almost immediately after the king had been crowned.

Even so the custom took some time to establish itself and it was still novel enough in 1755 for a gentleman to write in his diary 'brother Fretwell had a son baptized by the name of William Smith after his grandfather'.[2] Thomas Wright Lapish, who died 'of decline' in 1793, was a farmer's son in Saxton and the register reveals that he owed his middle name to his mother Mary Wright of Towton. It was a custom that would increase in importance through the nineteenth century. The baptism of Jackson Clark Shakelton in Leeds in 1691 is of interest because both his given names were surnames.

Few girls were given surnames as first names but occasional examples have been noted, especially in gentry families,[3] and, by the eighteenth century, it was not uncommon for girls to have two popular christian names, although these were often written and pronounced as one: Roseanna Appleyard was baptised in Rothwell in 1756 and Maryann Lawn in Garforth in 1787. Before long these were followed by combinations such as Sarah-Jane, Mary-Jane and Sarah-Ann, names that are said to have fallen into decline in the nineteenth century after becoming class stereotypes. However, Mary-Ann and Sarah-Jane recovered from that and enjoyed renewed popularity in the 1960s.

By the early nineteenth century the giving of two names was an established practice although, where counts have been taken, those given to girls outnumbered those given to boys. For example in Easingwold there were 125 cases recorded in the period 1813–37, out of a total of 1,358 baptisms; of these 76 were girls and 49 were boys. In Collingham the first example occurred in 1826, and only 5 were boys out of 22 recorded before 1837. There were 447 baptisms in that period.

In the same period it became more common amongst the gentry for a traditional first name to be followed by one that was rather more pretentious, and ministers were prominent among those who helped establish the custom in Yorkshire. For example in 1815–30 the Rev. Paley's five children were given the names Frederick Apthorp, Edward Graham, Temple Chevalier, Francis Henry and John Hewitt; Mr Beckwith, the vicar of Collingham, had a son called Augustus Ambrose and a daughter Annie Elizabeth Octavia. What Withycombe described in *English Christian Names* as 'a tasteless piling up of names' had begun and one of the earliest offenders was the Rev. William Wighton of Garforth: he named his son William Charles Allanson Barker (1785) and his daughter Eliza-Abigail Wilhelmina Sotheron (1786).

The strangest excesses though were often in ordinary families and it is difficult to know whether these were just tasteless or deliberately satirical. A publican in Meanwood called his first son Baron Roth (1868), the significance of which emerges only when it is linked with Child, the family's surname. Among his other children were a Prince Frederick Charles, a General Roberts and a Princess Beatrice. When Grace Strickland Catherine Steward Tankard was baptised in Kirk Hammerton, in 1774, the entry described her as 'the daughter of foolish Jonathan Brown'. It would be difficult now to find anything quite like these examples, for the upper classes are no longer the role models and naming excesses are of a different kind. However, I noted in the local newspaper that a man who celebrated 65 years of married life in 1987 rejoiced in the name Victor Diamond Jubilee Hardwick.

Diminutives and pet forms

Our traditional names have had pet forms and diminutives throughout their history and the role that these played in the development of surnames has already been touched on in Chapter 2. A few diminutives of the more common women's names had independent status almost from the beginning and they feature in Smith-Bannister's frequency lists of 1538–1700, although not among the most popular names: they include Beaton, Marion, Janet and Emmot. The lists contain no examples of diminutives such as Betty and Tommy and the circumstances in which these became names in their own right are not well documented.

We find occasional examples with diminutive –y endings in formal records from the early thirteenth century and we know from other sources that one or two were in common use colloquially from that time. Johney Topliff, a girl, was baptised in Snaith in 1560 and similar spellings occur throughout the seventeenth century, e.g. Jonye (1604), Johnnie (1651). We must look in the baptismal register for confirmation of their change in status, for the minister was the person responsible for sanctioning their use and baptismal entries in English are as close as we come to an 'official' list of these names. The topic seems to have attracted little serious attention, although the names are often commented on individually in dictionaries and Dunkling said, in *First Names First*, that the process began in the eighteenth century. He found examples of Betty, Nancy and Sally in name counts for the year 1700, although only Betty was recorded more than once.

Not surprisingly the evidence differs from parish to parish. In Leeds more than 20 different names of this kind were recorded in the period 1717–50. In the much smaller parish of Methley there were 9 in the period 1734–61, and in rural Thornton in Lonsdale there were 11 between 1755 and 1775. The majority of these were names of girls, and no male diminutives were recorded before the 1750s. Tomey Willson, a boy baptised in Rothwell in 1754, is the earliest example I have located, followed by Neddy in 1764. In many Yorkshire registers Betty and Fanny were the first girls' names of this type and both occurred frequently from c.1720. They were followed by Peggy and Molly in the 1720s, Nancy, Nanny, Mally, Matty, Sally and Nelly in the 1730s, Dolly in 1740 and Polly in 1758. Less usual names were Susy (1738), Katy (1748), Mabby (1764) and Elsie (1765).

Sometimes we cannot be sure which first name the diminutive refers to and in each case we have to take into account just when and where the example was recorded. 'My sweet Betty' in 1657 was a reference to Elizabeth, whereas 'Betty' in 1655 was Beatrice Mauleverer. 'Mary or Malley as she was commonly called' (1882) persuades us that Mally was then an alternative of Molly, but in Horbury register Pally was used for a boy in 1691 and a girl in 1795. In other registers Pally was usually for a girl, presumably an alternative for Polly, although even Polly could apparently be for Pauline. Patty is usually said to be for Martha and it was certainly an independent name long before Patricia was popular. Pat Warde (1723) though was certainly a man, known elsewhere as Patience Warde. There are too many similar examples to deal with here in depth but we certainly need to remember that Neddy could be for Edward or Edmund and Nelly for Ellen or Eleanor. The early references to Frank could be for both boys and girls but Frankey Beaumond of Emley (1735) was a girl.

This evidence has been drawn just from Yorkshire and it should not be presumed that it is typical of the country as a whole, although that may well be the case. One of the reasons for looking at names from a regional point of view is to emphasise how important the local perspective is and to encourage those who have an interest in such matters to carry out their own investigations.

The role of the individual

The earliest changes that took place in the name-stock were largely the result of choices made by individuals at the top end of the social scale, but those new names, no matter how adventurous they may have seemed to contemporaries, were still drawn from what might be called traditional sources: they were revivals rather than innovations, commemorating illustrious ancestors, saints and heroes. Even the names brought here from the Continent fell into those categories. That changed in the mid-sixteenth century when the gentry first began to use surnames as first names, for these were true innovations and they established the right of individual gentlemen to choose a name for which there was no precedent.

In the same century there were two further significant developments, both the work of the so-called Puritans. The significance of the names they drew from the Old Testament has less to do with the choices that were made, which could still be said to be traditional, than with the individuals making those choices, for these were farmers, clothiers, tanners and tradesmen, ordinary people who had no claim to gentility but were not among the poor either. Behind them, encouraging and prompting, were ministers, thought of by some as 'agents of social and political reconstruction' and by others as autonomous, 'advanced' intellectuals.[4] When those same ministers sanctioned virtue names and phrase-names they went one step further, for these were pure inventions; everyday vocabulary words given a new role.

The new-found freedoms were exercised gently enough to start with. The role of the godparents was still important as late as 1700 and traditions would continue to be maintained within families well into modern times. However the first signs of individual eccentricity can be traced to the seventeenth century, to the Civil War in fact. For example Castilian Morris was given his name during the siege of Pontefract Castle, when his father was a colonel in the Royalist army. He named his own son Castilian in 1687, when he lived on Briggate in Leeds, but seems to have had no connection with Castilian Cooper who was born in York in 1692. This boy was the son of the under-gaoler at York Castle. Of course the first Castilian may have inspired the second, and one or other of them seems likely to have influenced the girls' name Castiliana, used in the same period.

Such names are a godsend to the genealogist. Castiliana Copley was the daughter of Lionel Copley, a gentleman living in Wadworth. Her first marriage took place in 1675, to Sir John Beckwith or Beckworth, and the couple called their daughter Castiliana in 1676.[5] When her husband died in 1688 she moved to York where she was married to Thomas Maulyverer on March 31, 1692. Just 10 days later Mr Lonsdale of York called his first-born daughter Castiliana. The name is distinctive enough to identify this lady as she twice changed surname, but it also confirms Beckworth as a variant of Beckwith and suggests a possible family connection with the Lonsdales.

Another apparently unique choice was Abstrupus, a favourite with the Danbys who had an estate in the Farnley district of Leeds. The first Abstrupus was born in 1655, and both his son and grandson were given the same name, sometimes shortened to Abstrup. I have no evidence that Abstrupus was ever more widely used and its etymology remains obscure, although 'abstruse' might be a better word. Apparently less obscure are Vigorous, the name given to the son of an army officer called Edwards in 1703, and Anvilla, the daughter of a Barnsley blacksmith in the nineteenth century.

Juventus (or was it Inventus?) is another name which appears to have no precedent, but it may have been classically inspired, even if it was only a way of saying 'junior'. Juventus Brotherton first comes to our attention as an adult in York in 1693, at the baptism of his daughter Elizabeth, but he must surely be the Juventus Brotherton of Wakefield who was indicted at the quarter sessions seven years later for counterfeiting, caught in the act by Naomi Robinson as 'he held the mould' and 'Thomas Binns poured in the mettal out of a ladle'.[6] Considering those circumstances perhaps his name should be read as Inventus after all.

Such inventions were often gentry inspired but from the seventeenth century others were being coined at quite a different level. For example Exercise Hulley was a Quaker in Leeds in the 1690s, his name recalling the excesses of the Puritans, and then there were the names coined for foundlings and illegitimate children, such as Townesgood (1640), Fortuneatus (1656), Equal (1674) and Ignotus (1732). Soon afterwards we encounter genuine innovations by individuals who were neither gentlemen, sectaries nor parish overseers and again the meanings can be either obscure or transparent. In 1713 Henry Atkinson of Kippax named his daughter Teacher, which might seem obvious on the face of it but it was spelt Teasha and Tatia in later generations and I can offer no explanation of these. The inspiration, if not the motive, for a choice made by Henry Watson of Hull in 1749 is clear. He gave his son the extraordinary name Culloden but perhaps he was an extraordinary man since after the baptismal entry the minister wrote 'ignis fatuus', or will o' the wisp, perhaps in reference to his delusions.

Most names of this kind never spread far beyond the family but there are a few cases where what appears to be a local invention had more success. Admiral may be such a name, for the examples I have encountered all occur in the eighteenth and nineteenth centuries, in just one or two parishes that lie between Wakefield and Leeds. The first I have noted was Admiral Owin, baptised in Methley in 1752, but the name was used also by families called Pepper, Hanson, Lake, Ward, Hirst, Clarebrough and Brier, most of them from neighbouring Rothwell. It is not certain what lies behind its use but several of those families were watermen and others came from a locality called Fleet Mill, so either of these facts might have influenced the initial choice. In view of the date though we should perhaps consider whether Admiral Vernon was the inspiration, for he became a national hero in 1739 when he captured Porto Bello in Panama from the Spaniards. The locality Porto Bello in nearby Wakefield is evidence of his popularity.

A similar name in some ways is Squire, missing from most dictionaries, but said by Dunkling to derive from the surname and to have come into use in the nineteenth century. That may not be true in Birstall, where the name is recorded in the Firth family of Hunsworth in 1672, before any mention in the parish of the surname Squire.[7] There were still men called Squire Firth in that area in the mid-nineteenth century, by which time many other local families used the name, including the Woods, Booths, Marsdens Hemingways, Tordoffs, Barracloughs and Haleys. Slightly further afield there were examples in Halifax, Horbury and Rothwell, not to mention Leeds where Richard Squire called his son Squire in 1747. If this was not a surname it may be one of the earliest 'title' names, similar to Earl which has been popular with West Indians and black Americans.[8]

Such innovations had made little impact on the name-stock as late as 1800 but the precedents had been established and there were to be dramatic advances in the next century as social, religious and political change altered the face of Britain. One aspect of that revolution would be the ever-increasing influence of names from the other home countries (Scotland, Wales and Ireland), although that is difficult to identify in cases where the name already had a history in England, e.g. Brian, David, Michael, Nigel, Angela, Janet and Margaret. David, for example, reminds us that 'Taffy' was a Welshman and, as early as 1377–81, many of those who bore the name in English villages had surnames such as Walshman, Walsh and Gogh: some were more specifically 'ap Wylym', 'ap Gwyn' or 'ap Welyn'.

The nineteenth century

There is already available to us a good deal of information about first names in the nineteenth century, from the more idiosyncratic choices made by parents from the 1830s to the frequency of names for both sexes from 1870.[9] A recent publication by Stephen Archer throws new light on all aspects of this subject, although its title is at first misleading. His *Surname Atlas* is a CD-ROM which includes maps for all the more than 400,000 surnames that figure in the 1881 census, a marvellous contribution in its own right to surname studies. However, it also provides us with maps of all the 'forenames' used in that census, and this apparent afterthought illustrates many of the points I have been making about first name distributions and survival. Some of the information relating to individual names is astonishing: for example in 1881 there were just 6 males in Great Britain with the name Derek and 15 with its variant Derrick. More dramatically we can see at a glance that some first names were still confined to one district in 1881. Also in evidence are some of the obvious home-country borrowings that found their way into the frequency tables for England and Wales in the early twentieth century.

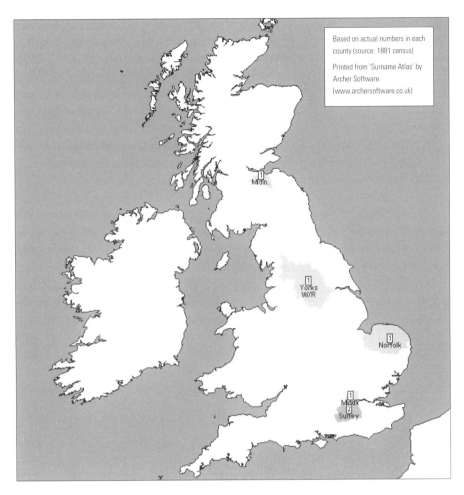

Based on actual numbers in each county (source: 1881 census)

Printed from 'Surname Atlas' by Archer Software (www.archersoftware.co.uk)

10 **The first name Derek (6)** This was a form of Theodoric, especially popular in the Low Countries. Most of the early examples are of Continental origin and it was rarely used by English people until the very end of the 1800s. Derrick was slightly more common in 1881 (15).

The frequency tables of 1925 and 1950[10]

Almost half the names in these tables in Dunkling and Gosling's dictionary would have been unknown in most communities just a hundred years earlier. There may have been a familiar look about the top male names in 1925, with John, William, George and James as the first 4, and Robert and Thomas also in the first 10, but Kenneth was already in seventh position and other Scottish names featured lower down the list, i.e. Leslie, Donald, Roy, Gordon and Douglas. By 1950 they had been joined by Graham, Colin, Keith, Malcolm, Ian and Stuart, making Scotland the most significant source of new names in the

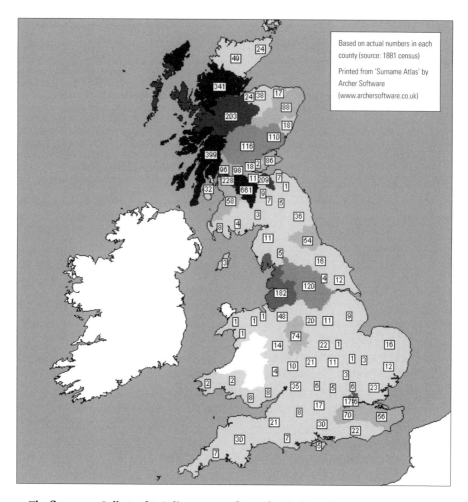

Based on actual numbers in each
county (source: 1881 census)

Printed from 'Surname Atlas' by
Archer Software
(www.archersoftware.co.uk)

11 **The first name Colin (4261)** Colin was a pet form of Nicholas and once common enough
in England to be the source of surnames such as Collins and Collinson. However, there is no
evidence that it survived and it is unrelated to the Scottish Colin which derives from the
gaelic *Cailean* (youth) and spread into England in the nineteenth century.

first half of the century. There was Scottish influence also in the popularity
enjoyed by Ronald and Norman, and probably in names such as Barry, Neil and
Patrick although here it would be difficult to determine what was Scottish and
what was Irish. Scottish influence where girls' names were concerned was much
less obvious, apparently confined to Elsie and Jessie in 1925, and Janet, Brenda
and Lesley in 1950.

The only one of these names to feature regularly in early English sources was
Patrick which was well represented in Westmorland and Northumberland in
1377. In other counties the Gaelic influence could be from Ireland and the Isle of

Man, rather than from Scotland, e.g. in 1379 Patricius de Irlond, Patricius Irysh and Patricius de Man. Both earlier and later than 1377–81 there were 'Patricks' in England who either had the by-name Scot or were described as Scot. In other cases a Scottish diminutive betrayed a man's nationality: Patrick Atkynson, who was mending walls on the Fountains Abbey estate in the mid-fifteenth century, was sometimes entered in the accounts as Patan Atkinson. Pattinson and Pattison are of course Scottish surnames.

Other Scottish first names must have sounded very strange to the Englishmen who had to write them down. In Honley, in the 1770s, a man called Kenneth Macpherson was working on the highways but his first name was recorded as 'Kenworth', a spelling which shows the influence of local place-names such as Hepworth, regularly pronounced and written as 'Hepporth'. Douglas too was in evidence in the north from the early seventeenth century but it usually referred at that time to a woman and was in some places confused with Dougald: Dowglass Brittaine was the daughter of a Rothwell bricklayer in 1756. Stuart and Stewart were recorded in Leeds from 1715, perhaps a reaction to the accession of the House of Hanover.

The most notable arrivals from Ireland in 1925 were girls' names, with Kathleen in seventh position and Eileen in tenth. These forms of Catherine and Helen were joined by Maureen in 1950 and they are credited with influencing the coining from Dora of Doreen which was particularly frequent in 1925. Also principally from Ireland were Sheila, which increased considerably in popularity between 1925 and 1950, Muriel which declined in the same period, and Theresa, making its first appearance in 1950. Girls' names from Wales were Gladys, Winifred, Jennifer and Gwendolen, but the only obvious boys' names from these sources were Kevin (Ireland) and Trevor (Wales).

Some of the new names in the tables were literally new, derived from plants such as Heather, Ivy, Lily, Rosemary and Violet. These first made an impression in the late nineteenth century, and may have been inspired by Iris, the goddess of the rainbow in Greek mythology, or by Rose. This had been known since the Middle Ages, but it came to be associated with the flower although it derived from a Germanic personal name. The only popular 'tree' name in this category was Olive, which also had a long history, but others such as Hazel and Holly were in regular use and the genre may have helped the Italian name Sylvia, through association with Latin 'silva' (wood). There may have been Continental influence also on Violet, usually said to date from the nineteenth century, but used in Scotland in the sixteenth century according to Withycombe (*English Christian Names*). I have found it in Yorkshire as Violetta (1645), Viallott (1706) and Violet (1752). The only 'month' was June and the solitary representative of the 'jewel' names, which date from roughly the same period, was Beryl, popular in 1925.

Other newly-coined or borrowed names are thought to have been inspired by novelists, notably Clive, Doreen, Eric, Janice, Pamela, Shirley, Vera and Wendy.

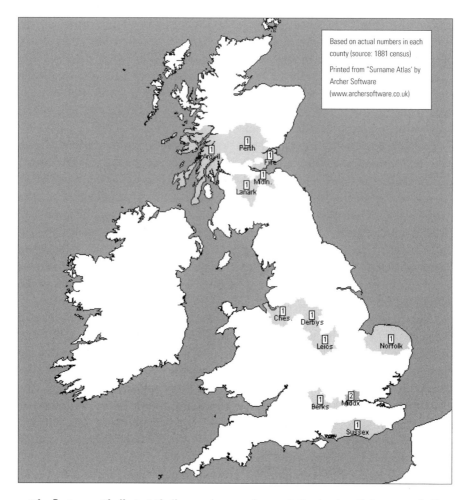

12 The first name Sheila (13) Sheila was almost unknown in England until the very end of the nineteenth century. It came here from Ireland and is an anglicised form of *Síle*, ultimately from Cecilia. The spelling Shiela occurred seven times.

The earliest of these is Pamela, a character in Sir Philip Sidney's *Arcadia* (1590) and the title of Richardson's epistolary novel in 1740–41. Charlotte Bronte is usually credited with having first used Shirley for a girl but she referred to it as a male name, and a man living in Rothwell in 1773 was called Shirley Lindley. The best known 'invention' in this category is probably Wendy in J. M. Barrie's *Peter Pan* (1904), which was apparently inspired by a child saying 'friendy-wendy'. Ethel, a short form of the Anglo-Saxon Etheldred, or similar names, became popular after two novelists used it in the 1850s.

Most of the other new names in these frequency tables were revivals of one sort or another. They included pet forms such as Betty, Carol, Jack, Linda, Sandra and Nora, the innovative Marilyn, possibly a linked version of Mary Ellen, the saint's name Hilary, and classical names such as Doris, Florence, Irene, Terence and Valerie. Jacqueline and Yvonne were borrowed from France, whilst Albert, Ernest and Frederick were from Germany, part of a trend that saw many other male Germanic names restored to favour, e.g. Alfred, Harold, Herbert and Raymond.

It is only when we make a direct comparison between the two frequency tables that we realise how fleeting the popularity of many names was by the twentieth century, particularly those for girls. For example 6 of the names in the top 10 in 1950 had no place at all in the top 50 just 25 years earlier, i.e. Susan, Linda, Christine, Carol, Jennifer and Janet. Annie had made way for Ann, Patricia had risen from forty-third to eighth and only Margaret maintained its popularity, in fourth place on both occasions. Fashion had also affected the top names of 1925, with Joyce, Dorothy, Doris, Betty and Eileen falling dramatically out of favour by 1950.

The changes were not quite so marked where boys' names were concerned but Albert was unplaced in 1950 having occupied tenth position in 1925, whereas Michael, Stephen and Paul rose from anonymity to high levels of popularity in the same period. The history of Brian is particularly interesting for it had been a localised name for centuries, with its popularity apparently confined to a very few families and their immediate affinities. Yet in 1950 it was the ninth most popular English name, having risen from forty-seventh position in 1925. The reasons for that reversal of fortune are not immediately obvious but influence from Ireland may have been partly responsible.

Notes

1. Marion Moverley has kindly sent me details of her research into Coverdale families.
2. *Yorkshire Diaries and Autobiographies in the Seventeenth and Eighteenth Centuries*, Surtees Society LXV (1875), p. 238.
3. For example, I have noted several examples of Holcroft in Lancashire, e.g. in 1683 Holcraft Hall of Mitton, C. Thornber, *Mitton Parish Registers, 1610–1719* (2001).
4. P. Collinson, *English Puritanism*, The Historical Association, General Series 106 (1983), p. 25.
5. *The Parish Register of Wadworth 1575–1837*, Yorkshire Parish Register Society CLXII (1997).
6. Wakefield Registry of Deeds, West Yorkshire Archive Service, Quarter Sessions Records QS4/19.
7. In west Yorkshire the surname was commonly written Swire because of the dialect pronunciation.
8. One local minister refused to baptise a child with the name Squire but accepted Duke because it was a local abbreviation of Marmaduke (personal communication from a Birstall family historian).
9. L. A. Dunkling, *First Names First* (London, 1978).
10. L. A. Dunkling and W. Gosling, *Everyman Dictionary of First Names* (London, 1984).

Conclusion

The late fourteenth century was the starting point for this inquiry into first names, principally because the publication of the poll tax returns makes it possible to compile accurate statistics of christian name usage in late medieval England at every level of society. These statistics testify to changes that had been taking place from c.1200 and they mark the emergence of the modern naming system. It was during the fourteenth century that English established itself as the national language, many of our surnames stabilised, and the population declined because of the Black Death. These matters all bear on one another to a considerable extent: they are the context in which one or two topics from this period were considered, notably the customs and problems associated with the popular use of pet forms and diminutives, and the derivation of surnames based on personal names.

However, the effective starting point of the investigation was the analysis of the first names recorded in 1377–81, which revealed that fewer than 50 male and female christian names were popular at that time. A slightly higher number were in occasional use but, even so, this is a very small total and many names that we may think of as perennial favourites were either exceptionally rare then or missing completely, for example, Mary, Susan, Francis, Anthony, Brian and Charles. In some cases the later popularity these enjoyed was the result of nation-wide fashions, such as the veneration of saints, the revived interest in the medieval romances, or the attraction of the Bible to sectaries. However where the popularity was more localised it could sometimes be traced to individuals, or to small, interconnected social groups, and that is a matter of considerable importance to family historians.

Individual names from different sources have been examined in greater depth in order to highlight the circumstances in which they were preserved or revived; some of these were remarkably distinctive, having their origins in the centuries before and immediately after the Norman Conquest. Special attention has been paid to their subsequent popularity and it can be seen how important the godparents' role was in that respect. From the fifteenth century at least this was the most important influence on name-giving until the eighteenth century, when the balance shifted to parental or family considerations. Important regional name-givers for the earlier period were identified, as were the special uses made of certain categories of first names by some gentry families. The inference there is that these families, and those who aspired to gentry rank, attached great symbolic value to their first names, and this seems to be an aspect of their history that has been largely neglected.

The significant development of the post-Reformation years was the emergence of wholly new first name practices. In the case of the gentry and aristocracy this resulted in surnames being used for the first time as baptismal names, a custom that eventually spread to all levels of society and was also made use of by unmarried mothers. More generally new names were drawn from the Bible, particularly from the Old Testament, although this custom had been anticipated long before that by some influential families like the Cliftons and Gillows. It was a new-found freedom for people at other levels of society and one consequence of that was the innovative use of virtue names and the more eccentric phrase-names. Most of these had only short histories but the Old Testament has remained a major source of inspiration, even if the use of the longer and more unusual names has declined.

The more general freedom of choice that began in the sixteenth century and developed more strongly as time passed has never been arrested and, from the nineteenth century, there have been innumerable additions to the national name-stock, a development that is reflected in borrowings from all the home countries and from many other parts of the world. We are only just beginning to appreciate the limitations and versatility of the names used in the fourteenth century. Not surprisingly our present attitude to naming and our familiarity with the popular names of recent centuries tend to distort our view of those earlier practices, and the failure of scholars to look more closely into the popularity of names in that period means that we have been badly informed about their history before the start of parish registers.

This study has revealed that there are many more distinctive first names than we at first imagined; that is to say many more names that are characteristic, for a certain period, of particular regions, smaller communities or individual families. We are familiar enough with the idea that names belong to regions when we consider the separate histories of the countries within the British Isles, but now we must accept that there are local patterns in England itself, although they are less immediately obvious. The names in these areas reflect different practices and influences, different political and religious affinities and even different individual aspirations and, once they are recognised, they are a means by which we can increase our understanding of local and family history within the national context.

The key to identifying such names is accurate knowledge about changing fashions in name-giving, however we define fashion, and accurate statistical information about first name frequency at regular intervals, even between one parish and another. These are aspects of the subject that have for too long been ignored and historians will benefit as more regional surveys are carried out. There are obvious benefits too for genealogists and it must be expected that they will be at the forefront of research in this relatively new field.

One of the most important themes in this book is the idea that every first name has its own history, no matter how commonplace it might now seem, and that some have very distinctive histories. Etymology is revealing about the linguistic origins of our names whereas 'meaning' is concerned with every aspect of their history, subject to regional and chronological influences. I am confident that the study of first names in this way will emerge as a major new field of research in local history.

First Name Popularity Nationally, 1377–81

In Chapter 3 there were frequency tables for both male and female names in 1377–81. In both cases 1,000 names from 10 different counties were counted and shown in rank order with their percentage share of the total. Here the actual numbers have been combined to produce national totals for the top 50 names and the degree of popularity is indicated. Not included are male names with totals under three and female names with totals under nine.

MALE			FEMALE		
John	3532	Extremely	Alice	1714	Extremely
William	1834	popular	Agnes	1433	popular
Thomas	945	Very	Joan	1239	
Richard	831	popular	Matilda	654	Very
Robert	741		Isabel	465	popular
Henry	334	Popular	Margaret	435	
Roger	306		Emme	409	
Walter	240		Marg'	281	Popular
Adam	178	Quite	Margery	279	
Nicholas	163	popular	Ellen	278	
Hugh	104		Julian	238	
Geoffrey	85		Cecile	229	
Simon	81		Christine	208	
Ralph	69		Katherine	178	Quite
Peter	62		Edith	142	popular
Stephen	50	Infrequent	Amice	125	
Gilbert	34		Elizabeth	112	
Philip	34		Beatrice	110	
Reginald	32		Magot	99	
David	29		Sarah	78	
Laurence	27		Sybil	74	
James	20		Felice	72	
Edmund	19		Christian	72	
Alan	16		Avice	71	
Denis	15		Denise	64	
Michael	15		Is'	62	
Alexander	15		Isolde	60	
Matthew	12		Lucy	46	Infrequent
Andrew	12		Petronille	39	
Edus (?)	10		Rose	36	
Giles	8	Rare	Mariot	34	
Benedict	8		Mabel	30	
Edward	7		Lettice	30	
Luke	6		Constance	27	
George	6		Anne	24	
Gregory	6		Idony	24	
Clement	6		Eve	22	
Elias	5		Annabel	21	
Bartholomew	5		Marion	20	
Martin	4		Eleanor	19	
Jena	4		Ibot	18	
Nigel	4		Mag'	18	
Randolph	3		Evita	14	
Madok	3		Clemence	13	
Maurice	3		Agatha	12	
Griffin	3		Helwise	11	
Gervase	3		Godelena	11	
Eyvyn	3		Lora	10	
Hamond	3		Mary	9	Rare
Stacey	3		Margr'	9	

First Name Profiles, 1377–1700

These tables present a profile of a name's frequency for the period 1377–81 to 1700. The rank order in 1377–81 is taken from the conflated total of 10,000 for the 10 counties surveyed. The asterisk indicates that more than one name shares that position. The other figures are from the frequency tables in Scott Smith-Bannister's *Names and Naming Patterns* pp. 191–201, where the author explains his adaptation of Spearman's rank-order correlation.

MALE NAMES

NAME	1377–1381	1538–1549	1550–1559	1560–1569	1570–1579	1580–1589	1590–1599	1600–1609
Abraham			35.5	42	37.5	34.5	42	32.5
Adam	9					47.5	42	
Alexander	25*	35	35.5	32.5	35	30		31
Allen	24		29.5	36.5	32.5	47.5		
Andrew	28*		25.5	34	19	23.5	23.5	20.5
Anthony		24.5	15.5	19.5	14	10	12	14
Arthur		35	21.5	49	43.5	38.5	46	39.5
Bartholomew	38*	24.5	29.5	22		42		34.5
Benjamin							42	45
Bernard				49		47.5		47
Charles				30.5	32.5	32.5	29	26.5
Christopher		14.5	17	12	13	13.5	13	13
Cuthbert						42	42	
Daniel		35	44.5	49	30	34.5	23.5	25
David	20	35			43.5	47.5		42.5
Edmund	23	11	18	19.5	16.5	17	23.5	17
Edward	33	8	7	7	8	6	6	6
Ellis	38*		44.5	42		47.5		
Francis		16	14	13	10	12	11	10
Gabriel			44.5					
George	34*	9	9	10.5	7	8	8	7
Gilbert	17*			42		38.5		39.5
Giles	31*		35.5				50	39.5
Gregory	34*	35	29.5	32.5	35		38	
Henry	6	7	6	6	6	7	7	8
Hugh	11		19	17	18	21	31	26.5
Humphrey			21.5	27.5	21.5	19	29	34.5
Isaac					49		35.5	37
Jacob							50	
James	22	10	10.5	10.5	9	9	9	9
John	1	1	1	1	1	1	1	1
Jonas								
Jonathan								
Joseph				49	49		26.5	24
Joshua								
Laurence	21	18.5	25.5	36.5	27.5	27.5	42	36
Leonard		24.5	44.5	30.5	21.5	30	50	28
Mark		35					33.5	45
Martin	40*			36.5	21.5	36.5	38	42.5
Matthew	28*	12.5	21.5	23	15	13.5	17	12
Michael	25*	24.5	29.5	25	30	23.5	16	16
Miles						32.5	35.5	
Nathaniel					35		23.5	29.5
Nicholas	10	6	8	8	11	11	10	11
Peter	15		10.5	16	24	23.5	19	19
Philip	17*	18.5	13	14.5	25.5	23.5	26.5	32.5
Ralph	14			19.5	12	15	15	18
Reynold	19		44.5	42	37.5	36.5	38	
Richard	4	4	4	4	5	5	5	4
Robert	5	5	5	5	4	4	4	5
Roger	7	18.5	12	9	27.5	16	14	23
Rowland				27.5	49	19	33.5	
Samuel		35	35.5	27.5	30	26	19	15
Simon	13	24.5		14.5	21.5	19	29	29.5
Stephen	16	14.5	35.5	27.5	25.5	27.5	21	20.5
Thomas	3	2	3	2	2	3	3	2
Timothy								
Valentine		24.5	35.5		49		32	
Walter	8	12.5	15.5	19.5	16.5	30	19	22
William	2	3	2	3	3	2	2	3

1610–1619	1620–1629	1630–1639	1640–1649	1650–1659	1660–1669	1670–1679	1680–1689	1690–1700
46	34	25	24	35	31	19	26.5	18.5
					44.5	40.5		43
32	29	42	30	35	23.5	33.5	33	37
	41							
22.5	18.5	27.5	20.5	16	18.5	30.5	30	26
12	14.5	22	15	26.5	22	24	20	22.5
37	38.5	33.5					46	
50			44.5	46.5				
46	31	33.5	29	24	15	15	15.5	14
41.5	34	30.5	44.5					
26	26	23.5	19	15	12	12	14	13
13.5	17	14	16	14	17	16.5	23.5	21
	44		33	39.5	49.5	36	49	43
21	23	23.5	17	19	26.5	21.5	19	15
37	46	38.5	39	39.5	35	36	39.5	28.5
13.5	16	15.5	18	17	30	30.5	32	28.5
6	6	6	8	8	8	8	8	9
34	42	50	37.5	42.5	49.5			
11	10.5	12	12	13	13	13	12	12
50	46	46		42.5	34	38	44	
9	8	7	6	7	7	6	7	6
				46.5		44	49	
41.5								
7	9	8	9	11	9	11	11	11
31	31	50	31.5	46.5	44.5	33.5	39.5	
29.5	28	46	48.5		49.5		39.5	
46		35.5	35	29	26.5	29	31	30
		38.5			37	44	37	39.5
8	7	9	7	6	6	7	6	7
1	1	1	1	1	1	1	1	1
50	46		41		40.5			36
50	38.5	26	34	21	20	25.5	17.5	24
22.5	13	11	11	10	11	10	10	8
		50	23	21	16	14	15.5	16
37	46	38.5			42.5			39.5
41.5		35.5		41			49	
34	40	46	40	35	37	40.5	39.5	
41.5	42	42		46.5		48.5		
16	14.5	15.5	22	24	26.5	23	17.5	18.5
20	20.5	19.5	20.5	26.5	23.5	27	25	27
41.5	36.5	38.5	44.5	46.5			49	
29.5	25	19.5	27	21	32	28	28	
10	10.5	13	13	12	14	18	13	17
18	20.5	17	25.5	24	18.5	21.5	22	25
25	22	27.5	28	29	21	25.5	26.5	32
16	18.5	18	14	18	29	20	21	20
							49	
4	4	4	4	4	5	5	4	4
5	5	5	5	5	4	4	5	5
24	24	29	31.5	35	49.5	36	42	31
41.5	36.5	42	44.5					
16	12	10	10	9	10	9	9	10
27	34		37.5	32			35	34
19	31	21	25.5	31	26.5	16.5	23.5	22.5
3	2	3	2	3	3	3	3	3
			48.5	29	33	48.5	35	34
34			44.5		49.5			
28	27	30.5	36	35		48.5	44	34
2	3	2	3	2	2	2	2	2

FEMALE NAMES

NAME	1377–1381	1538–1549	1550–1559	1560–1569	1570–1579	1580–1589	1590–1599	1600–1609
Abigail								
Agnes	2	3	5	3	4	5	5	8
Alice	1	4	3	4	5	7	7	5
Amy		39.5	43.5	29.5	31		36	41
Anne	35*	5	7	5	6	3	4	3
Avice	24	30	28		50			
Barbara			21	25	31	29.5	26	30
Beatrice	18				50	42		37.5
Bridget		16	14	23.5	20	19.5	22	18.5
Cecile	12	16	33	20.5	28	24	31	33.5
Charity		30			35	42		50.5
Christian	23*	16	14	15	21.5	25	41.5	44.5
Clemence	44		14	22	17	32.5		35.5
Constance	34		43.5	32		42		50.5
Deborah								
Dorothy		13	15.5	13	12	11	12	12
Edith	15	10	24	16.5	21.5	28	26	41
Eleanor	40	11.5	11	12	10	12.5	13	13
Elizabeth	17	2	1	1	1	1	1	1
Ellen	10	18	12	18.5	15	17	16	14
Emme	7	30	24	29.5	23	42	32.5	47
Esther								
Faith			43.5					
Frances		24.5	21	23.5	18.5	16	17	16
Gertrude			43.5					
Grace		30	28	26	28	29.5	18	17
Hannah								35.5
Hester							38.5	23
Isabel	5	11.5	15.5	11	11	10	10	10
Jane		8	8	9	8	8	8	6
Janet		22.5	43.5	51	45	36	20.5	26
Joan	3	1	2	2	2	6	6	7
Joyce		30		16.5	18.5	18	24	25
Judith			43.5	40	40	27	23	23
Julian	11			32	40	36		
Katherine	14	14	10	8	9	9	9	9
Lucy	28	30	33	45.5	25	42	29	29
Lydia								
Mabel	32*			45.5	35	21.5	29	28
Margaret	6	6	6	6	3	2	2	4
Margery	9	9	9	10	13	14	15	18.5
Marion	39		28	35.5	25	32.5	45.5	
Martha				40	25	26	19	20
Mary	49*	7	4	7	7	4	3	2
Patience								
Petronille	29	39.5		32				
Phyllis			43.5	51		32.5	32.5	33.5
Priscilla							41.5	31.5
Prudence								47
Rachel		39.5	18.5	45.5	31	42	34	41
Rebecca			51			42	29	31.5
Rosamund								
Rose	30	39.5	28	40	35	42	45.5	37.5
Ruth					50			
Sarah	20		43.5	40	16	15	14	15
Susanna		30	17	14	14	12.5	11	11
Sybil	21	30	43.5	35.5	45	32.5		
Thomasin		30	18.5	35.5	35	21.5	26	21
Ursula		22.5	43.5	35.5	45	23		44.5

1610–1619	1620–1629	1630–1639	1640–1649	1650–1659	1660–1669	1670–1679	1680–1689	1690–1700
44	36	40.5	39.5	28	29	41.5	25.5	34.5
8	8	10	11	14.5	16	18	16	17
7	5	6	6	7	8	9	9.5	12
34.5	30.5	29.5	27	43.5	33	36.5	36	46
3	3	3	3	3	3	3	3	3
22	24.5	26	25	21	23	21	23	23
		40.5	47	43.5	43.5		44	46
19	20	19.5	21	22.5	26	24	21.5	32
27	29	45.5	39.5	43.5	37.5			
	38	44	47				44	
36.5	34.5	37.5	35	33	41	33.5	40	41
39.5								
					47			
50.5	38	40.5	28.5	28	24	31	27.5	29.5
10	10	12	10	11	14	10	12	15
39.5		37.5	47					46
14	16	15	15	12	10	14	17	18
1	1	1	1	2	2	2	2	2
17	17	17	17	19	21	22.5	21.5	20
44			43					
39.5	41	35.5	37.5	35	47	29	34	25
	49							
18	17	18	18	18	18	16	15	13
50.5								
15	13.5	16	16	17	15	17	13	14
31.5	19	19.5	19	14.5	17	12	9.5	8
28	27.5	23	23	24	20	41.5	24	36.5
12	13.5	14	13	16	12	15	18	16
5	6	5	5	4	5	5	5	5
36.5	32.5	34		43.5		38	40	
6	7	8	9	9	13	11	14	10
25	23	25	30.5		37.5	27.5	31	31
21	24.5	24	24	25	22	20	20	21
11	11	11	12	13	11	13	11	11
44	41	45.5		31	43.5	33.5	46.5	46
		35.5	35	28	34.5	36.5	32.5	29.5
39.5	45	27	28.5	30	37.5			
4	4	4	4	5	6	6	6	6
20	21	22	22	22.5	27	22.5	25.5	33
	45							
16	15	13	14	10	9	8	8	9
2	2	2	2	1	1	1	1	1
34.5	38	45.5			41		40	34.5
50.5		40.5	32.5	37.5				
	45			43.5	37.5	41.5	40	
47								
31.5	30.5	32		26	30.5	25.5	27.5	22
23	22	21	20	20	19	19	19	19
50.5						41.5	44	41
50.5			32.5	33	47		36	26
	45		26	37.5	25	25.5	29	27
13	12	7	7	6	4	4	4	4
9	9	9	8	8	7	7	7	7
50.5	49		47					
29	27.5	29.5	30.5	33	29	33.5	30	28
33	41	49	37.5		47			46

Select Bibliography

S. Archer, *The British 19th Century Surname Atlas* (2003), CD-ROM

D. Attwater, *The Penguin Dictionary of Saints*, 2nd edn (London, 1983)

C. W. Bardsley, *Curiosities of Puritan Nomenclature* (London, 1880, reprinted 1996)

W. Coster, *Baptism and Spiritual Kinship in Early Modern England* (Aldershot, 2002)

J. C. Cox, *Parish Registers of England* (London, 1910, reprinted 1974)

L. A. Dunkling, *First Names First* (London, 1977)

L. A. Dunkling and W. Gosling, *Everyman's Dictionary of First Names* (London, 1984)

D. H. Farmer, *The Oxford Dictionary of Saints,* 3rd edn (Oxford, 1992)

C. C. Fenwick, *The Poll Taxes of 1377, 1379 and 1381: Part 1 Bedfordshire–Leicestershire* (Oxford, 1998)

C. C. Fenwick, *The Poll Taxes of 1377, 1379 and 1381: Part 2 Lincolnshire–Westmorland* (Oxford, 2001)

H. B. Guppy, *Homes of Family Names in Great Britain* (London, 1890)

P. Hanks and F. Hodges, *A Dictionary of First Names* (Oxford, 1990)

G. F. Jensen, *Scandinavian Personal Names in Lincolnshire and Yorkshire* (Copenhagen, 1968)

P. McClure, 'The Interpretation of Hypocoristic Forms of Middle English Baptismal Names', *Nomina* 21 (1998)

P. McClure, 'The Kinship of Jack: I, pet forms of Middle English personal names with the suffixes – kin, –ke, –man and –cot', *Nomina* 26 (2003)

P. H. Reaney, *The Origin of English Surnames* (London, 1967)

P. H. Reaney and R. D. Wilson, *A Dictionary of English Surnames*, revised 3rd edn (Oxford, 1997)

G. Redmonds, *Surnames and Genealogy: A New Approach* (Boston, USA, 1997)

B. Seltén, *The Anglo-Saxon Heritage in Middle English Personal Names: East Anglia 1100–1399* (Lund, 1979)

S. Smith-Bannister, *Names and Naming Patterns in England 1538–1700* (Oxford, 1997)

E. G. Withycombe, *The Oxford Dictionary of English Christian Names*, 3rd edn (Oxford, 1977)

Christian Names Index

Family Names Index